HOUSE AND HOME

House and home are words routinely used to describe where and how one lives. This book challenges predominant definitions and argues that domesticity fundamentally satisfies the human need to create and inhabit a defined place in the world. Consequently, house and home have performed numerous cultural and ontological roles, and have been assiduously represented in scripture, literature, art, and philosophy. This book presents how the search for home in an unpredictable world led people to create myths about the origins of architecture, houses for their gods, and house tombs for eternal life. Turning to more recent topics, it discusses how writers often used simple huts as a means to address the essentials of existence; modernist architects envisioned the capacity of house and home to improve society; and the suburban house was positioned as a superior setting for culture and family. Throughout the book, house and home are critically examined to illustrate the perennial role and capacity of architecture to articulate the human condition, position it more meaningfully in the world, and assist in our collective homecoming.

Thomas Barrie, AIA is Professor of Architecture at North Carolina State University, USA. His scholarship focuses on alternative histories of architecture and, in particular, the interrelationship of a culture's religious beliefs and socio-political agendas, and the communicative and ritual roles of the built environment. He is the author of *The Sacred In-Between: The Mediating Roles of Architecture* (2010) and *Spiritual Path, Sacred Place: Myth Ritual and Meaning in Architecture* (1996), and co-editor of *Architecture, Culture, and Spirituality* (with Bermudez and Tabb, 2015).

HOUSE AND HOME

Cultural Contexts, Ontological Roles

Thomas Barrie

Routledge
Taylor & Francis Group
LONDON AND NEW YORK

First published 2017
by Routledge
2 Park Square, Milton Park, Abingdon, Oxon OX14 4RN

and by Routledge
711 Third Avenue, New York, NY 10017

Routledge is an imprint of the Taylor & Francis Group, an informa business

British Library Cataloguing-in-Publication Data
A catalogue record for this book is available from the British Library

Library of Congress Cataloging-in-Publication Data
Names: Barrie, Thomas, author.
Title: House and home : cultural contexts, ontological roles / Thomas Barrie.
Description: New York : Routledge, 2017. | Includes bibliographical references and index.
Identifiers: LCCN 2016039811| ISBN 9781138947160 (hb : alk. paper) | ISBN 9781138947184 (pb : alk. paper) | ISBN 9781315670232 (ebook)
Subjects: LCSH: Architecture, Domestic--Themes, motives. | Home.
Classification: LCC NA7125 .B37 2017 | DDC 728--dc23
LC record available at https://lccn.loc.gov/2016039811

ISBN: 978-1-138-94716-0 (hbk)
ISBN: 978-1-138-94718-4 (pbk)
ISBN: 978-1-315-67023-2 (ebk)

Typeset in Bembo
by HWA Text and Data Management, London

To my parents, who gave me my first and everlasting home.

CONTENTS

FIGURES

FIGURE CREDITS

Chapter 1

1.1 *Adam and Eve Expelled from Paradise*, Paul Gustave Doré: engraving, 1865; public domain/Wikimedia Commons.
1.2 Navaho forked pole hogan symbolism: from Peter Nabakov and Robert Easton, *Native American Architecture*, 1989, Oxford University Press.
1.3 Mongolian ger: photo, P. Lechien, 2011; Creative Commons CC0 1.0 Universal Public Domain Dedication.
1.4 *Summer*, John Henry Twachtman: oil on canvas, late 1890s; public domain/ the Phillips Collection, Washington, DC/ Wikimedia Commons.
1.5 Castlerigg stone circle: photo courtesy of Andrew Crompton.

Chapter 2

2.1 *Harbor with Fog (The Embarkment of Ulysses)*, Claude Lorrain: oil on canvas, 1646; Louvre, Paris, France. Erich Lessing/Art Resource, New York.

Chapter 3

3.1 *Baucis and Philemon*, Rembrandt: oil on canvas, 1658; public domain/ National Gallery of Art, Washington, DC/Wikimedia Commons/Widener Collection.

Chapter 4

Chapter 5

5.1 Tomb of the Leopards, Tarquinia, Italy: public domain/Wikimedia Commons.
5.2 Neolithic longhouses: from Michael Parker Pearson and Colin Richards, *Architecture and Order: Approaches to Social Space*, London, 1994, Routledge.
5.3 Hopewell ceremonial house: National Park Service, Harper's Ferry Center Commissioned Art Collection, artist Louis S. Glanzman.
5.4 Great Circle, Newark Earthworks, Newark, OH: drawing, Thomas Barrie.

Chapter 6

6.1 *Diogenes*, John William Waterhouse: oil on canvas, 1882; public domain/Art Gallery of New South Wales/Wikimedia commons.
6.2 Isla Negra, Chile: photo, Thomas Barrie.
6.3 Carl Jung's house, Bollingen, Switzerland: photo, Thomas Barrie.
6.4 Plan, Heidegger's Black Forest hut: from Adam Sharr, *Heidegger's Hut*, 2006, MIT Press.
6.5 Martin and Elfride Heidegger in front of the hut: *Martin Heidegger and Ms. Elfride on deck chairs in front of the hut in Todtnauberg*, photo by Digne Meller Marcovicz, bpk/Art Resource, 1968.
6.6 Well at Heidegger's Black Forest hut: *Heidegger's hut and the fountain in Todtnauberg*, photo by Digne Meller Marcovicz, bpk/Art Resource, 1968.
6.7 Martin Heidegger at the well: *Martin Heidegger fetching water at the well at the cottage in Todtnauberg,* photo by Digne Meller Marcovicz, bpk/Art Resource, 1968.
6.8 Thoreau's cabin at Walden Pond: from Lester Walker, *Tiny Houses, or How to Get Away From It All*, New York, 1987, The Overlook Press.
6.9 Thoreau's cabin at Walden Pond : *On Walden Pond*, N.P. Santoleri, courtesy of the artist.

Chapter 7

7.1 Frank Lloyd Wright's house and studio: public domain/Library of Congress, Prints and Photographs Division, Washington, DC/Wikimedia Commons.
7.2 Schröder House, Utrecht, Netherlands: public domain/Wikimedia Commons.
7.3 Villa Savoye, Poissy, France: photo, Thomas Barrie.
7.4 Schindler-Chace House, Los Angeles, CA: photo, Timothy Sakamoto.
7.5 Glass House, New Canaan, CT: photo, Thomas Barrie.

7.6 Mother's House, Chestnut Hill, PA: public domain/Wikimedia Commons.
7.7 House VI, Cornwell, CT: photo, Thomas Barrie.
7.8 The Cabanon, Roquebrune-Cap-Martin, France: public domain/Wikimedia Commons.

Chapter 8

8.1 Villa Capra, Vicenza, Italy: photo, Thomas Barrie.
8.2 Chiswick House, London, England: photo, Thomas Barrie.
8.3 Stourhead Gardens, Wiltshire, England: photo, Thomas Barrie.
8.4 Clapham Common, London, England: *View of NE End of Clapham Common*, lithograph, by kind permission of Lambeth Archives Department.
8.5 Monticello, Charlottesville, VA: public domain/Wikimedia Commons.
8.6 Llewellyn Park, West Orange, NJ: public domain/after Alexander Jackson Davis, lithograph, 1857, Metropolitan Museum of Art, New York, Harris Brisbane Dick Fund, 1924, OASC.
8.7 Levittown, Long Island, NY: Levittown History Collection, Levittown Public Library.

ACKNOWLEDGMENTS

I am passionate about the potential of architecture to materialize and communicate the most significant questions people ask about the world and their place in it. This has led to longstanding research and design interests in house and home. Over many years, my own homes have been the locus for exploring and materializing ideas that matter the most to me. At the School of Architecture, NC State University, where I direct the *Affordable Housing and Sustainable Communities Initiative*, I regularly teach graduate community-based design studios focused on affordable housing. Studio conversations about the pressing needs for well-designed, affordable housing have naturally elicited questions regarding the cultural contexts and ontological roles of house and home. Consequently, I created a graduate seminar entitled *The Ontology of Home*, where student research and probing discussions helped clarify many of the topics covered in this book.

My students have been instrumental in prompting and advancing my scholarship, but so have colleagues and friends. I have presented papers on many of the topics included in this book at the *Architecture, Culture, and Spirituality Forum*'s annual symposia, and its supportive scholarly community of academics and practitioners challenged and refined my thinking on the subject. Peer reviewers also insightfully critiqued my work – Bob Mugerauer's and David Leatherbarrow's suggestions during a formative period opened up new areas of inquiry, and Robin Dripps' and Richard Etlin's reviews of separate chapters helped clarify my positions. I offer sincere and special thanks to Lindsay Jones and Ben Jacks who thoroughly reviewed the final manuscript, and whose expertise and critical acumen helped me to see what otherwise I would have not. Barbara Brenny, Visual Resources Librarian at the College of Design, skillfully located images that had eluded me. A scholarly leave from NC State provided much needed time to complete this book, and I sincerely thank Robin Abrams for her support. A visiting position at The Catholic University of America during that time resulted in many productive conversations with colleague and friend, Julio Bermudez.

Throughout years of travel, research, and writing, my family, Lisa, Ian, and Simon, have encouraged and supported my passion and work. Our house and home is the center of my world – one I may depart from, but always return to.

PROLOGUE

The problem of house and home – topics, themes, and analytical methods

What could be the problem of house and home? These two words are easily and routinely used to describe where and how one lives. *House* is the place that shelters one's *home* within which the events of their lives take place. But, are these two terms – the first prosaic, the second poetic – so clearly distinguished? And, how can home, a word that conjures so many variable wishes, attributions, and meanings as to suggest indeterminacy, be defined? It is, to state the obvious, a broad subject, complicated by the fact that everyone is embedded in the domestic and consequently, either consciously or unconsciously, has opinions about it.[1]

House and home are big subjects and this is a small book, and thus topical and theoretical boundaries are required. I include a broad range of topics, sources, and examples, but problematize the domestic in selective and specific ways. For example, even though house and home may be ubiquitous, ephemeral, and ever-changing words, they fundamentally signify the human need to create and inhabit a defined place in the world. In this context, house and home have performed numerous cultural and ontological roles: shelter, symbol, ritual space, and social construct; taken numerous forms: primordial dwelling, house of god, house tomb, modernist exemplar, and cultural icon; and have been assiduously represented in scripture, literature, art, and philosophy. Furthermore, while I incorporate the difficulty, complexity, and contradictions of the subject, my inquiry is narrowed by a focus on literary examples, theoretical texts, and fields that have specifically addressed the architectural implications of the domestic. This is all in service of explaining interrelationships of culture, ontology, domesticity, and house and home.

A people's beliefs and artifacts are reliably explained as emerging from their particular culture. Cultural determinants legitimately reveal differences between cultures, but can miss their commonalities. In this book, culturally specific explanations of house and home are incorporated, but I also seek congruities. Cultural artifacts are like spoken language – the motivations to create them its structure. A preeminent human motivation is to find meaning in an often inscrutable world. Of course, in everyday life people are largely unreflective, but when they reflect, which most mature cultures do, a perennial human trait is revealed – humans are meaning-seeking beings. I am principally interested in what beliefs and artifacts humans construct when they consider the world and their place in it – ontological questions of why they exist and how they came to be, and their purpose and how to fulfill it. An underlying theme of this book is how humans think about the world and the roles that house and home have played in this reflective activity.

This book is a scholarly study that aims to contribute to knowledge regarding the complex, charged, and deeply human domestic environment, and perhaps inform how it might more effectively fulfill our needs. It needs to be said that it does not provide poetic celebrations of home or personal reminiscences of its qualities. It goes without saying that most, if not all, have experienced the comfort of returning home after a difficult day, the intimacy of a shared meal, the pleasure of folding their bodies into bed, and the joys of waking to a sun-filled bedroom – as well as the sadness of leaving a loved home, the discomfort of family strife, the loneliness of a house after a failed relationship, and the eeriness of a sleepless night – without having a presumptuous author describe how it feels or what it means. The experience of place has a role in this study, but principally because thinking and awareness are often intertwined.

One might assume, given the ubiquity of house and home in our lives and language, that the subject would have produced a plethora of architecturally-specific scholarly work – but it has not. However, the history of architectural theory does include a diversity of proscriptive and prescriptive writings on houses and homes. Beginning with the oldest surviving theoretical text, Marcus Vitruvius Pollio's *The Ten Books on Architecture*, architects have often been compelled to assert what house and home should, and should not, be. As is well known, Leon Battista Alberti had quite a lot to say about houses in his own ten books on architecture, and some have argued for his continuing influence. There are also established traditions of house style and pattern books in Anglo-American culture. Equally familiar are the variety of writings and, in some cases, manifestos, by modernist theoreticians that ranged from the practical to the visionary and positioned the domestic as particularly redemptive to society.

Few studies on house and home attempt to analyze, compare, and synthesize a more inclusive territory. Scholarship on the anthropological, psychological, and socio-political aspects of domesticity have largely dominated the subject.[2] And there are, of course, no shortage of studies on vernacular dwellings, on the histories of concepts about, and artifacts of, house and home, some of which find their place in this volume, and an abundance (or excessive) number of books on famous houses, regional house styles, and so-called home improvement, which do not. Considerably less addressed are the symbolism, meaning, ritual use, cultural significance, and ontological roles of home, which is the overall subject of this book.

All of which poses the inevitable question, what in particular is meant by the terms *house* and *home*? Scholarship on house and home typically entails cataloguing the etymological roots of these words, a convenient beginning but, certainly, not ending point. The Anglo Saxon *ham* is the most phonetically close to *home*, as are the Old Norse *Heima*, Dutch *hejm*, and German *heim*. *Domestic* is from the Latin *domus*, but the Romans also referred to home as *mansio*, meaning a place of rest, which appears in French as *maison* and in English as *mansion*. For Greeks a house was *domos*, but home was *oikos* and held a range of meanings regarding the activities it housed.[3] All refer to a place of habitation. Indeed home, habitation, to inhabit and even habit, which share the same etymological roots, suggest the quotidian activities associated with home. A similar term is dwelling, which is used as a noun (a specific place where we live), and also a verb (the act of living in a specific place).[4]

Distinctions are often made between house and home. One study states, "Whereas the house is generally perceived to be a physical built dwelling for people in a fixed location, the home, although it may possess the material characteristics of a built dwelling, implies a space, a feeling, an idea, not necessarily located in a fixed place;"[5] another, "'house' means shelter, and implies edges, walls, doors, and roofs… home does not require any building."[6] Amos Rapoport complained that house and home were often indiscriminately interchanged. He coopted Nikolaus Pevsner's formula for distinguishing building from architecture to suggest that home = house + "×," with "×" comprising elements such as security and control; family and self-expression. However, he also insisted that house and home are more qualifying terms, with the latter generally employed to describe places we like, the former those we don't, and concluded that the term home is actually not needed at all, as house or dwelling can easily suffice.[7]

Moreover, often cited is that even though animals may build shelters, as in bird nests and beaver lodges, only humans deliberately plan them. In the words of an anthropologist, "The house is *made*, rather than merely constructed."[8] As Karl Marx opined, "The architect builds the cell in his mind before he constructs it in wax," an intellectual activity that "distinguishes the worst architect from the best of bees."[9] A house provides shelter and houses people's lives, but a home is what they create in a house, the myriad of elements of living that, though changeable over time, define and represent their lives. Accordingly, home exceeds mere shelter similar to the idea that the soul exceeds the body that houses it.[10] And, just as "language accomplishes thought," house and home express what they are believed to be.[11]

While all these definitions may be useful, they are insufficient regarding the various meanings and attributions of house and home. Many are recent, and it is likely that at one time, because the domestic was everything in a people's world, there was no need for a special term to distinguish it from other areas of life. In the past, as it still is now, home was a location, the place where one's life was oriented, and where one situated the lives of others. In the words of T.S. Eliot, "Home is where one starts from."[12] People typically ask strangers where they live and share where they do, as a means of introduction. It nearly always refers to a specific place with unique meanings and connotations. Ruth McElroy observes, "Home is always embedded in another map of spatialized meaning,"[13] and its orienting roles can be observed in many of its associated expressions – homecoming, home base, and even home page. As simply stated in Henry Bishop and John Payne's popular nineteenth-century song "Home Sweet Home", "Be it ever so humble, there's no place like home!"

House and home are also places of action, the setting for the habitual, quotidian, and significant life events, which consequently contribute to shaping its meaning. Paul Oliver contributes an essential point that the home is "the theatre of our lives, where the major dramas of birth and death, of procreation and recreation are played out, and in which the succession of scenes of daily living are enacted, and re-enacted in the process of dwelling."[14] Dolores Hayden also offers the observation that a home is a means of self-expression and identity, but also "a vessel of memories, a refuge from the outside world, a cocoon where we can feel nurtured and let down our guard."[15] These perspectives may be true, but what is more important is how the agency of house and home do so, how their significance, or understandings of them, may have changed over time, and how different cultures may have different inflections or interpretations of similar conditions or phenomena. Histories of traditional dwellings or cultural domesticity may usefully situate the house and home in time, place, and culture, but they are not necessarily histories of the cultural and ontological significance of home. This is an important distinction. Of equal importance is distinguishing between what a culture may attribute to the house and home, and what they actually provide, as there are cases where they are not the same.

Also, it should not be assumed that pervasive valuations of house and home are uniform or can be uniformly applied to other cultures. Predominant Western values regarding family and home are relatively recent, and differ in significant ways from preceding beliefs and practices.[16] In Classical Greece the home, at least for men, was of secondary importance to the public realm. Men had their needs met in their households so they could fulfill their responsibilities to the polis, or space of political discourse. The Greek house was one of a hierarchy of power, where the man had authority over his wife, children, and slaves, and persuasion by violence was accepted. In contrast to the home, where there was no freedom, in the *polis* men related to each other as equals. For Greeks, and similarly Romans, the most important activities of life – especially regarding universal things – took place in the polis, which was focused on community and the future. According to Hannah Arendt, "The *polis* was for the Greeks, as the *res publica* was for the Romans, first of all their guarantee against the futility of individual life, the space protected against this futility and reserved for the relative permanence, if not immortality, of mortals."[17]

Home is also a malleable term often employed in service of particular agendas. Rowan Moore points out that, "the multiple meanings of 'home,' its ability to contain in four letters concepts of family, life, building, belonging, longing, house, village, land, property, shelter both physical and spiritual, both container and thing being contained, lend it to exploitation."[18] It is typically used to describe where we were born or raised, our "home town," indicating its profound and enduring ontological significance. To speak of one's "homeland" is to describe a unique place to which one is inextricably bound that includes others who presumably share one's values, and it is evoked when people feel threatened by outside cultural, political, or military forces. In this manner, "home" is naturally exclusive, it bounds people's lives, individual and collective, from family to nation, and in doing so can render everything else other, different, lesser, and even hostile.

Just as one needs to be circumspect defining house and home, a similar caution should be exercised regarding identifying particular examples as appropriate, useful, or important. House and home appear throughout literary, religious, and philosophical traditions, and the history of art may be distinguished by representations of home. Consequently, there is no shortage of examples, but just because the house is presented, even predominantly, that doesn't mean it has something essential to say. The predominance of representations of house and home simply indicate their importance. Therefore, one needs to be deliberate and selective in choosing which examples to identify and discuss, and be clear regarding the reasons why they were.

★★★

Given this, how can a productive scholarly study about a subject so broad and difficult, if not impossible, to be dispassionate about, be effectively crafted? First of all, it is essential to situate the subject – to take a position. My overarching position is that architecture and the built environment are particularly potent communicative media with the capacity to embody content and, however varying, express it over time. Overall, I emphasize the ontological and symbolic functions of architecture, and its assignation and capacity to articulate humans' position in the world – specifically expressed through house and home. I may analyze specific examples in detail, but also address the subject according to how house and home have been described, positioned, proscribed, and otherwise prescribed. In other words, I am equally interested in the roles they have been assigned and expected to play, as what they actually do.

In this context, my approach is phenomenological in spirit, if not in practice, but more on the ontological side of the house than the experiential one often dominant in architectural theory. My primary theoretical goal is how – and why – values, meanings, and significance are constructed, and thus ontological and symbolic considerations are emphasized. Consequently, Phenomenological Hermeneutics is applied to address the phenomena of the multiple aspects of the subject, in recognition that "we have only to interpret something when its meaning is not clearly laid down or it is ambiguous."[19] Because cultural artifacts, like language, are subject to multiple interpretations, I utilize aspects of hermeneutic retrieval to analyze, from a contemporary perspective, a broad array of direct and related material and scholarly evidence.

Even though the comparative nature of Ontological Phenomenology informs my positions, I avoid its more universalizing schools of thought, and do not overemphasize unitary attributions regarding house and home's capacity to shelter, orient, comfort, and nurture. As such I agree with Henri Lefebvre's assessment that the domestic, especially in the hands of Gaston Bachelard and Martin Heidegger, often "passes everywhere for a special, still sacred, quasi-religious and in fact absolute space,"[20] where totalizing pronouncements inure it to critical analysis. For example, traditional concepts of house and home, such as "center of the world" and "model of the cosmos", though easily identifiable, are changeable. Humans can be predictably adaptable, and a people may have resolute beliefs of this type but, due to calamity, displacement, or other affects, can shift their centers and models. That is, symbol systems are not always fixed or static, but can change at times of disjunction or disruption.[21] Hermeneutical comparative methods are employed to navigate disparities of this type, and to examine, analyze, and synthesize pertinent literary, historical, socio-political, and cultural-religious influences, and critically interrogate and explicate scholarly source materials. The goal, at least in part, is to mediate between "totality and infinity,"[22] as a means to establish a "critical holism,"[23] and perhaps derive some appropriate congruencies.

These scholarly approaches and methodologies recognize that it is in between the diverse perspectives regarding culture and its material artifacts that some dependable and useful perspectives and knowledge might be accessed. From a hermeneutical perspective an appropriate question is: what do the material artifacts of cultures *mean* to us today? In which ways do they still *speak* to us? Or even: what do we *ask* them to say? Theory is put in service of such questions, as a means to frame and contextualize material evidence in a manner that allows them to speak for themselves. Reception theory has a role here, especially reception histories of particular aspects or examples that reveal their variability of content and importance over time.

All of these positions, to varying degrees and utilizing a broad range of theoretical and material sources, are applied to the special case of the domestic. I position the broad nomenclature and examples of house and home as potent cultural artifacts that have played multiple roles throughout the history of human habitation including: expressing cultural hegemonies; enforcing cultural beliefs and hierarchies; communicating social status; embodying concepts of self and family; facilitating rituals; and accommodating fundamental and ontological needs. However, it is neither a history of home, nor an ethnographic study of houses, even though it includes aspects of these scholarly approaches, but a comparative study of the subject where cultural critique, cross-disciplinary interrogation, and formal and organizational analysis find their place. It does include, but is not overly reliant on, socio-political, gendered, and psychological analyses of domesticity for its arguments. All to present, in a variety of ways and through a broad range of examples, how house and home have been tasked with a diverse and diffuse range of cultural and ontological roles, often exceeding other creative medias.

★★★

All that being said, what are the dominant themes of house and home that I set out to address? First of all, to further define the subject, I discuss its obverse – homelessness – and the special roles often assigned to architecture generally, and the domestic specifically, to ameliorate this condition. I also incorporate how humans, as meaning-seeking beings, search for ways to understand the enormity of the world, and their place in it. As such, culture, as a communal construct and activity, is positioned as the ground from which architecture, as a primary cultural artifact, emerges. Consequently, in addition to seeking meaning, the all too human desire for certainty, power, and dominance find their place in expressions that range from territorial claims and social hierarchies of some traditional homes and villages, to assertive religious dictates and declarative modernist theories. Consequently, I present how the domestic, and in particular the "first house" and other formative constructs, were often appropriated to authenticate particular theories regarding the fundamental tasks of architecture.

Another theme is the capacity of the domestic to establish cultural and historical authority. The domestic roots of sacred architecture are presented to illustrate how the domestic and the sacred were often conflated, and to what end. Similarly, ubiquitous house tombs, especially those for the ruling elite, reveal how architecture generally, and the domestic specifically, were employed to express and perpetuate a ruler's power and their culture's hegemony. The vocality of architecture, and its capacity to express beliefs, assertions, and dictates is a consistent interest and theme of this book. However, I am equally interested in the ways humans project their desires onto the domestic, and assign it roles to satisfy them. This is particularly evident in the domestic retreat, but also can be observed in modernist houses and suburban subdivisions.

Throughout, my focus is on how house and home have been conceived and represented – what humans, peoples, and cultures, across time, have thought regarding what their houses and homes should be, do, say, and accommodate. This includes recent and contemporary beliefs about houses and homes, and their historical roots, and why they can be so assertive, intractable, and enduring. Additionally, concepts, histories, representations, meanings, and implications of house and home are employed to explicate particular aspects of architecture and the built environment. Last, I recognize that house and home are far from a fixed subject, but a means by which the roles the built environment plays in representing the human experience can be effectively conceptualized.[24] All of which, at times, leads to considerations regarding the broader tasks of architecture and the built environment.

★★★

Throughout the book, I ask the overarching question, what, and in what ways, have humans asked the home and, by extension, the built environment, to *do* for them? Considerations of the roles house and home are asked to play, and the questions they are assigned to address, are a means to incorporate a diverse and even conflicting range of issues. John Cheever observed that he wrote to make sense of his life. Architecture, like literature, is a predominant cultural output and, as such, can, does, and has served related cultural purposes of materializing our all too human condition. In these contexts, examinations of the cultural and ontological functions of house and home reveal their multifarious presumptions, prescriptions, nostalgia, and idealizations. Consequently, productive inquiries and appropriate positions regarding how house and home can more effectively serve our needs, in all of their forms, may be established, including, it must be said, how they cannot.

Even though this study is ambitious in scope, it is, nonetheless, incomplete, with many examples or subjects omitted. It is also speculative and selective, as any scholarly study must be, but also strives to explain the choices that were made, and why. The etymological origin of the word *speculate* is the Latin *speculari*, to "watch over" or "explore," and is related to *specula*, which is a watchtower. The speculative approaches I employ aim to critically watch over and explore the diverse and diffuse subject of house and home. Theory is employed as a means to establish a critical distance and render history more accessible and understandable. I also have a distinct interest in the analysis of case studies, in confidence that built form has unique and perhaps authoritative things to say, while also recognizing, as one scholar has asserted, "It is by no means clear that literature is less embodied than architecture, or that architecture is less visionary than literature."[25]

House and home are two words that call into question, or illustrate, the roles of architecture. The former is clearly a place – material and instrumental – the latter a placeless idea, cultural construct, and historical object. Considerations of house and home as fundamental human needs may assist the framing of questions regarding the broader tasks of architecture, such as placemaking and identity, separation and connection, and shelter and symbol. For example, house and home materially embody and present the relationship between one and other – oneself, other beings, and the world. That this fundamental condition, and the questions it raises, has been such a ubiquitous concern of Western philosophy underlines a particular depth of the subject. Moreover, how the house is conceptualized, how it *speaks* and what it *says*, reveals particular aspects about the culture that created and described it. Even though at times I illustrate the tasks of architecture through examinations of house and home, I am not interested in essentializing, but in culturally, ontologically, and materially contextualizing them. I pose a range of questions and, in attempting to answer them, hope others will gain expanded understandings.[26]

It is most likely obvious that this book is not a handbook on how to design better houses, though I would be gratified if that proved to be a collateral result. Instead, its applications can be understood as secondary. That is, if the multifarious concepts, beliefs, histories, and uses of house and home are better understood, consequently domestic and built environments that are more authentically aligned with enduring and contemporary needs may be created. But, perhaps most importantly, house and home are examined and presented to illustrate the perennial role and capacity of architecture to articulate the human condition, position it more meaningfully in the world, and assist in our collective homecoming.

1

HOMELESSNESS AND HOMECOMING

Cultural contexts, ontological roles, and the task of architecture

The American poet Wallace Stevens writes:

> There was a muddy centre before we breathed.
> There was a myth before the myth began:
> Venerable and articulate and complete.
>
> From this the poem springs; that we live in a place
> That is not our own and, much more, not ourselves
> And hard it is in spite of blazoned days.[1]

Humans have consistently sought to understand the world – its beauty, mysteries, fecundity, and threats – and been troubled by its capricious and indifferent nature. When Stevens describes a world that is "complete" and exists independent of humans, he evokes an ontological condition of estrangement – even homelessness. But when he suggests that the "poem springs" from the recognition that the world is "not our own and, much more, not ourselves," he assigns a unique role to poetry to address the human condition. Could not the built environment, like poetry, be similarly positioned as an essential means used by humans to articulate their understanding of the world and their place in it? And, if so, isn't the house, as a preeminent cultural artifact

FIGURE 1.1 *Adam and Eve Expelled from Paradise*, Paul Gustave Doré

in the history of human habitation, a potent medium to do so? The home, as observed previously, is a complex word typically charged with multifarious and often deeply personal meanings. However, as I will suggest, in its most potent renditions – or aspirations – home, and the house, essentially served as the locus for people's corporal lives, while providing the settings to transcend them. That is, house and home may be mere shelter but can also embody a sense of being in the world and express understandings of the world and, in doing so, facilitate a homecoming to the world. And, if homecoming is something attained, then its obverse, homelessness, is what is experienced when one is without home.

Homelessness

The condition of homelessness, and the desire for homecoming – for founding and inhabiting a home in its broadest definitions – has enjoyed significant attention, especially in the West. Even though homelessness is often described as a modern condition of alienation, it appears in other Western philosophic, religious, and literary traditions. Plato's "Allegory of the Cave" in *Book VII* of *The Republic* presents the isolation of humans trapped in the sensible world and human existence as one of exile and imprisonment in incarnate life.[2] The "strange prisoners" Socrates shows Glaucon are held not only by chains but ignorance. Centuries later, Christian Gnostics would mourn humanity's bodily imprisonment and estrangement from the original condition of true being. In the Judeo-Christian tradition, humans are often characterized as lost, wandering and homesick for an elusive god. This dislocation is evocatively described in *Genesis* as the lost Eden; man eats from the tree of knowledge and subsequently is alienated from the paradise garden where such separation does not exist.[3] In *Psalms*, David depicts himself as a "sojourner on earth," and cries, "How long wilt thou hide thy face from me?" (Ps 119:9 and 13:1), a plaintive expression of exile from the divine.

At the beginnings of the modern era, questions regarding the relationship between humans and the world were embedded in confrontations with scientific discoveries and attendant social and cultural displacements. The mathematician, physicist, and Christian philosopher Blaise Pascal wrote in *Thoughts* that in contemplating the universe, "The eternal silence of these infinite spaces fills me with dread,"[4] articulating the mystery and even terror of alienation in the cosmos. The seventeenth-century German mathematician, astronomer, and astrologer Johannes Kepler was profoundly affected by his discoveries that dramatically changed understandings of the universe and earth's position within it. As the science of the universe has expanded in the twentieth and twenty-first centuries, the result has been a type of existential loneliness and a longing for other intelligent creatures, or homes in other planetary systems. Scientists have listened for extraterrestrial radio signals, and sent their own, and searched for earth-like exoplanets. So far, they have found only silence and emptiness.[5]

Stevens observes in the same poem, "The death of one god is the death of all,"[6] echoing Holderlin's lament[7] that the gods have "fled" the modern world. When more open and dynamic societies replace closed, static, traditional ones, and religion becomes a choice not an intrinsic condition, what remains is relative individuality and cultural autonomy. The hegemony of non-dogmatic thought and recognition of an autonomous human rationality, which some say began with Socrates, also resulted in the loss of certitude of belief of humanity's place in the universe typically provided by religion. Martin Heidegger identified the capacity of humans to view the world from a separate, individual perspective as a source of anxiety. When one is no longer enclosed within the limits of their world, in the homely (*heimlich*), then broader perspectives appear. In seeking to understand the world, one must paradoxically stand apart from it, and this separation from the familiar is felt as anxiety. For Heidegger, homelessness was an enduring philosophic theme. "Uncanny homelessness" (*unheimlich*) was the condition of estrangement from the familiar, provoking a mood of homesickness. Sigmund Freud described it as fear and dread resulting from estrangement where the familiar has become strange. For Freud, it was the shadow of repressed emotions or a secret revealed, and could initiate psychological integration.[8] Heidegger, consistent with the ontological phenomenology he advanced, was interested in how it might affect homecoming.[9]

The West has typically positioned itself as exceptional, where the modern condition of alienation is situated in its preoccupations with mechanization, rationality, and a certain type of cosmopolitanism. But, even though its specific postulations of ontological homelessness may be remarkable, they are certainly not unique. Instead, in a variety of ways, estrangement from the world is found pan-culturally and trans-historically. In the East, however, homelessness can offer certain rewards. Hindu asceticism values the stage of life where the householder renounces the ways of the world in favor of the homelessness of the *sadhu*. Mendicant monks who eschewed any stable dwelling distinguished the practices of early Buddhism. The Buddha in *The Dhammapada* states:

> Let the wise man leave his home life and go into the life of freedom. In solitude that few enjoy, let him find his joy supreme: free from possessions, free from desires, and free from whatever might darken his mind.[10]

In some cases, the condition of homelessness can be redemptive. World mythology contains a panoply of stories regarding hero-redeemer figures and the necessity of leaving home to gain insights and benefits for others. The Buddha must renounce the comforts and sensual pleasures of his palaces to achieve enlightenment; Muhammad's solitary vigils in the cave on Mount Hira are required to receive the revelations of god; the seventeenth-century Japanese poet Matsuo Basho must wander homeless to access the insights he records; and American Plains Indians embarked on solitary vision quests to pass from one stage of life to another. The hero's journey is one of separation from the familiar and a journey to the unknown, followed by a return "home" with insight or knowledge gained along the way.[11]

The Buddha and his disciples were deeply concerned with how to live in the world, and their simple huts were emblematic of the renunciant and essential lives they cultivated.[12] The Buddha even described enlightenment as dissolution of the final house:

> Vainly I sought the builder of my house
> Through countless lives.
> I could not find him.
> How hard it is to tread life after life!
> But now I see you, O builder!
> And never again shall you build my house.
> I have snapped the rafters:
> Split the ridgepole
> And beaten out desire.
> And now my mind is free.[13]

This is very different from Greek and Christian place and time situated narratives. Instead, the Buddha and his disciples believed enlightenment was made possible by abandoning home and all it represented. The religious scholar Jonathan Z. Smith named these complementary visions of the world "locative" and "utopian,"[14] and the geographer Yi-Fu Tuan observed that religion either embeds a people in a specific place, or frees them from it.[15]

And so, paradoxically, in these brief examples the abandonment of home is a very different kind of homecoming. But these symbolic journeys are only one part of the homecoming enterprise. For Heidegger, poetry was a means to confront and reconcile an imperious and impenetrable world.[16] Wallace Stevens positions poetry as "the supreme fiction," the ultimate construct to render the inexplicable familiar, an art that through artifice materializes the immaterial. Stevens explains:

> What makes the poet the potent figure that he is, or was, or ought to be, is that he creates the world to which we turn incessantly and without knowing it and that he gives to life the supreme fictions without which we are unable to conceive of it.[17]

In other words, poetry reveals what otherwise would remain hidden. However, the arts have also been essential agencies to assist this ontological task and, of all the arts, architecture has been particularly charged with creating legible, dependable, and meaningful places – a home in the world.

Vitruvius, in his observations on the origin of the dwelling house, states that it was the unique human capacity to stand "upright and gazing upon the splendour of the starry firmament," to realize and consider their place in the universe, that was, in part, the impetus for the birth of architecture.[18] In other words, the recognition of a certain kind of estrangement from the world was catalytic of creating one of their own making. Consequently, humans have demanded that architecture not only shelter them from the storms of the environment but the storms of existence as well.[19] Karsten Harries argues that poetry and myths, as well as other art forms such as architecture, serve to "so re-present the world that it no longer seems indifferent to our needs, arbitrary and contingent, but is expressed as a place we call home."[20] According to Harries, architecture has a special and perhaps preeminent role, which "answers to the human need to experience the social and natural world as a non-arbitrary meaningful order."[21]

All of this suggests that one of the functions architecture has been asked to serve is to ameliorate humanity's homeless condition. In the poem "Anecdote of the Jar," Stevens describes how even a simple object, once placed in the "slovenly wilderness," brings a particular kind of order, rendering it "no longer wild."[22] Norman Crowe argues that the human quest for order and stability in an often capricious and unpredictable world produced the need for a "new nature" of the "domicile and the settlement." Cicero characterized human habitation as a second world:

> We enjoy the fruits of the plains and of the mountains, the rivers and the lakes are ours, we sow corn, we plant trees, we fertilize the soil by irrigation, we confine the rivers and straighten or divert their courses. In fine, by means of our hands we essay to create as it were a second world within the world of nature.[23]

As Crowe states, "With Eden left behind," humans needed a "new garden, one permanently positioned in the world of time and place."[24] Harries and others have suggested that the domestication of the environment served to recover the Eden or paradise that had been lost. But, conversely, acts of appropriation, congruent with the making of architecture, promise not so much a return to paradise, but a creation of one's own.[25]

However, even though the simplest of domiciles and settlements may have served as a "new nature," they were also positioned as part of nature, with alignments to cardinal points, celestial bodies, and environmental features that served to link them to the orders of the natural world. Paul Oliver argues that the vernacular houses of traditional societies were organized and materialized as a means to harmoniously situate their collective culture in the world, while also symbolically creating it. Myths that depict the origins of the world and a people's place within it served to valorize the house as a primordial and enduring model. Consequently, it also housed the religious beliefs and daily activities of indigenous peoples. Oliver explains:

> As the roof under which so much of this is acted and re-enacted in the daily, yearly and life cycles, the dwelling readily becomes the symbolic model for the greater universe of time and space in which they are seen to exist.[26]

The cultural contexts of the house

The concept of culture only dates from the nineteenth century, and its definitions have varied ever since. Paul Oliver defines culture as "the totality of values, activities and products, including buildings, of a society which give meaning and direction to the lives of its individual members."[27] I use the term *culture* to describe the ground from which the figures of house and home emerge and are embedded. *Cultural contexts* are predominant values and beliefs, and social and behavioral structures that, however varied and different, have shaped the forms, uses, and meanings of the house. Indigenous cultures typically are place-based and time-situated – often a people's locale was believed to occupy the center of the world and place of creation. Settlements and houses were often seen as the world, or served to create or represent the world of their makers. Religion and other cultural constructs informed and enforced predominant beliefs that the world was divinely ordered, and a culture was responsible for maintaining said order. This was not always the case but when it was, architecture and the domestic were participants and often principal players in satisfaction of these cultural claims. Consequently, they served to embody and express preeminent cultural values.

Fixed worldviews, and ideologies for maintaining them, are not limited to traditional societies, but find more direct expressions in them. Humans may be meaning-seeking beings, but they also seek safety and power. Ideology and its material means are primarily used to convince and coerce others to believe and act in prescribed ways. The house often played essential roles in power relations – from gendered hierarchies in individual houses, to styles that reflected social status, to settlements whose layouts enforced social, political, and economic

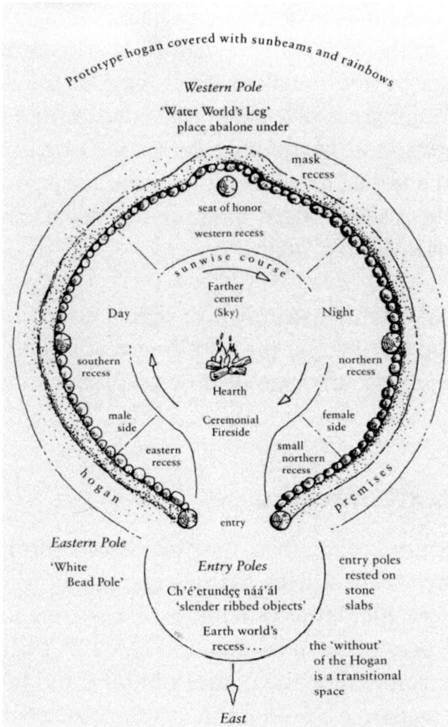

FIGURE 1.2 Navaho conical forked pole hogan symbolism

FIGURE 1.3 Mongolian ger

hierarchies. Houses may be the ultimate foil for ideological agendas because of their embeddedness in everyday life and distinction from religious and civic buildings. One scholar termed this the "silent complicity of architecture" in maintaining power relations.[28]

Specific cultures present problems of understanding to non-natives, as their motivations and values can be in a foreign language, hidden, or contextually or historically changeable. Scholars faced with an inscrutable culture can fail to distinguish their own cultural prejudices from the motivations and artifacts of their subjects. Another challenge is that examinations of house valorizing cultures often reveal that people may not always, or even often, think about and conceptualize their houses. Instead, building cultures are more governed by place, tradition, and ritual, and grounded in experience and awareness.

To illustrate these issues, I briefly turn to a few examples of traditional house building cultures, beginning with the houses of the Navaho peoples of the American Southwest. In the Navaho Blessingway myth, their traditional dwelling, the hogan, was a divine gift, its form and organization representing the predominant features of their environment. Hogans were (and still are) circular and oriented to the cardinal directions with each quadrant assigned particular ritual and quotidian functions. They were organized according to a binary system that distinguished male and female, earth and sky, and sun and moon. The roof represented the sky, the smoke hole the sun, and the walls boundaries of the cosmos. At its center was the hearth symbolizing a family and cosmic center. The hogan also ordered their lives and enforced prescribed (and proscribed) behaviors, including the "sunwise path" where one always moved through the space in a clockwise direction.[29] However, as Gary Witherspoon has argued, the Navaho believed that language was the creative agency of their world.[30] As such, the hogan was not so much the means to create their world as it was to cosmically and ritually align with it.

Other examples recall the formal and symbolic organization of the hogan, but are otherwise different. The ger is the traditional dwelling of Mongolia, but has discrete iterations throughout a vast territory stretching from Mongolia to the Caspian Sea. Gers are circular in plan and are cosmically oriented, with a hearth at their center and a smoke hole above. They also evidence binary organizations and assignations, but their symbolizations serve hybrid animist and Buddhist beliefs. The dwellings of the Dogon peoples of northern Africa are also organized according to a binary system. Even villages were built in pairs to represent heaven and earth.[31] However, Dogon dwellings reflected a sacred order according to particular anthropomorphic associations. Clearly there are cultural differences between the hogan, ger, and Dogon settlements, but also congruities in ontological aspirations to create dwellings that structured beliefs and rituals, while also aligning with or revealing their world.[32]

FIGURE 1.4 *Summer*, John Henry Twachtman (detail)

In some cultures, building practices eventually become canonized in written texts, providing accessible evidence of their motivations and means. This is the case in the building traditions of India, arguably one of the oldest codified building cultures. Beginning in the sixth century, texts outlined precise proportions for the disposition and proportioning of temples and cities, which also found applications in houses that were similarly organized and consecrated by priests.[33] Corollaries are found in building manuals of China and Japan, their esoteric practices often requiring the intervention of trained practitioners to correctly position dwellings.

The ontological function of home

Ontology is a specific but also general, interpretable, and adaptable word. Its Latin etymological root, *ont-logia*, or the science or study of "being," provides a modest definition. Philosophical ontology seeks to conceptualize and situate existence and the human condition. I use *ontology*, or, specifically, *ontological*, to describe inquiry or acts that serve to make sense of the world and one's place in it. Whereas culture is site, artifact, and time specific, ontology is general and concerned with the conditions of being and ways of understanding them. However, artifacts, and especially architecture, are ontological subjects because they materially and experientially exist, but also disclose existence. In Hans-Georg Gadamer's words, a building should, "draw to itself the wonder and admiration of the viewer. At the same time it should fit into a living unity and not be an end in itself."[34]

Phenomenology has had an enduring interest in the ontological function of house and home. Heidegger's philosophical construct of "dwelling" served to consider ways of deeply engaging the world and consequently disclosing its nature. Christian Norberg-Schulz, who was primarily an interpreter of Heidegger, equated "dwelling" with a "return to things," or engagements with the essentials of existence, and his arguments are often illustrated by domestic examples.[35] For Gaston Bachelard, home was deeply connected to the "unforgettable house" of childhood. He described the "oneiric house" as a place saturated with memories, dreams, and symbolic meaning, and asserted that the "house is one of the greatest powers of integration for the thoughts, memories and dreams of mankind."[36] All made significant contributions to the ontology of home, and continue to influence theories regarding the roles house and home can play to initiate or facilitate humanity's homecoming to more authentic, integrated ways of living.

However, these writers can also express a certain nostalgia, where the home stands in for notions regarding previous, superior, and preferred ways of living. In a variety of ways, they all identified qualities of domesticity that one suspects are close enough to their specific cultures and experiences to be compromising.[37] And their often idealistic conceptions of what home should, and should not, be displayed an exclusivity that bordered on the unsympathetic to a broader spectrum of human needs and identities. Emmanuel Levinas was particularly critical of what he viewed as Heidegger's provincialism of place: "One's implementation in a landscape, one's attachment to *Place*, without which the universe would become insignificant and would scarcely exist, is the very splitting of humanity into natives and strangers."[38] Rowan Moore's approbation that home has the risk of being exploited for ideological purposes may apply here, without diminishing the contributions these thinkers made to establishing and furthering important thinking on the ontological function of house and home.[39]

One area where phenomenologists have been effective is in articulating how house and home may serve to structure one's psychic being in the world. Bachelard advanced this concept when, referencing the Swiss psychiatrist Carl G. Jung, he attributed the different places and vertical layers of the house to a psychic structure.[40] Others similarly described the house as an amalgam of the psyche. Claire Cooper Marcus states:

> The unconscious often chooses houses, buildings, and secret rooms as symbols. The basement or cellar is often a metaphor for the unconscious, of something hidden that needs to be explored, whereas the attic or roof or opening to the sky often reflects a desire to explore transpersonal realms or spiritual dimensions.[41]

For W.H. Auden, the "Cellar underneath the house, though not lived in, Reminds our warm and windowed quarters upstairs that Caves, water-scooped from limestone were our first dwellings," and a place of unnamed fears, but the attic a place of safety and dreams, "a schooner on which a lonely only Boy sails north or approaches coral islands."[42]

In Jungian psychology, when the house appears in dreams or psychoanalysis it typically refers the "self," and Jung in his autobiography described in detail a dream where different levels and rooms revealed different aspects of his psyche and suggested a direction for his research. Later Jung built a highly symbolic house on Lake Zurich at Bollingen, where its stages of construction represented milestones of his life and psychological development, and when completed was a "symbol of psychic wholeness."[43] The contemporary philosopher Thomas Moore positions home as:

> An emotional state, a place of the imagination where feelings of security, belonging, placement, family, protection, memory, and personal history

> abide. Our dreams and fantasies of home may give us direction and calm our anxieties as we continually look for ways to satisfy our longings for home.[44]

For Moore, feelings associated with truly being "at home" are among the most significant and meaningful. Being at home is associated with "enchantment," of being connected, centered, even rapturous and ecstatic. One is literally under the "spell" of the numinous, the mysterious, and the meaningful.[45]

The ontological roles of the house are revealed by a diversity of examples. The Navaho considered the building of one's hogan to be a prerequisite to navigating the world. One had to build the "home place" before one could proceed with the next stages of their lives.[46] In Japanese literature of the medieval period, the hermit scholar's retreat held a preeminent position as a place that both centered one while providing connections to the larger world. The title of the thirteenth-century *Record of the Ten-Foot-Square Hut*, by Kamo no Chomei, refers to a room of these dimensions where the Buddhist sage Vimalakirti was said to have accommodated tens of thousands of devotees.[47] For the author, his austere mountainside retreat similarly grounds him in a place while revealing a vaster world beyond it. The attribution of sacrality to the home also appears in some examples of sacred architecture, but in this case dwellings house, and thus situate, the god or gods and render them accessible. Some building texts, such as the Indian *vastu*, include detailed descriptions regarding the locations, orientations, organizations, materials, and proportions required for the god(s) to dwell there. Funerary architecture also includes many examples that utilized domestic symbols. In elite tombs, these symbolizations served to solve the crisis of the death of ruler-gods, and guarantee their continuity and, by extension, the people under their protection. In the funerary architecture of Pharaonic Egypt, the house of the deified, eternal ruler not only materialized his continued participation in the affairs of his culture but also provided a setting where it was commonly believed he might be accessed. These dual functions were also predominantly performed in the mortuary architecture of cultures as diverse as Neolithic Europe and American Indians, further illustrating the capacity of the house and home to embody a diverse range of ontological content.

The special roles of architecture

I have discussed how house and home have expressed cultural beliefs and performed ontological roles. To do so, architecture needs to possess a certain kind of discursive capacity. That is, people receive symbolic content from, but also ascribe meaning to, the spaces and imagery of architecture. On one hand, descriptions of exchanges of this type assign a degree of animism to the

FIGURE 1.5 Castlerigg stone circle, Cumbria, England

built environment but, on the other, recognize that humans actively structure their understandings by directly engaging in a dialogue with their subjects. The discursive capacity of architecture has been a longstanding interest in phenomenology, but also finds a place in more general theories of architecture. Herman Hertzberger writes about the special capacity of art, and by extension architecture, to change one's understanding of a particular place and their relationship to it: "Not only do painters succeed in rendering the space of our reality, the opposite is also true, that reality is a rendering of the painter's space. We also experience space as we know it from images given by painters."[48] What does he mean by this? Isn't it about the transformative potential of art to change the ways one sees the world? Gadamer argues that creative artifacts have an enduring capacity to engage and even positively change one, and that art and design can be a means to articulate and provide new perspectives to life's most important questions.[49] In a similar manner, the embodied and experiential capacities of architecture and the built environment may be understood to affect one in ways that are instructive, even life changing.

There are many examples where architecture communicates symbolic content and materializes ontological meaning, but with varying goals of elucidating, inspiring, convincing, or even coercing. However, even though assessing what architecture *does* may be a fruitful enterprise, it is problematic due to its largely subjective nature. It is more reliable to consider what architecture is *asked* to do because of the availability of objective written and material evidence to inform this inquiry. As it turns out, throughout history, architecture has been *asked* to do quite a lot. As a predominant cultural artifact, architecture has often been tasked with embodying and articulating what a culture values most, and its material evidence is equally a mirror and a lamp, reflecting and illuminating the culture that produced it.[50] From the earliest of sacred works, the media of architecture served as an intermediary between humans and the gods they worshipped, or the knowledge they sought. Examples from the history of sacred architecture can be comparatively understood as serving to recreate and reveal a world that otherwise, it was believed, would have remained hidden. They are heroic and heartbreaking in their expressions of the perennial human quest for understanding and meaning.[51] That said, architecture, *per se,* doesn't actually mean anything at all – it is assigned meaning as part of the roles it is asked to play.[52] In these contexts, architecture can be conceptualized as an active agent, engaging its users in a variety of perceptual, visual, and experiential ways.[53]

The tasking of architecture to replicate or reveal the world and situate one's place within it can be understood as a quest for making a home in an inherently unstable world. Acts of building have served to connect people with themselves and their place in the cosmos, while simultaneously revealing the vast contexts of which they were a part. This double mediation – individual to architecture and architecture to the world – presents the essential roles that architecture has been asked to play generally, and has often materialized specifically. Throughout history, architecture has proven to be effective in materializing, communicating, and eliciting the values of a culture and the ontological aspects of the human condition.

★★★

During their lives, most people inhabit and pass through a number of houses, beginning with the first "house" of the womb. They live in the house or houses of their parents or guardians, and eventually move out (but never completely) to live with roommates or alone as they find their way in the world. Finding and creating the first home one can truly call one's own is typically an important milestone. Then there are the houses people rent or own and the homes they make as they move to new jobs or opportunities, cohabit with a partner, marry or divorce, raise or adopt children, and eventually where they grow old. At some point they may live with their children or move to care facilities, before the inevitable death of their bodies. All are temporary and impermanent (especially because, unlike most animals, people often live in dwellings that previously housed others), but throughout are "home."

Home is the center of most people's lives, the place they may depart from, but to which they always return. As a bulwark against the uncertainly of their lives, it serves as the hub of their personal world, and its safety and stability are essential to their sense of wellbeing. The feeling of "being at home" describes a condition of ease and comfort, and so it is not unusual that people (at least in the West) tell guests to make themselves "at home." All of which explains why descriptions of home and its value have enjoyed preeminent status in the arts. In the *Odyssey*, Odysseus, having been released by Calypso after she finds him "sitting upon the beach with his eyes full of tears, and dying of sheer homesickness," is shipwrecked on the Phaeacian coast. Naked and despondent, he is found by the maiden Nausicaa, and tells her, "There's nothing better in this world" than a "happy peaceful home," where "man and wife should be of one mind in a house," [54] recalling his home in Ithaca and his wife Penelope.

Home is the place of the most intimate relationships, as expressed in the Burt Bacharach and Diane Warwick song, "A house is not a home, when there's no one there to hold you tight."[55] But home is not simply a physical container of people's lives, but one they appropriate, personalize, and express themselves through. They may rent or buy a house or housing unit, but it is through occupation and personalization that the house becomes a home.[56] Inhabiting a home establishes an identity in the world, while also communicating one's self-definition to others. The Spanish writer Vicente Verdú reflected that the house is "between reality and desire, between body and dream, between what is possible and what remains to be longed for."[57] The house has also been described as a "third skin," an outer layer that, in addition to a person's body and clothing, provides a center for their lives while also projecting their self-image. It is where people orient themselves in the world and, through the quotidian rituals of domesticity, they are oriented.

As noted earlier, the spiritual path, paradoxically, often requires renouncing home. The novelist Peter Matthiessen suggested that a restless unease prompts embarking on this journey; a journey, however, that is also a return. Matthiessen reflects, "Yet one senses that there is a source for this deep restlessness; and the path that leads there is not a path to a strange place, but the path home."[58] For Heidegger, true homecoming was through an understanding of one's essential homelessness, one's being in the world, and one's place in finite and infinite space and time. This was his call for living an authentic life.[59] Heidegger upends the common definitions of architecture as more than mere shelter, and suggests that through the domestic act of sheltering, much like Stevens' jar in Tennessee, worlds formerly occluded may be revealed. However, this is no easy task with simple answers and singular means. Stevens recognizes this when, at the end of the poem introduced at the beginning of the chapter, he invokes the poet and the sky at war, a metaphor for the human struggle to understand the world and themselves. Each offer particular perspectives on the roles house and home may play in assisting humanity in a continuous homecoming to their shared humanity.

So home, as it turns out, is not really so much about how it is often reflexively conceived and imagined. It is not as much about a place, as it is finding a place in the world. It is not as much about a physical abode, as it is a home collectively inhabited. And yet, it is about a place, about people placing themselves in that which they can only truly know, or from which they can come to know.

2

A HOME IN THE WORLD

House and home in literature

I have outlined a broad range of subjects, theories, sources, and perspectives regarding house and home. I next turn to the specific subjects of homelessness, homecoming, and the roles and representations of houses and homes in select examples of literature. That home, and the search for home, are ubiquitous subjects in literature is obvious. However, how they are represented, why, and to what ends, is less so. I do not have documentary or literary criticism aspirations, but instead will discuss how house and home have presented a diversity of content, illustrated by works from a variety of literary traditions and periods. I have chosen them because they offer unique, immaterial evidence of the cultural and ontological roles of house and home. As such, they may reveal what material artifacts cannot, and thus make essential contributions to this study.

Homelessness and the search for home

It is no surprise that numerous descriptions of homelessness and the search for a home appear in literature, especially in Western twentieth-century examples. In the Western literary tradition, one often finds preoccupations with the ontological condition of homelessness, and themes of leaving and, in some cases, returning home. Oedipus, born into the Royal House of Thebes, is a wanderer, his antidote to the Delphic Oracle's prophecy that he will kill his father. He does eventually find a home, but, as is well known, it is short-lived and ends in tragedy. There is much in Homer's *Odyssey* about homelessness and the quest for home. Cast adrift in the world following the Trojan Wars, Odysseus wanders for ten years, unable through a range of impediments attributed to

FIGURE 2.1 *Harbor with Fog (The Embarkment of Ulysses)*, Claude Lorrain

the gods, to return home, poetically describing the disorientation and terror of being homeless. Often he suffers from nostalgia, the pain of longing for home, increasing as his impediments grow. Even upon returning home he must appear as a stranger, symbolizing the degree of his estrangement from home.

Herman Melville's *Moby Dick* is an equally epic tale. However, there is no nostalgia, but instead compulsion to escape home, and a quest to capture the unknowable and unobtainable. It begins with the desperation of the protagonist, who reflects:

> Whenever I find myself growing grim about the mouth; whenever it is a damp, drizzly November in my soul; whenever I find myself involuntarily pausing before coffin warehouses, and bringing up the rear of every funeral I meet; and especially whenever my hypos get such an upper hand of me, that it requires a strong moral principle to prevent me from deliberately stepping into the street, and methodically knocking people's hats off – then, I account it high time to get to sea as soon as I can. This is my substitute for pistol and ball.[1]

At the end, the narrator Ishmael clings to a coffin in the vortex of the sunken whaler *Pequod*, the sole survivor of its ill-fated journey, a metaphor for an individual's aloneness in the world.

Emily Dickinson pictures another type of individual estrangement in an uncanny, imagined un-homecoming:

> I Years had been from Home
> And now before the Door
> I dared not enter, lest a Face
> I never saw before
> Stare stolid into mine
> And ask my business there.[2]

Dickinson's poem ends with the narrator fleeing "gasping from the house." In Robert Frost's "The Death of the Hired Hand," home is a sad last resort for Silas, who returns to the only place he considers home and is reluctantly taken in by Mary and Warren. Frost writes, "Home is the place where, when you have to go there, they have to take you in."[3]

The novels of Thomas Wolfe often describe the quest for home, and all that it implies, as a rather futile enterprise, and homelessness as a perennial condition. His fiction has been characterized as fixated on themes of loneliness, the isolation of the individual, the inexorable passage of time, the search for stability in a world that offers little, and death.[4] He writes at the beginning of *Look Homeward Angel: A Story of the Buried Life*:

> Naked and alone we came into exile. In her dark womb we did not know our mother's face; from the prison of her flesh have we come into the unspeakable and incommunicable prison of this earth. Which of us has known his brother? Which of us has looked into his father's heart? Which of us has not remained forever prison-pent? Which of us is not forever a stranger and alone?[5]

The profound alienation in Wolfe's novels is crystallized in the prologue to the posthumous 1940 novel, *You Can't Go Home Again*, and establishes some of the novel's preoccupations:

> It seemed to him that all man's life was like a tiny spurt of flame that blazed out briefly in an illimitable and terrifying darkness, and that all man's grandeur, tragic dignity, his heroic glory, came from the brevity and smallness of this flame.[6]

The novel's young protagonist, George Webber, is an aspiring writer who has moved from a small town in North Carolina to New York City, where he completes his first, and eventually well received, novel. However, anger over its depictions of his hometown, and the death of his Aunt Maw who raised him, results in the severing of his ties to home: "He saw himself as a creature homeless, uprooted, and alone, with no door to enter, no place to call his own, in all the vast desolation of the planet."[7]

On the train returning home for his aunt's funeral Webber reflects, "He never had the sense of home so much as when he felt he was going there. It was only when he got there that his homelessness began,"[8] a recurring theme of the novel. At the end of the novel, Webber delivers its eponymous line, "You can't go home again," and then explains:

> You can't go back home to your family, back home to your childhood … back home to a young man's dreams of glory and of fame … back home to places in the country, back home to the old forms and systems of things which once seemed everlasting but which are changing all the time – back home to the escapes of Time and Memory.[9]

Wolfe's pronouncement has become a common expression that means many things, but principally that one can never return to the singular meaning and comfort childhood once provided. Indeed, the process of growing up and leaving home is analogous with Wolfe's pronouncement. The journey from the home of childhood and search for one's own home entails crossing the threshold to the unknown and the unpredictable, and entering an ontological condition of homelessness.

Modern estrangements

An individual's navigation of their life's stages and challenges presents ontological questions. In Wolfe's novel, loneliness is presented as "the central and inevitable experience of every man."[10] However, cultural contexts also exert effects. T.S. Eliot's "The Waste Land" is often cited as an anthem of the twentieth century's disaffections and dislocations. Modernism, as a response to modernization, has often been characterized as prompting estrangement from, and loneliness for, a world that has been lost. Marshall Berman suggested that modernism itself was the "struggle to make ourselves at home in a rapidly changing world."[11] In Rainer Maria Rilke's only novel, *The Notebooks of Malte Laurids Brigge*, modern estrangement and isolation are predominant themes, but also, similar to Wolfe, the swift transit of time and ephemerality of human life. The narrator is also a young man who has moved to the city, this time Paris, where he lives in poverty with aspirations to write something of importance and meaning. Recorded in his diary are sketches of crowds, of numberless faces of the poor and the lost, and of rooms stained with human occupation. In one scene, Malte comes across a remaining wall of a demolished Parisian townhouse with traces of the rooms on each floor imprinted on an adjoining building:

> You could see the walls of rooms on the various floors, with wallpaper still adhering, and here and there a fragment of the floor or ceiling… The stubborn life of those rooms had refused to be stamped out. It was still there, it clung to the nails that were left, it stood on the remaining hand's-breadths of floor, it had crept under the corner joists where there was still a little of the interior. You could see it was in the paint, which it had gradually changed, from year to year: blue into mouldy green, green into grey, and grey into an old, stale, putrescent white.

Its exposed surfaces, layers, structure, and services reveal the ephemerality but also uncanny endurance of human existence:

> There they all hung, the midday mealtimes and the illnesses and the breath exhaled and the smoke of years and the sweat from armpits that makes clothing heavy and the flat reek of mouths and the clamming odour of perspiring feet.

Malte is so affected he cannot remain, but "broke into a run the moment I recognized that wall," horrified that it revealed something that was "at home in me."[12]

In James Salter's novel *Light Years*, a married couple Nedra and Viri Berland grasp home as a means of stability in their modern lives. They live in a house near the Hudson River outside Manhattan, commuting there for work and shopping, their lives conforming to many notions of comfort and stability. But Viri, an architect, yearns for fame, for one building that will last, "that would appear in photographs of his time, the famous building he had created and that nothing – no criticism, no envy, not even demolition – could alter,"[13] and each are troubled by the passage of time that is beyond their control and the ephemerality of memory.[14] Their lives, however, appear placid, securely bounded by the rituals of raising young daughters, entertaining friends, and even pursuing separate affairs. The couple is "special, devout, they prefer to spend time with their children, they have only a few friends."[15]

One chapter opens describing Nedra and the house together, as if inseparable, as she is preparing for the arrival of dinner guests:

> I am going to describe her life from the inside outward, from its core, the house as well, rooms in which life was gathered, rooms in the morning sunlight, the floors spread with Oriental rugs that had been her mother-in-law's, apricot, rough and tan, rugs which though worn seemed to drink the sun, to collect its warmth; books, potpourris, cushions in colors of Matisse, objects glistening like evidence, many of which might, had they been possessed by ancient peoples, have been placed in tombs for another life: clear crystal dice, pieces of staghorn, amber beads, boxes, sculptures, wooden balls, magazines in which were photographs of women to whom she compared herself.[16]

However, later, after Viri and Nedra have divorced, the house serves as a metaphor for his loss:

> Viri was left with the house. Every object, even those which had been hers, which he never touched, seemed to share his loss. He was suddenly parted from his life. That presence, loving or not, which fills the emptiness of rooms, mildens them, makes them light – that presence was gone.

One evening when he returns to the house after dinner with his daughter, "it stood lighted and empty like some hotel in the outskirts, open but lost."[17]

These examples are often nostalgic, but also express escaping from home, the difficulty or even futility of returning home, and the ontological effects of modern culture. Throughout, home remains elusive, even in Salter's detailed descriptions of Viri and Nedra's house. In the following, home is very much present but, instead of ontological ennui, it is imbued with emotion, anxiety, and even danger. In some cases, houses even become central, malevolent characters.

Anxious homes

In *The New House*, Maya Angelou also describes the "stubborn life of rooms," through descriptions of the ephemerality and continuity of a house that is clearly not new, but newly occupied. She asks:

> What words
> have smashed against
> these walls:
> crashed up and down these
> halls:
> lain mute and then drained
> their meanings out and into
> these floors?
>
> What feelings, long since
> dead:
> streamed vague yearnings
> below this ceiling
> light?[18]

Angelou's poem depicts the transience of human habitation but also, when she writes "in some dimension, which I cannot know, the shadows of another still exist,"[19] the endurance of emotions and emotional lives in houses. Home can also be unnerving and even sinister, a phenomenon that is part of most childhoods and their memories. Children's stories often recount domestic anxieties – Hansel and Gretel from *Grimm's Fairy Tales* expect succor in the old woman's house while she sees them as sustenance. Marcel Proust, in *Swann's Way* from the seven-volume *Remembrance of Things Past*, describes the generalized anxiety of a young boy at his family's summer home in Combray. Much of the opening chapter entitled "Overture" is devoted to detailed descriptions of his bedroom, and his fears of going to bed and need for his mother's goodnight kiss to allay them. The stairs he ascended away from his mother and father, and their guests, he "always passed with such dismay," and "gave out a smell of varnish which had to some extent absorbed, made definite and fixed the special quality of sorrow that I felt each evening."[20]

Once in his room:

> I had to stop every loophole, to close the shutters, to dig my own grave as I turned down the bed-clothes, to wrap myself in the shroud of my nightshirt. But before burying myself in the iron bed which had been placed there because, on summer nights, I was too hot among the rep curtains of the four-poster, I was stirred to revolt, and attempted the desperate stratagem of a condemned prisoner.[21]

Each night he nervously waits for the comfort of his mother's kiss. His "sole consolation when I went upstairs for the night was that Mamma would come in and kiss me after I was in bed."[22] For this young, anxious boy, the goodnight kiss was like an "act of Communion in which my lips might drink deeply the sense of her real presence, and with it the power to sleep."[23]

The anxiety of Proust's character was internal, but houses themselves can assume terrifying personalities such that they become principal characters in some novels. In *To Kill a Mockingbird*, the classic southern novel by Harper Lee set in Maycomb, Mississippi, a house three doors down from where the narrator, a young girl called Scout, lives with her brother Jem, father Atticus, and their maid Calpurnia, plays a central role. The Radley Place is where a couple and their strange son, Boo, live in isolation and dissipation, symbolized by the dilapidated and forlorn condition of the house:

> The Radley Place jutted into a sharp curve beyond our house. Walking south, one faced its porch; the sidewalk turned and ran beside the lot. The house was low, was once white with a deep front porch and green shutters, but had long ago darkened to the color of the slate-grey yard around it. Rain-rotted shingles drooped over the eaves of the veranda; oak trees kept the sun away. The remains of a picket drunkenly guarded the front yard – a "swept" yard that was never swept – where Johnson grass and rabbit-tobacco grew in abundance.[24]

One summer, the two children have a new playmate, Dill, who is fascinated with the Radley Place, as are many in the small town. The house drew Dill "like the moon draws water, but drew him no nearer than the light-pole on the corner, a safe distance from the Radley gate," where he would stand "staring and wondering."[25] The couple rarely emerges – Boo never – and there are many stories about what occurs inside the dissipated house. Its imagined horrors focus on the believed-to-be insane Boo, who "went out at night when the moon was down, and peeped in windows."[26] This does not dampen the children's macabre curiosity and one day, dared by Dill, Jem races into the yard and slaps the side of the house. All breathlessly race to the safety of their own porch, where Scout observes, "The old house was the same, droopy and sick, but as we stared down the street we thought we saw an inside shutter move. Flick. A tiny, almost invisible movement, and the house was still."[27]

In this particular passage, the house is an animated character. In Romantic novels and stories of the nineteenth century, with their themes of dread and foreboding, houses assume even more complete characterizations. Anthony Vidler describes the Gothic horror story:

> Its favorite motif was precisely the contrast between a secure and homely interior and the fearful invasion of an alien presence; on a psychological level, its play was one of doubling, where the other is, strangely enough, experienced as a replica of the self, all the more fearsome because apparently the same.[28]

In these contexts, the two following examples contrast the domestic conventions of safety and comfort by presentations of the opposite.

Edgar Allen Poe was perhaps the most dedicated and successful in describing a particular kind of domestic anxiety. In *The Fall of the House of Usher*, a "mansion of gloom" serves as the primary character of a claustrophobic tale of dread and disorder. It begins with the narrator's boyhood friend asking him to visit his country estate. Roderick Usher has been suffering from a "mental disorder which oppressed him," and hopes that his old friend can alleviate his suffering. The narrator recalls, "with the first glimpse of the building a sense of insufferable gloom pervaded my spirit." The house seems to watch him with malevolent "vacant eye-like windows," and once he enters its Gothic archway, he observes that the "atmosphere" of the house "had no affinity with the air of heaven." Throughout, the house is presented as actively affecting its inhabitants – an evil character poisoning their bodies and souls. For Roderick Usher, "the physique" of the house had gradually produced the "morale of his existence," imprisoning him as effectively as a dungeon. His twin sister, Lady Madeleine, who has been gradually wasting away, is close to death and the narrator feels as if he "breathed an atmosphere of sorrow."[29]

The story reaches its conclusion when Lady Madeleine dies and is entombed in a windowless stone cell at the center of the house that in "feudal days" was a dungeon. Seven or eight days later the narrator lies sleepless in bed, affected by the "bewildering influence" of his room and its furnishings. Usher appears in his room where, after both hear disturbing noises, Lady Madeleine, having been entombed alive, arrives bloodstained, falls on her brother, and dies. The story ends with the narrator's escape, punctuated (conveniently) by the literal fall of the House of Usher into its lake.

In Nathaniel Hawthorne's *The House of the Seven Gables*, the house also plays a leading role. The Pyncheon House is a principal character in Hawthorne's "Gothic Romance," its gloomy and foreboding presence creating and expressing the dread and terror that pervade the novel. The narrator recalls the inauspicious building of the house: land wrested from a poor man through charges of witchcraft, and a curse from the condemned man on the gallows. The house serves as a metaphor for the power, conservatism, and hypocrisy of the privileged, and the tension and anxiety of conflicting cultures.

The day Colonel Pyncheon opens his new house it appears "withdrawn from the line of the street, but in pride, not modesty," and the townspeople approach it like a "congregation on the way to church."[30] Before the party commences, however, the Colonel is found dead in his study of mysterious causes, and afterwards the "rustiness and infirmity of age gathered over the venerable house itself."[31] The narrator recounts: "The aspect of the venerable mansion has always affected me like a human countenance," and that the house "was itself like a great human heart, with a life of its own, and full of rich and somber reminiscences."[32] Its prideful seven gables "pointed sharply to the sky" and surrounded the "spiracles of one great chimney." The deep projection of the second floor "gave the house such a meditative look, that you could not pass it without the idea that it had secrets to keep, and an eventful history to moralize upon."[33]

The Colonel's sister Hepzibah inherits the house and lives there alone until she is joined by her brother Clifford, who was released into her care after being imprisoned for a murder he didn't commit, and Phoebe, a young relation. Like Rodrick Usher, the house holds Hepzibah and Clifford prisoner. Even when they finally manage to leave, spontaneously taking a train trip, they cannot escape: "This one old house was everywhere! It transported its great, lumbering bulk, with more than railroad speed, and set itself phlegmatically down on whatever spot she glanced at."[34]

The story concludes with another mysterious death. Hepzibah's cousin, Judge Pyncheon, who, for his own gain, was responsible for Clifford's conviction, dies in the house while waiting for Clifford's return. He sits dead in the parlor of the empty house, which, animated by the wind, "creaks again, and makes a vociferous, but somewhat unintelligible bellowing in its sooty throat."[35] However, the novel ends on an uncharacteristically happy note – Phoebe is engaged to Holgrave, a boarder and mystic, who foresaw the impending events, and all leave the house to live in the "elegant country-seat of the late Judge Pyncheon."[36] Even though the house's appearance changes after the family's emancipation (including flowers growing in a space between the gables), like an unredeemable character it must be abandoned for its inhabitants to find a new and presumably happier life.

Homeliness

Other writings provide counterparts to the homelessness depicted by Wolfe and others, or the unease and anxiety of Gothic novels and stories. In the *Odyssey*, even though Odysseus' home becomes disordered during his absence, it endures, and after he returns order is restored. His house represents *oikos*, the Greek conflation of home, sanctuary, family, and the natural order of the world – its courtyard and rooms, surrounded by fields, a self-contained cosmos. Its symbolic center is Odysseus' bed, built around an olive tree, symbolizing the continuity of the goddess Athena and the reconciliation of war and peace.[37]

In Japanese literature of the medieval period, the rustic hut was the opposite of a self-contained world, but instead, through austerity, represented spiritual engagements with the world. It served as a means to embody and express the virtues of the simple life based on Buddhist principles, and to house sages who had renounced the ways of the world to focus on spiritual considerations. Kamo no Chomei, the author of *Record of the Ten-Foot-Square Hut*, retired to a self-built rustic hut on Mt. Hino near Kyoto. He recounts a number of his houses, and the calamities and disappointments of his life before he retired alone to his essential hut. He poetically describes the impetus and goals of his dwelling where his days were spent in contemplation, recitation of Buddhist chants, and playing a *koto* and *biwa*[38] – his hut providing the bare essentials to do so:

> Now that I have reached the age of sixty, when life fades as quickly as dew, I've put together a lodging for my final days. I'm like a traveler who prepares shelter for one night, or an aging silkworm spinning its cocoon. The size is not even one hundredth that of the house where I lived in middle age. You might say that, as my years have grown in number, my houses have gotten smaller and smaller.[39]

Po-Chü-i was a celebrated Chinese poet of the T'ang Dynasty who, for a short period of time, lived in a simple dwelling in the mountains.[40] A devout Buddhist, he built his dwelling close to nearby Buddhist temples where he practiced meditation. His *Record of the Thatched Hall on Mount Lu,* named for the hut of an earlier famous poet, portrays the house's virtues of austerity and authenticity:[41]

> By the spring of the following year the thatched hall was finished. Three spans, a pair of pillars, two rooms, four windows – the dimensions and

> expenditures were all designed to fit my taste and means. I put a door on the north side to let in cool breezes so as to fend off oppressive heat, made the southern rafters high to admit sunlight in case there should be times of severe cold. The beams were trimmed but left unpainted, the walls plastered but not given a final coat of white. I've used slabs of stone for paving and stairs, sheets of paper to cover the windows; and the bamboo blinds and hemp curtains are of a similar makeshift nature. Inside the hall are four wooden couches, two plain screens, one lacquered *ch'in*,[42] and some Confucian, Taoist, and Buddhist books, two or three of each kind.[43]

Towards the end of his essay, Kamo no Chomei returns to themes of impermanence and the enduring qualities of his hut: "Only this temporary dwelling of mine has remained tranquil and safe from harm."[44] Similarly, Po-Chü-i reflected, "One night here and my body is at rest, two nights and my mind is content, and after three nights I'm in a state of utter calm and forgetfulness, I don't know why it's like this, but it is."[45]

Comfort and sensual pleasure are also central to homeliness. In a famous passage from *Swann's Way*, Proust describes the olfactory and gastronomical delights of the *petites madeleines* his mother serves with tea one cold winter day, and in doing so presents a picture of domestic bliss.[46] *La Petite Maison,* an eighteenth-century novella by Jean-François de Bastide, more directly pairs sensual pleasure and architecture.[47] The setting is a garden pavilion on the banks of the Seine where the Marquis de Trémicour has invited Mélite with a plan of seduction. The tour of the house by the Marquis presents its architectural styles, craft, and virtues resulting in Mélite's increasing pleasure. When first seeing the house, Mélite lets out a "gasp" of pleasure that increases when they enter the salon, which was "so voluptuous… that it inspired the tenderest feelings, feelings that one believes one could have only for its owner."[48] Indeed, the story presents a strange *ménage à trois* where the house is equally an object of desire and participant in erotic seduction.[49]

In other novels, the house symbolizes the achievement of personal aspirations or fulfillment of cultural dictates. In V.S. Naipaul's *A House for Mr. Biswas*, Mohun Biswas strives to overcome his post-colonial homelessness by searching for his own house and the solid identity it represented.

> He had thought deeply about this house, and knew exactly what he wanted. He wanted, in the first place, a real house, made with real materials. He didn't want mud for walls, earth for floor, tree branches for rafters and grass for roof. He wanted wooden walls, all tongue-and-groove. He wanted a galvanized iron roof and a wooden ceiling.[50]

Special houses in English novels

It was in the English novel, however, that the house becomes a more fully realized object of personal and cultural support and desire. According to Richard Gill, the country house is "peculiarly English" and uniquely distinguished from its continental counterparts. The English nobility and gentry typically maintained a house in the city to serve their responsibilities there, but reserved their most affection for, and ascribed the most meaning to, their country estates. Home for this class of English society was the country house, not the city domicile, with the former starring in some of the most recognized works of English literature, including many novels named for the houses they featured. For Gill, "it is obviously much more than a literal setting: it is the chosen emblem of what the author considers humane order and enduring values."[51]

In this type of English novel, the house is often presented in detail to illustrate particular attributes of its owners and the stable society they represented. Of these, themes of order, probity, and cultural hierarchy and continuity often take center stage. The country house is often characterized as symbolizing the dominance of the upper classes and their essential role in guaranteeing the values of English culture. As such, their wealth was often conspicuously displayed in an otherwise circumscript society. In the words of Josh Silvers and Toby D. Olsen, the "country house was equally proof of prosperity and necessary for its continuation."[52] In a society that valued knowledge of literature, arts, and architecture, the houses also communicated the good breeding, social standing, and superior taste of their owners. Well-mannered houses reflected and enforced a well-mannered society. Country estates stood alone in the landscape – solid, enduring, "well-dressed," and adhering to the architectural manners of their time, while materializing their command of them, doubles of the personages they housed and embodied. Consequently, they also served as symbols of community, and the axis of the hierarchy of classes the houses, literally and figuratively, oversaw.

The nineteenth-century American novelist Henry James, who applied his experiences of English country homes to his novels, wrote in *English Hours*:

> Of all the great things that the English have invented and made part of the credit of the national character, the most perfect, the most characteristic, the only one they have mastered completely in all its details, so that it becomes a compendious illustration of their social genius and their manner, is the well-appointed, well-administered, well-filled, country house.[53]

For James, the country house was a "symbol, one of the most attractive variants of the 'great good place.'"[54] James' descriptions and characterizations found particular expression in *A Portrait of a Lady*, with its ordered and Edenic house Gardencourt.[55] E.M. Forster's early twentieth-century novels are similarly centered on country houses. In *Howards End*, titled for a country house in Hertfordshire of the same name, the house is positioned as a main character, though often off stage, in the social and class relations that play out in the novel. In this case the house, owned by a family of the new middle class, does not so much symbolize cultural values as it does their conflicts in a time of change.

But, it was the nineteenth-century novelist Jane Austen who arguably most successfully employed the country house for symbolic effects. In *Pride and Prejudice*, the maturation and eventual marriage of Elizabeth Bennet depends on houses. In particular, her opinions of her suitor, Fitzwilliam Darcy, a wealthy man from a patrician family, change from distain and revulsion, to admiration and love, principally following her visit to his country estate. Throughout the novel, a variety of houses are cast as characters that express certain aspects of their inhabitants and their place in the cultural hierarchy. Elizabeth is the second of five daughters and lives at the undistinguished Longbourn. Her family is loving and stable, but their coming travails are foreshadowed by the reader's knowledge that the house is entailed to a distant male cousin and therefore will not be inherited by the daughters. Early in the novel a new neighbor, Charles Bingley, appears after he has rented the nearby Netherfield, his status as "new money" "acquired by trade,"[56] reflected in the conditions of his tenancy. Also nearby is Rosings, the estate of Lady Catherine de Bourgh, its impressive house and grounds representing its owner's "old money" status, and its demeanor her condescension and arrogance. When Elizabeth visits for the first time, her companions effuse about its fineness, and one, Sir William, when they are admitted to its entry hall is so "awed by the grandeur surrounding him," he "had just enough courage to make a very low bow, and take his seat without saying a word."[57]

It is Darcy's house in Derbyshire, however, that gets the leading role. Elizabeth, though she has rejected his proposal of marriage, accompanies her aunt and uncle on travels that include stopping at his family estate, Pemberley. Even though Elizabeth has rejected him for, among other reasons, his arrogance, she experiences a change of heart when she sees Pemberley. At this point in the novel, Elizabeth has discovered that her negative assumptions of his character have proven untrue, but she still does not recognize her love for him. This dramatically changes as they approach the house, where she "saw and admired every remarkable spot and point of view."[58] The house, in Elizabeth's words, is "large" and "handsome," and its rooms "long and handsome," which she sees "with admiration of his taste." The housekeeper reinforces these sentiments when, as they tour the house, she effusively comments on Darcy's "sweet-tempered" and "generous-hearted" character. When she learns that he and

Elizabeth have met, they agree that he, like the house, is very handsome. Elizabeth concludes, "to be mistress of Pemberley might be something!"[59]

The order, graciousness, and beauty of the house is set against extensive grounds and woods, "ten miles round," that reflect and complement the house's grandeur. While Elizabeth and her party are touring the gardens, Darcy unexpectedly arrives and thus begins the couple's rapprochement and eventual mutual confessions of love. After their engagement, Elizabeth's older sister inquires how long she has been in love with him, to which she replies, "It has been coming on so gradually that I hardly know when it began. But I believe it must date from my first seeing of his beautiful grounds at Pemberley."[60] And so, just as Elizabeth gains possession of a superior man, she also attains a superior house through her discernment of the merits of each.

The later *Mansfield Park* also casts a number of houses for roles that illustrate the social standing and character of their owners and, perhaps most importantly, convey the virtues of cultural stability and continuity. Calvin Trilling argued, "No other great novel has so anxiously asserted the need to find security, to establish, in fixity and enclosure, a refuge from the dangers of openness and chance."[61] The noise and disorder of the heroine Fanny's parents' house in Portsmouth, which she left at ten when she joined her relations' household at Mansfield Park, and visits when she is an "out" (available for marriage) young woman of eighteen, illustrates how cultured she has become. Like houses in *Pride and Prejudice*, the Portsmouth house serves as a foil to illustrate the virtues of Mansfield Park.[62] Fanny describes her parents' house as "an abode of noise, disorder, and impropriety. Nobody was in their right place, nothing was done as it ought to be."[63] After being there for almost two months:

> She could think of nothing but Mansfield, its beloved inmates, its happy ways. Everything where she now was was in full contrast to it. The elegance, propriety, regularity, harmony – and perhaps, above all, the peace and tranquility of Mansfield were brought to remembrance every hour of the day by the prevalence of every thing opposite to them *here*.[64]

She reflects, "Portsmouth was Portsmouth, Mansfield was home."[65]

Mansfield Park ends similarly to *Pride and Prejudice*. Fanny recognizes her love for her cousin Edmund, and after their marriage, her uncle sees her as the "daughter he wanted," and legitimate heir to Mansfield Park. Throughout both Austen novels, London is a distant presence, a corrupting influence and, in Fanny's words in *Mansfield Park*, "very much at war with all respectable attachments."[66] By contrast, the countryside and, in particular, its gracious houses, represents the best of human nature and symbolizes the stable and admirable qualities of

English culture. Pemberley and Mansfield Park are assigned distinct personalities and perform as active characters that, like beneficent personages, represent the highest cultural values and perform roles as agents that reveal life's most essential truths. Indeed, in many of the previous examples, the house serves as a principal character – sensually attractive, malevolent, vain, arrogant, stable, comforting, authoritative, and even ethical.

★★★

The previous examples reveal different aspects, and varying cultural goals and ontological roles, of house and home. Ontological homelessness is preeminent in Melville and Wolfe, but also finds complementary expressions in other examples. The human quest for stability and safety is highlighted by their subversion in the Gothic stories and novels. As such, they highlight the desire for familiarity, homeliness, and comfort by presenting their opposite. They may also reflect the cultural anxieties of their time. Anthony Vidler attributed the phenomenon and popularity of the Gothic horror story to the social and cultural changes and uncertainty of its times: "At the heart of the anxiety provoked by such alien presences was a fundamental insecurity: that of a newly established class, not quite at home in its own home."[67] In Jane Austen's novels, the established upper class were not insecure about what they had gained, but what they might lose. They buttressed their position through houses, where the cultural stability of country estates took center stage to enforce class distinctions and cultural hegemonies. The ambiguity of Salter's novel is simply not present in Austen's country houses. As such, her novels provide unique access to the culture she lived in, and the roles houses were assigned to represent and enforce its values.

Of course, the home is often a backdrop in Austen's novels and a stage for the human relations it houses. The affective capacity of the house is more explicit in Gothic stories, with special evil powers its assigned roles. But, affective qualities of the domicile can also be positive, as in sexual atmosphere of the pavilion in *La Petite Maison*, where its voluptuous spaces are metaphors for places of pleasure. The spiritually imbued settings of the simple hut in classical Japanese and Chinese literature provide other renditions of propitious houses. They recall the simple huts of the early Buddhist community, but are also ephemeral. It is as if they, like the spiritual goals of their creators, will eventually dissolve into, and meld with, the unconditioned realm of enlightenment. In the Eastern and Western examples, ontological homelessness and homecoming, and their domestic counterparts, are very different. The contrast between the Buddhist-imbued hut and the culturally expressive English house is obvious, even though both had aristocratic roots.

William Maxwell, in the novel *So Long, See You Tomorrow*, describes themes of change and homelessness set in houses that serve to frame them. After the mother of the main protagonist, a young boy, dies, his life changes. First he and his father live in a rental house farther from town, where the walk home from school changes from the familiar to the dangerous, "beyond 9th Street" where two young thugs, "coal miners' sons," wait to taunt and beat him. They mercilessly torment him in the schoolyard, and in plain sight where "no hand was ever raised in my defense," a picture of alienation and vulnerability. His father re-marries and begins construction on a house outside of town, where most afternoons the boy meets a friend to play among the house's half-finished walls. In contrast to the inevitability of the boy's school experiences, the house suggests new possibilities:

> The agreeable feeling, as I went from one room to the next by walking through the wall instead of a doorway, or looked up and saw blue sky through the rafters, that I had found a way to get around the way things were.[68]

Maxwell presents the hope for an improved life through a new home. The house under construction is a metaphor for a work-in-progress life that leads to better things. There is also the promise of attaining a cultural foothold through creating a new house in Naipaul's novel. In both novels, the house is a palpable presence – in others, it is an off stage, ephemeral one, or even unattainable condition. Throughout, the house and home play starring roles in describing the human condition, relations, and psychology, not only symbolically or metaphorically, but in their physical presences and experiences. That the home should play such an important function in literature is not surprising. The depth and breadth of its roles, however, is, and illustrates how architecture can affect our emotions, materialize our psyches, and express our desires.

3

ORIGINS

Stories and theories about the first house

In the previous literary examples, house and home were metaphors for alienation and homelessness, receptacles of emotions, sinister characters, sensual settings, and symbols of stable cultural structures. Home, as I observed, has also been presented as transformative. In the myth of Philemon and Baucis, a pious old couple welcomes Jupiter and Mercury, disguised as wayfarers, into their simple hut after the other inhabitants of Phrygia had turned them away.[1] Even though they are very poor, the couple invite the gods to their hearth and generously attend to and feed them. Eventually the visitors reveal themselves and punish their neighbors by flooding the valley. At Philemon and Baucis' request, their primitive hut transforms into a temple they tend until their deaths – the simple hut now a sacred setting.[2]

In this myth, the essential dwelling signals its transformative capacity. I now turn to the subject of the simple, formative hut, and the ways it was deployed to establish cultural, ontological, and theoretical positions regarding the primary functions and values of domesticity. This is particularly evident in myths, beliefs, and histories about the origins of architecture. That the house plays a leading role in these narratives is logical given the primacy of dwellings in most traditional cultures. Origin myths typically provide dependable lineages and establish immutable truths to lend authority to a people's cultural structures and territorial claims. They also served ontological roles by situating a people in a stable past and a specific place. The origins of a people are common mythological subjects, and religions have often depended on origins to establish their historical authority. However, stories about the origins of dwellings also find an important place in the history of theory where they similarly served as authoritative sources to bolster theoretical arguments. I will argue that from the "first house" depicted in creation myths and the "primitive hut" used in architectural theory, to the first home of childhood and the spiritually portentous hermit's retreat, the original house has enjoyed a preeminent position.

It is important to recognize that one etymological root of *architecture* is *arche-tecture*, or "form of origin," belying its assignation as a formative cultural force, and suggesting its foundation in archetypes (a related term) or fundamentals.[3] In the case of the "first" or original house, the origins of architecture are often coterminous with the first shelters and reveal the original, or archetypal home.[4] Joseph Rykwert argued that there has been a consistent interest in the paradigmatic "primitive hut," as he and others termed it, and its essential relationship with the origins of architecture generally and the origins of the house specifically. He suggested that the primitive hut "seems to have been displayed by practically all peoples at all times, and the meaning given to this elaborate figure does not appear to have shifted much from place to place, from time to time."[5]

Also pertinent to the subject is how the believed or formulated origins of dwellings depended on a range of projections regarding their intrinsic capacity to satisfy individual and collective ideals. In Jungian psychology, "projections" are unconscious acts where elements of the psyche, typically those unwanted parts that have been repressed, are attributed to others. However, projections can include many areas of the psyche and are often pronounced enough to render personal relationships highly symbolic. In Carl Jung's words, we project "our own psychology into our fellow human beings. In this way everyone creates for himself a series of more or less imaginary relationships based essentially on projection," and "in these imaginary relationships the other person becomes an image or carrier of symbols."[6] The key term is "imaginary relationships," because it suggests that what one sees in others is largely a reflection of what is projected onto them. Whether these projections are the contents of the unconscious psyche, or are conscious aspirations, assignations, or desires, matters little in the context of recognizing that others, and other things, become receptive objects for structuring self-conceptions. Might not the same be said about a person's or people's relationships with home, which, as I have noted, is not simply a place but a symbol?

That said, why have the origins of architecture and the original dwelling been such a perennial and persistent subject? One answer may be their ability to receive and communicate a range of cultural and ontological content. The conceptualization of dependable beginnings and historical continuities, and the

FIGURE 3.1 *Baucis and Philemon*, Rembrandt

FIGURE 3.2 *The Interior of a Hut of a Mandan Chief*, Karl Bodmer

presentation of propitious fundamentals and dependable – and unchanging – models, serves to situate a culture in place and time. Cultures have used origin histories to validate territorial claims based on the beginnings of a people, and structure narratives regarding place and a people's relationship to it. In some cases, it was an instrument by which to authoritatively establish the participation of the divine in the affairs of its people. The Solomaic Temple is described in detail in Jewish scripture as the "house of the Lord," and it represented god's accessibility to his "chosen people" from their beginnings, establishing Jerusalem as the center of their world. Another culturally-affirming origin history is the *Casa Romuli*, the legendary house of the founders of Rome. The simple straw and mud hut, typically situated on the Palentine Hill, was the dwelling of Romulus and Remus after their adoption by the shepherd Faustulus. Here is a potent combination of primitive man, a she-wolf raising the brothers, living in an essential dwelling, and eventually founding a city and a culture.

Communal origins and home

The suggestion that origin myths should be a means to explicate house and home appears at first to be dubious.[7] Isn't mythology, by its very construct, created stories with, at best, tenuous relationships to history? What, if any, dependable content can it convey? Questions like this presume that history is preferable but, while history may be efficacious in describing the conventions, activities, and artifacts of a culture, it can be deficient in explicating its motivations. And history, like myth, is constructed in a manner that often reveals its own prejudices and agendas. When it comes to origins, myth may explain phenomena that are largely inaccessible to history. Like symbolism generally, myth has the capacity to disclose perspectives that are largely independent of its narrative. In essence, it provides an excess of meaning.

Traditionally, mythology provided dependable explanations of how to build and why to do so. A myth's authority was established by its capacity to render the past eternally present. These aspects of the functions of origin myths are accessibly evidenced in the myths of American Indians regarding the building and ritual uses of their domiciles. The domestic architecture of American Indians offers examples of dwellings serving multiple cultural and ontological roles, many of which were described in myths. According to Peter Nabakov and Robert Easton:

> The buildings of Native Americans encoded not only their social order, but often their tribal view of the cosmos. Many Indian narratives tell of a "Distant Time" or a "Myth Age" when a "First House" was bestowed upon

> a tribe as a container for their emerging culture. Some tribes have likened the creation of the world itself to the creation of a house, strengthening the metaphoric correspondence between dwelling and cosmos. Thereafter Indian peoples held the ritual power to renew their cosmos through rebuilding, remodeling, or reconsecrating their architecture.[8]

However, not all American Indian houses had this cultural and ontological status. The Paiutes, for example, were known to have built relatively simple shelters, which were simply abandoned when no longer needed.[9] But when American Indian dwellings were culturally and ontologically important, which many often were, they were tradition-bound in form, construction, materials, and use. They often were models of the cosmos and, as such, it was auspicious for dwellings to replicate original models and inauspicious to deviate from them (though developments and improvements were possible). The origin myth of the Mandan of North Dakota conceptualized the world as a colossal earth lodge with the sky held up by four posts. This "first house" served as a model of the universe, or everything important in the universe, and was symbolically recreated in their earth lodges that were round with a square marked by four posts at their centers.

The hogan, as noted earlier, played important cultural and ontological roles for the Navaho. Hogan means "home place," and in Navaho myths its form, organization, and orientation were given to the first man and woman by the "Talking God."[10] The Navaho believed the hogan was originally fashioned by god as a home for god, and replicated the conical forms of mountains they considered sacred. There were two original types, male and the female, both of which were believed to recreate the divinity of the natural world through the modeling of significant landmarks. The male conical forked pole hogan, for example, was constructed exactly as instructed by the "Talking God" using five major poles, the ends of which were typically adorned with feathers and served as the "eyes" of the hogan.[11] Moreover, the building of a hogan was a person's first step in ordering their life – one had to "build" before one could "plan." Thus the creation of one's house was also an original act, essential to the establishment of a productive relationship with the cosmos and others, and a precondition for a meaningful life.[12]

Individual origins and home

Karsten Harries suggests that most people have "creation myths" related to their first homes. He recounts his love of a "certain-washed out red," which he associated with the red hawthorn tree. The color elicited feelings of "special well-being" that were inexplicable until he discovered that a large hawthorn tree was in the garden of a house in Jena, Germany where he spent the first summer of his life. It is not important that he remembers nothing else about this house. In fact, for Harries it represents a more generalized association of an original house and the desire to reconstruct the past in a manner that renders the present more accessible and meaningful. Acts of reclaiming an original past intend and serve to "schematize our idea of the archetypal home," in a manner that can stabilize and inform actions in the present.[13]

Memories associated with childhood houses can deeply inform views of the world, and powerfully influence attitudes about domesticity. Phenomenology's interest in ontological experiences of the world includes sympathies with the importance of origins. For Bachelard, the "first house" of an individual's origins is a significant component of self-definition: "The house we were born in has engraved within us the hierarchy of the various functions of inhabiting." He calls this the "unforgettable house."[14]

It is also where architects, either consciously or unconsciously, begin their considerations of house design. According to the Swiss architect Peter Zumthor, memory plays an essential role in his work. He recalls from childhood his aunt's naturally conceived kitchen and presents it as emerging from the natural order of the world:

> I remember the sound of gravel under my feet, the soft glean of the waxed oak staircase, I can hear the heavy front door closing behind me as I walk along the dark corridor and enter the kitchen, the only really brightly lit room in the house… Everything about this kitchen was typical of a traditional kitchen. There was nothing special about it. But perhaps it was just the fact that it was so very much, so very naturally, a kitchen that has imprinted its memory indelibly on my mind.

Zumthor's story illustrates the capacity of architecture to structure one's consciousness, but also how architecture is structured by conscious, or unconscious, memories. He concludes: "The atmosphere of this room is insolubly linked with my idea of a kitchen," and that "Memories like these contain the deepest architectural experiences that I know. They are the reservoirs of the architectural atmospheres and images that I explore as an architect."[15]

The formative dwelling in architectural theory

The formative dwelling has enjoyed a mythical status in theory similar to the divinely embodied dwellings of traditional cultures. Congruent with the goals

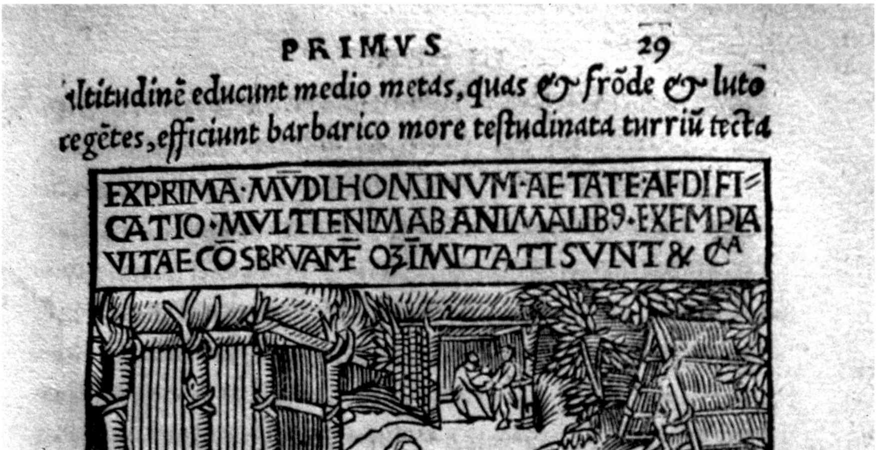

PRIMVS 29

altitudinē educunt medio metas, quas & frōde & lutō
tegētes, efficiunt barbarico more testudinata turriū tecta

Phriges vero qui in cāpestribus locis sunt habitātes ꝓ
pter inopiā syluarū egētes materia, eligunt tumulos natu
rales, eosq; medios fossura exinaniētes, & itinera perfo

FIGURE 3.3 *Origin of the Dwelling House*, Vitruvius

of mythology, its deployment served as a means to historically situate particular principles of architecture and present them as irreducible fundamentals. The formative dwelling was often employed during transitional periods in which previously unified values became unstable and the renewal of architecture deemed necessary.[16] Because of attributions regarding its formative origins, it often served as an unassailable foil,[17] and it was adaptable to a variety of complementary positions – idealistic, materialistic, deterministic, and evolutionary.

Vitruvius, in addition to self-deprecating addresses to Augustus, often prefaced the chapters of his *Ten Books on Architecture* with mythical accounts or references to the "ancients," presumably as a means to situate his subjects in formative and fundamental contexts. Vitruvius' origin stories are particularly prominent in his descriptions of the origins of the Doric, Ionic, and Corinthian orders. The latter begins with the grave of a young "maiden of Corinth" and reads like a Greek tragic myth. An acanthus plant magically spreads to "bend into volutes" from underneath a tile placed to hold offerings, and is discovered and replicated by the sculptor Callimachus. Clearly a myth, it claims history to establish an authoritative construct for architecture.[18]

In *Book II*, Vitruvius created a mythical account of the origin of the first "dwelling house" that would prove to be formative itself – a ubiquitous source and reference point for origin stories that followed. He describes the discovery of fire, which leads to language, and then deliberate assembly and social interaction, cumulating in the birth of architecture. As presented by Vitruvius, primitive men first created shelter to modify and improve their environment; next, they attributed it with the establishment of a meaningful place; and last, they connected it with the divine. In his story, the creation of the house is conflated with the establishment of language, political discourse, and civilization. He goes on to describe how as their construction skills increased, "they next gradually advanced from the construction of buildings to the other arts and sciences, and so passed from a rude and barbarous mode of life to civilization and refinement."[19] In Vitruvius' brief exposition, the house is not mere shelter, but emblematic and catalytic of culture – a center from which civilization was conceived and born, and even as a metaphor for civilization itself.

There is a strain of Platonism in Vitruvius' presentation of archetypal origins.[20] According to Robin Dripps, Vitruvius moves "outside history" to present his theories as "mythic and archetypal." Consequently, by means of a conflation of "history and myth," he establishes an "ideal" and thus constructs an authoritative position.[21] But, when he mentions that men were naturally imitative, illustrated by examples of less developed architecture in the Roman Empire, he also creates a culturally evolutionary history of Roman architecture.

Vitruvius' original dwelling story is also about ontological placemaking in an otherwise indeterminate world, sentiments that appear in stories by other theoreticians. However, throughout the formative dwelling's lengthy lineage, it plays diverse and even contradictory roles.

Leon Battista Alberti, who took many of his cues from Vitruvius in his own ten books on architecture, also described the origins of architecture, but in a curiously truncated manner. He introduces the subject in *Book I* in a very promising manner by stating, "what follows may be taken as the correct account of the whole matter," but what follows is a very modest presentation on the origins of the house. He states, "in the beginning," men sought a harmonious place to dwell and quickly partitioned their dwellings to satisfy certain functions – "sleeping," "hearth," and "other spaces" for "different uses."[22] He then vaguely suggests that the "goddess Vesta, daughter of Saturn, or the brothers Heurialus and Hiperbius, or Gallio, or Thraso, or the Cyclops Typhincius" may be deserving of credit for the first dwellings.[23] Apparently satisfied that an authoritative foundation has been established, he leaves origins and turns to descriptions of the principal components of architecture.

Not all promulgators of fundamentals needed the primitive hut. Henry Wotton's recasting of the Vitruvian triad in *The Elements of Architecture* made no mention of it. Bannister Fletcher noted that architecture began with caves, huts, and tents, but added nothing else. Many did, though, but often for distinctly different, and typically ideological, reasons. Gottfried Semper, in *The Four Elements of Architecture* of 1851, pinned his theories of architecture more firmly to origins than Alberti, and presented a story remarkably similar to Vitruvius' when he wrote:

> The first sign of human settlement and rest after the hunt, the battle, and wandering in the desert is today, as when the first men lost paradise, the setting up of the fireplace and the lighting of the reviving, warming, and food-preparing flame. Around the hearth the first groups assembled; around it the first alliances formed; around it the first rude religious concepts were put into the customs of a cult. Throughout all phases of society the hearth formed that sacred focus around which the whole took order and shape.[24]

Similar to Vitruvius, Semper's formative hut is a place where human discourse and culture were born, and where ontological understandings of the world and one's place in it were articulated. According to Mari Hvattum, Semper argues that the primary impetus of human constructs is "to make sense of the world."[25] But Semper's self-created myth, like some of his eighteenth-

and nineteenth-century contemporaries, is more self-consciously constructed as a means to empirically argue that four primary elements comprise architecture – the hearth, roof, enclosure, and mound.[26] The Caribbean hut he discovered at the Great Exhibition of 1851 in London became a model for his evolutionary position where the four elements result from intrinsic human needs and the rituals of construction to serve them.[27]

His contemporary, Eugène Viollet-le-Duc, also created an origin myth, but in this case to lend authority to his materialist and evolutionary theories of architecture, and valorize the medieval. In *The Habitations of Man in All Ages*, two figures, Doxius and Epergos, discover a crude, primitive tribe (illustrated by their inadequate shelters and diet that includes reptiles). Epergos, touched by their "misery," demonstrates how to build an improved hut by first bending down two saplings and tying them together at their tops, and then weaving an enclosure with other light branches. It is coated with mud and the floor of the round hut beaten smooth. Afterwards, all of the Nairriti (as he names them) want a hut just like this original. The logical and structurally based shelter mimics the structural logic of the medieval (or at least as Viollet-le-Duc saw it), and lends authority to his argument as to what constitutes an authentic architecture.

Le Corbusier had ideological goals of his own in his apocryphal version of an architectural creation myth in *Towards a New Architecture* of 1923:

> Primitive man has brought his chariot to a stop, he decides that here shall be his native soil. He chooses a glade, he cuts down the trees which are too close, he levels the earth around; he opens up the road which will carry him to the river or to those of his tribe whom he has just left; he drives in the stakes which are to steady his tent. He surrounds his tent with a palisade in which he arranges a doorway. The road is as straight as he can manage it with his implements, his arms and his time. The pegs of his tent inscribe a square, a hexagon or an octagon. The palisade forms a rectangle whose four angles are equal. The door of his hut is on the axis of the enclosure – the door of the enclosure faces exactly the door of the hut.[28]

This is a curious story from a self-defined apostle of ahistorical, progressive modernism, but one that is understandable as a deployment of origins to lend authority to a theoretical position. Le Corbusier's "hut" recalls the Biblical tabernacle, and he goes on to describe how these formative dwellings became the first temples. More importantly, he constructs the story to argue that, from the very beginning, geometry and proportion governed the making of architecture, intuitively arrived at by humans free from the limitations of history and style. When he states "there is no such thing as primitive man; there are primitive

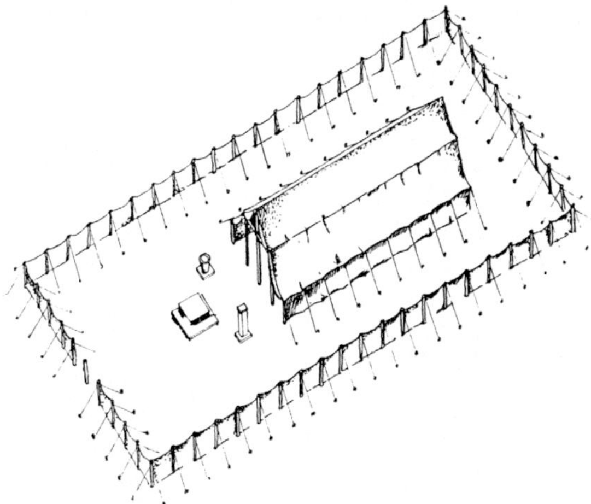

FIGURE 3.4 Le Corbusier, primitive hut

FIGURE 3.5 Marc-Antoine Laugier, *The Primitive Hut*, engraving by Charles Eisen

resources. The idea is constant, in full sway from the beginning,"[29] he historically validates his deterministic theories generally, and his Modulor proportioning system specifically. For Le Corbusier, origin and original were synonymous.

Equally paradoxical, and perhaps the most well-known use of an idiosyncratic and ideological origin myth, is Marc-Antoine Laugier's influential *An Essay on Architecture*. In the first chapter, appropriately entitled "General Principles of Architecture," he imagines a formative, four-posted and roofed hut to illustrate prototypical elements of the column, entablature, and pediment. Laugier wrote during a time when a search for origins was obsessively pursued by many disciplines. His myth is in service of rationally establishing irrefutable principles of architecture, and arguing for the superiority of classical architecture.[30] Consequently, his "thought experiment"[31] alludes to the essential conditions of the natural world and logically leads to championing classical architecture. Thus when he argues, "All the splendors of architecture ever conceived have been modeled on the little rustic hut," he presents an *arche-tecture* of archetypes, situated in timeless origins, as unassailable models.[32] When Laugier exclaims, "let us never lose sight of our little rustic hut!" he means it much more literally than Vitruvius' or Semper's more philosophical tracts. Indeed, he concludes this section by extolling the virtues of the Maison Carrée, the Roman temple in Nîmes, "where everything… accords with the true principles of architecture."[33] Laugier's valorizing of the classical through the deployment of myth has more to do with his particular prejudices and their cultural grounding than they do about its origins. In his mythical construct, the primitive hut is actually modeled on the classical temple, and not the other way around.[34]

Like Le Corbusier, and arguably Viollet-le-Duc and Laugier, Frank Lloyd Wright also created a version of an origin myth to support his formal and stylistic arguments. In his story, there were originally two types of men: cave dwellers and those who lived in tents on the open plains. The former "troglodytes" were inferior, superstitious, and subservient city dwellers – the plains people were freethinking, independent, and democratic country dwellers. He confidently, and without qualification, recounts the following "history."

> Go back far enough in time. Mankind was divided into cave-dwelling agrarians and wandering tribes of hunter-warriors… The static cave dweller was ancient conservative. Probably he was more brutal, if not more ferocious, with his heavy club when occasion arose than the mobile wanderer with his slender spear. The cave dweller became cliff dweller. He began to build cities. Establishment was his idea. His God was a malicious murderer. His own statue, made by himself more terrible than himself, was really his God; a God also hiding away. He erected this God

> into a mysterious covenant. When he could he made his God of gold. He still does.
>
> But his swifter, more mobile brother devised a more adaptable and elusive dwelling place – the folding tent. He, nomad, went in changing season from place to place, over the whole earth, following the laws of change: natural to him. He was the Adventurer. His God was a Spirit: like the wind, devastating or beneficent as he was himself.[35]

Wright's self-constructed history says more about his anti-urban sentiments and sentimental beliefs in the authenticity of the American Midwest than they establish any credible construct of the beginnings of architecture; nor do they describe any particular ways to create an authentic house based on models from the past. They do serve to introduce the Prairie Style house Wright created for his imagined superior "man," one that was centered on the archetypal hearth but also open to the surrounding, redemptive countryside.

In origin myths of these types, dependable beginnings establish dependable foundations. Moreover, often implicit (if not explicit) is that the creation of the formative dwelling happens naturally. The architecture emerges as a complete and perfect exemplar, untarnished by intellectualization or cultural impositions. Adolf Loos may have acidly dismissed the decorative habits of foreign cultures as degenerate but, in a 1910 essay entitled simply "Architecture," he extolls the virtues of local peasant dwellings on a lakeside. They are equated with a type of god-given naturalism when he writes:

> May I take you to the shores of a mountain lake? The sky is blue, the water green and everywhere is profound tranquility. The clouds and mountains are mirrored in the lake, the house, farms and chapels as well. They do not look as if they were fashioned by man, it is as if they came straight from God's workshop, like the mountains and trees, the clouds and the blue sky.

He goes on to attribute the insufficiency of newer dwellings created by "architects" to their separation from nature and the divine. The peasant, on the other hand, enjoys such essential connections, primordial and immediate like those of animals. He continues:

> The peasant wanted to build a house for himself, his kin and his cattle, and he has succeeded. As his neighbor and his ancestor succeeded. As the animal succeeds, guided by his instincts. Is the house beautiful? Yes, just as beautiful as the rose and the thistle, the horse and the cow.[36]

FIGURE 3.6 *Scholar's Dwelling in the Mountains*, formerly attributed to Ma Yuan

Similar arguments appear in Frank Lloyd Wright's *The Natural House* of 1954 regarding the virtue of an original relationship to the world. He recounts how when he was eleven years old, he was "sent to a Wisconsin farm to learn how to really work," an experience that would "keep me from ever finding satisfaction in anything superficial," and producing a "determination to search for the qualities in all things."[37] He presented the self-titled prairie style as naturally emerging from the Midwestern landscape in a manner that, like Loos' peasant dwellings, reflected the natural life of its inhabitants.

Louis Kahn's often vaguely stated theories were focused on formative beginnings of an almost primordial and archetypal "order." When he simply states, "order is," he also shares the convictions of others that true architectural principles emerge naturally. And, in Christopher Alexander's theories regarding an essential and authentic architecture, as articulated in *The Timeless Way of Building* and *A Pattern Language*, the "quality without a name" suggests a type of timeless ideal. Alexander argues that once these vaguely primordial but authoritative elements are understood, the architecture will naturally make itself. More significantly, his models are remedies for the insufficiencies of the contemporary built environment.

The spiritually imbued hermit scholar's retreat

To greater or lesser degrees, the theoreticians I cited relied on dependable lineages from a presumably more stable and authentic past to provide antidotes for a culturally and ontologically deficient present.[38] An example of a medieval Japanese Zen Buddhist temple and its entry path illustrates a particular appropriation of origins, lineages, and the primitive hut, and further explicates the topics and themes I have explored. In Zen Buddhism, the austere hermit scholar's retreat was often depicted in landscape paintings as the setting for an authentic life and a threshold to the unconditioned realms of enlightenment. These metaphorical dwellings were also situated in myth. They were typically characterized as the formative dwellings of the first monasteries – founded by enlightened monks as spiritual retreats but eventually joined by the huts of acolytes.[39] Histories of the extensive and culturally important Rinzai Zen Buddhist monastery Daitoku-ji in Kyoto unequivocally describe its founding by Daito Kokushi as a remote hermitage in the mountains, a specific but not unique history, or myth, as it were.

Japanese literature from the medieval period also features accounts regarding the virtues of the primitive and portentous abode. Kamo no Chomei, after recounting the calamities of his time, asks, "What place can you live, what activities can you pursue, in order to ensure a haven for your body and bring

FIGURE 3.7 Entry path, Koto-in, Daitoku-ji, Kyoto, Japan

even a moment of peace to your mind?" His answer is to build an austere dwelling in the mountains:

> My present place is quite unlike any ordinary dwelling. It measures only ten-feet square and less than seven feet in height… Since I came here to hide my traces in the depth of Mount Hino, on the east side of my hut I have extended the eaves out for three feet so as to provide a place for firewood and cooking. On the south I constructed a bamboo verandah, with a shelf for vases and other Buddhist articles at the western end. The north side I blocked off with a partition, and adorned it with an image of Amida, the bodhisattva Fugen by his side; a copy of *The Lotus Sutra* is placed before them. Along the east edge of the room I've spread soft fern fronds to make a place to sleep at night. In the southwest corner I put up a hanging shelf of bamboo with three leather-covered boxes on it. These are for my books on Japanese poetry and music and for selections from the Buddhist writings such as the *Ojoyoshu* (Essentials of Salvation). Beside them stand my koto and my biwa… Such is the layout of this little temporary dwelling of mine.[40]

For the author, his dwelling was reciprocal with an ephemeral and impermanent world, and where the Western paradise of the Amida Buddha could be contemplated. Teahouses of the medieval period also displayed utopian sentiments of spiritual transformation. They took cues from rustic farmhouses, emulating their simple constructions and materials, including a type of clay daub wall, to achieve a highly codified aesthetic. The restraint of their design and application of authentic materials was associated with *wabi-sabi*, an aesthetic of studied imperfection particularly expressed in celebrated ceramic tea bowls. The highly choreographed rituals of the tea ceremony were bounded by carefully defined aesthetic parameters designed to achieve a natural informality. They were a spiritual practice of sorts, which was adopted by the military aristocracy of this time. According to Okakura Kakuzo, a well-known source of medieval "teaism," tea masters "wished to create the attitude of a newly-awakened soul still lingering amid shadowy dreams of the past, yet bathing in the sweet consciousness of a mellow spiritual light, and yearning for the freedom that lay in the expanse beyond."[41]

If the first monasteries symbolized remote hermitages of enlightened beings, then a journey or pilgrimage to access them and what they promised was required. That the pilgrimage to the sacred abode of a Zen master came to be symbolically represented by the *hojo*, or abbot's quarters, of Japanese Zen Buddhist temples, particularly in their entry paths and gardens, is an expected if not inevitable outcome. Akin to the poetic "dewy path" of teahouses, it elongated the experience of entry by articulate thresholds and spatial sequences designed to engender kinesthetic and haptic experiences in service of spiritual preparation. Koto-in, a sub-temple of Daitoku-ji, recalls formative models by a skillfully choreographed series of articulate paths, spaces, gateways, and thresholds that lead to the *hojo*.[42]

Hojo translates as "one jo" (tatami) square, a reference to a prototypical teahouse but also to a legendary mythical space where the Buddhist sage Vimalakirti, mentioned earlier, was said to have accommodated a multitude. The simple hut, carefully positioned and ritually attained, marks a sacred center while also establishing connections to vast Mahayana cosmologies. The representation of a sacred abode of an enlightened master asserts that the monastery is a spiritually propitious place, and establishes the unique capacity of the *hojo* to render history, and the promise of enlightenment, ever-present. And so, this concluding example illustrates how an origin myth potently informed the house's creation, and structured the rituals and meanings it housed.

★★★

A lengthy treatise by Epergos concludes Viollet-le-Duc's book, including a statement that could have introduced it. "The time has come for us to say to humanity: investigate thy beginnings: thou wilt learn thy aptitudes, and wilt be able to pursue that path of true Progress to which thy destiny calls thee...."[43] That time, it appears, has come numerous times in the history of architecture and theory. As Rykwert reminds us, "The return to origins is a constant of human development and in this matter architecture conforms to all other human activities."[44] Examining architecture's roots in, and references to, formative domestic structures can productively contextualize its various roles, agendas, and materializations. According to the historian E. Baldwin Smith, "Architecture was on the way to becoming something more than mere construction when simple huts acquired in the imagination of men the significance of a type, an ideal, a concept, to which was associated meaning and importance."[45] That is, the human search for meaning has origins in the domestic.

However, preoccupations with the origins of architecture and its situation in the domestic can seem anachronistic in contemporary discourse, and the mythical cave, tent, and hut fictions from eras that needed them.[46] Histories and theories that enlist the formative hut for support are often suspect, as they reveal mere, and even arbitrary, constructs in service of particular stylistic, polemical, or political agendas. Laugier presented the "little rustic hut" as a timeless exemplar, but his theories were deeply rooted in the preoccupations of his time with nature, natural man, and the sources of human history, and reflected matters of taste more than principles.[47] The formative hut also becomes problematic when traditional dwellings are presented as meaning-imbued exemplars in service of Western cultural chauvinism.[48] And, even though the trope of origins and the original house has been a consistent theoretical interest, not all upheld its value, especially in eighteenth-century reconsiderations of the classical. Quatremère de Quincy may have presented the cave, tent, and hut as fundamental types, but he also challenged the *arche* of architecture and attendant historical continuities. For Quatremère, "If there is an art that hides its origins, it is *architecture*," and "There is nothing more difficult, even with the help of history and traditions, than to fix the *first beginnings* of human inventions."[49]

So what can be gained by understandings of the phenomenon of the formative hut in cultural and theoretical histories? First, they reveal the human quest for certainty, and dependable sources for culturally affirming and ontologically productive architecture. As such, they are congruent with the search for meaning through artifice. As previously noted, humans stand "Upright and gazing upon the splendor of the starry firmament" in Vitruvius' "The Origin of the Dwelling House," an ontological position from which to comprehend the enormity, precariousness, and unpredictability of the cosmos. But, even though they stand apart from nature, in Vitruvius' account it is clear they are also part of it. Consequently, by imitating idealized nature, the original hut reflects divine sources.[50] The persistence of origin stories evidence the need for, and capacity of, architecture to house the ontological position of humans in the world and explicate their relationship to it. Accordingly, the original dwelling in some accounts has the capacity to effect spiritual transformation – Philemon and Baucis' hut becomes a temple, the *Casa Romuli* a place of worship, and the *hojo* a portentous setting for enlightenment. For Bachelard, the primitive hut is a metaphor for "youthful certainty of being," where life can be started anew and a more authentic one created.[51]

To varying degrees, the formative dwelling has reflected the search for dependable lineages of architecture, the desire for immutable truths, and the need to restore humanity to a previous (and better) state. Origins can also be characterized as other stories about the house and, like the stories of the previous chapter, may reveal particular motivations and projections regarding the domestic. In Quatremère's *Dictionnaire*, the "hut" may be the "first adumbration," but can "find a place in the dictionary of architecture only in an abstract and theoretical respect."[52] Theoretical concepts, not material origins, were his interests. Consequently, he asserts that origins are best applied as theories, or means to insightfully interrogate the past. Even though many writings on the formative hut are more about their time than the timeless, the ideals they embraced demand attention because they reveal the tension in any age between historical continuities and the needs and spirit of the present.[53] Without historical memory, people risk being adrift, cut off from their cultural foundations and rendered ontologically homeless. That origins and primitive huts speak more about the desire to reclaim cultural and ontological certainty than they deliver is secondary to recognizing the timeless, and original, human quest to do so.[54] Even the beginnings of architectural theory assume significance in the persistence of Vitruvius' description of the first dwelling house.

Rykwert states:

> The primitive hut – the house of the first man – is therefore no incidental concern of theorists, no casual ingredient of myth or ritual. The return to origins always implies a rethinking of what you do customarily, an attempt to renew the validity of your everyday actions, or simply a recall of the natural (or even divine) sanction for your repeating them for a season.[55]

Because origin myths regarding the formative hut and the beginnings of architecture exist independent of history in Vitruvius' account, they transcend the mere instrumentality of shelter. In this manner, they suggest a higher purpose for houses and homes, and for architecture itself. For Dripps, "language plays a critical role" in Vitruvius' account, which suggests that architecture "might have an autonomous existence independent of external contingency,"[56] and, like language, architecture is a means by which humans have structured their understandings of existence. In this manner, origins, the original house, and the primitive hut can be understood as particular, and particularly potent, renderings of how house and home have been tasked with materializing certainty in an uncertain world.

4

SACRED DOMESTICITIES

Houses for divinity, divinity of home

Origin myths often served to valorize cultural and theoretical positions by situating the formative dwelling in dependable histories. This chapter presents the ways in which house and home were often positioned in the sacred. From the earliest days, humans needed shelter, and even though in some instances they were minimal, impromptu, or temporary, many settlement-building cultures built architecturally significant houses. As dwellings were elaborated over time, they transcended mere shelter and, through form, size, location, orientation, and decoration, embodied symbols that communicated a diverse range of cultural and ontological content. The house, as the center for kinship groups, also at times became the center of religious and social life. In some cases, the house represented the cosmos and assumed sacred functions for peoples who believed they were responsible for maintaining the orders of the world. Social hierarchies were often paired with responsibilities of this type, and houses tasked with serving them. This was not always the case, but when it was, kinship determined where one lived and settlements were arranged hierarchically, with houses of rulers distinguished by their location, form, or decoration. Dwellings could also be created for divinities, and were designed and materialized to represent them, and provide spaces for their worship. In this chapter, I will present houses for divinity, the incorporation of sacred settings in houses, the house as cosmogram and cosmogony, and the house and settlement as socio-political constructs, to further contextualize the various roles, agendas, and materializations of house and home.

Traditions and lineages

The categories I have just outlined are a means, but not an end, to organize historically and culturally diverse examples. With this caveat, and as means to further contextualize the subject, I will introduce a number of historically deterministic theories regarding the interrelationship of house and sanctuary. Recalling the lineages of origin myths and how they served to establish authority through historical constructs, some have proposed historical lineages that trace significant sacred architecture to domestic roots. Two in particular illustrate these approaches: the historian E. Baldwin Smith's "palace–temple concept," and a palace–house theory by the aristocratic scholar Lord Raglan.[1]

Smith argued that the temple was a logical result of developments from house to palace to temple. Regarding lineages of Egyptian architecture, he stated, "The house, in its simplest and ancient beginnings, was man's first architectural effort. The concept of the house must, therefore, underlie all subsequent architectural needs,"[2] and turning to Roman, Byzantine, and Islamic examples argued:

> It is axiomatic that from the remoter time when men began to visualize their deities as like themselves in need of shelter, and then began to see in their rulers either priest-kings or god-kings, the palace and temple developed as interrelated forms of architecture. In every theocratic society, where the royal dwelling was revered as a sacred edifice, temples were customarily built like palaces, or palaces like temples.[3]

According to his argument, the first sanctuaries evolved from the houses of the priests or rulers, who were often the same. As a place of consultation and judgment, power, prestige, and mystery, and the setting for rituals, large and small, enacted to ensure the health and longevity of rulers (and by extension their subjects and world), the house assumed significance as a primal and portentous place. Even religious rituals can be understood as emanating from early domestic devotional acts of serving the ruler-god.[4] Accordingly, the reciprocity of the sacred and secular in ancient cultures suggests that the transition from the house of the ruler-god to that of the god-ruler was a logical and natural one. Mircea Eliade stated a similar but more general concept when he suggested, "Religious architecture simply took over and developed cosmological symbolism already present in the structure of primitive habitations."[5]

Not long after Smith proposed his theory, Lord Raglan penned a counterargument that it was, in fact, the other way around. His palace–house theory insisted that all began with palaces for divine rulers; only later were houses built, which took their cues from their predecessors. As evidence, he cites the absence of houses in some primitive cultures and the prevalence of temples in most cultures. Because early cultures had limited material and technological means, people primarily applied them to the dwellings of their most important personages – deified rulers. He went on to suggest that because many cultures devoted considerable reverence for the sacred fire, early sanctuaries were created to house it – and not humans – an early form of a house for god. Additionally, because the needs and activities of the gods were preeminent, temples, and also tombs, were created as the eternal residences of ruler-gods.[6]

E. Baldwin Smith also proposed another intriguing theory, this time regarding lineages of domed houses and temples. He suggested that early houses were circular in plan and covered by expediency by curved roofs of whatever light and flexible materials were available. According to his argument, the dome, an essential architectural element of particular lineages of Hindu, Christian, and Islamic sacred architecture, evolved from the earliest domestic architecture. Eventually (or inevitably), it came to potently conflate the home as an ontologically imbued center, and the domed sanctuary as the center of the cosmos.[7] Even though not consistently applicable, there are many examples of dwellings that support Smith's thesis. In some cultures tents, pit houses, and earth lodges display formal and symbolic similarities, with the floor typically representing the earth, the ceiling the sky, and the walls the cardinal points. Ananda Coomaraswamy corroborated Smith's theory with one of his own, which was that Indian domical sacred architecture evolved from primitive, wooden, domed huts.[8] Certainly, the dome has enjoyed preeminence in the history of global sacred architecture – the symbolic potency of Hindu temples, Mughal tombs, Ottoman mosques, Roman civic and religious architecture, and Christian churches, martyria, and baptisteries is unimaginable without it.

Historical continuities of domical dwellings and domed sanctuaries may be difficult to establish, but their capacity to symbolize ontologically potent places is more dependable. Dome and *domus* ("house" in Latin and Greek) are etymologically related suggesting common domestic beginnings.[9] In some cases round, vaulted houses, as discussed earlier, represented a people's world. This symbolization also appears in mature, sacred architecture. In *Isaiah*, the world is a domical space created by god, who "established heaven as a vaulted chamber and stretched it out as a tent to dwell in" (Is 40:22).[10] Associations between the dome and domesticity find particular expression in Byzantine churches where an omnipotent Christ is often shown at the center of the dome. Christ Pantocrator (Christ Almighty or the Sustainer) occupies the apex of a dome in the inner narthex of St. Savior in Chora, an early sanctuary built outside the city walls of Byzantine Constantinople. His ancestors, beginning with Adam, surround him in a series of concentric rings.[11] Here the Christian conceptualization of

FIGURE 4.1 Mosaic, dome, inner narthex, St. Savior, Chora, Istanbul, Turkey

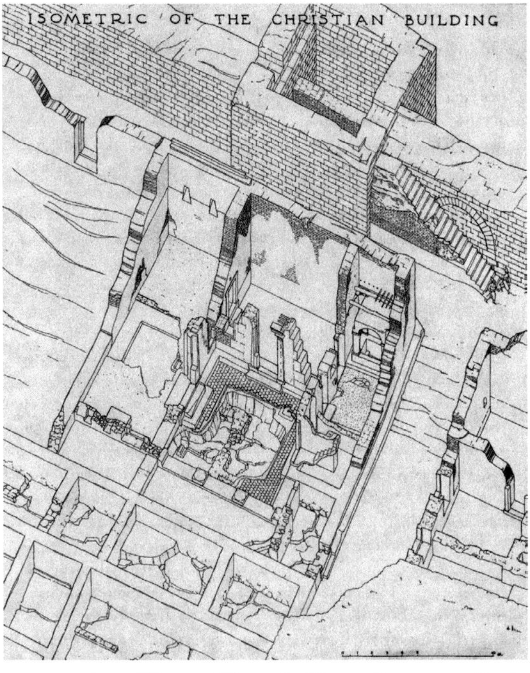

FIGURE 4.2 Reconstruction, House Church, Dura-Europos, Syria

the *Domus Dei*, the house of god, includes its patrilineal history dating from the beginning of time, and the architectural manner by which they are to be housed. Moreover, representations of Christ as Pantocrator symbolized his role as central and essential to the founding and sustaining of the world. At its center, Christ, the *pater familias* of the house of god, performs a sustaining role for humankind, similar to what the head of the Roman household did for his family, and the emperor did for the Roman Empire.

Another possible congruence between house and temple is the Greek megaron and the classical temple. The *megaron* was an early domicile that comprised a central hall with a hearth at its center and a front porch created by extended side walls. Norman Crowe outlined an evolution over time and numerous transformations of the Mycenaean megaron to the Classical Greek temple.[12] In his lineage, the simple becomes complex – the house of the deity a replication and elaboration of domestic models. Furthermore, recalling William Chamberlain's eighteenth-century deterministic theory, he argues that stone eventually replaced the original wooden constructions, providing a further materialization of the enduring house of god.[13] In this case, the endurance of architecture signifies the endurance of the gods and, by extension, the culture that depends on them.[14] Archeological evidence of substantial megaron palaces have been found in the Mycenaean cities of Troy, Pylos, and Mycenae where large hypaethral halls housed a central hearth, which was used for ceremonies and sacrifices, an offering table, and the king's throne.[15] Their form and organization suggest a logical development to the later prostyle and peristyle temples, where the great hall and throne of the king transformed to become the *cella* for an enthroned statue of the deity. As in the megaron palace, early temples also may have included a hearth before it found its more typical location in the forecourt of the temple.[16]

The development of the first Christian churches suggests other intriguing lineages. Early Christians worshipped in small groups in private homes, and their "house churches" adapted domestic architecture to facilitate the nascent rituals of the formative faith. Much has been written about the first "domus ecclesia," and lineages from the house church to early atrium churches routinely suggested. Often cited is a third-century CE house church in Dura-Europos, a Hellenistic city on the banks of the Euphrates in present-day Syria and an important center of the young faith.[17] Here a two-story atrium house, with a vestibule fronting the street leading to a peristyle courtyard, was transformed into a place only for worship. The uses of some of the rooms is unclear, but it has been established that one room was converted to a baptistery and two joined together for the sanctuary. The atrium served as a classroom for the catechumens, the unbaptized who were forbidden from entering the sacred

FIGURE 4.3 Old St. Peter's, Rome

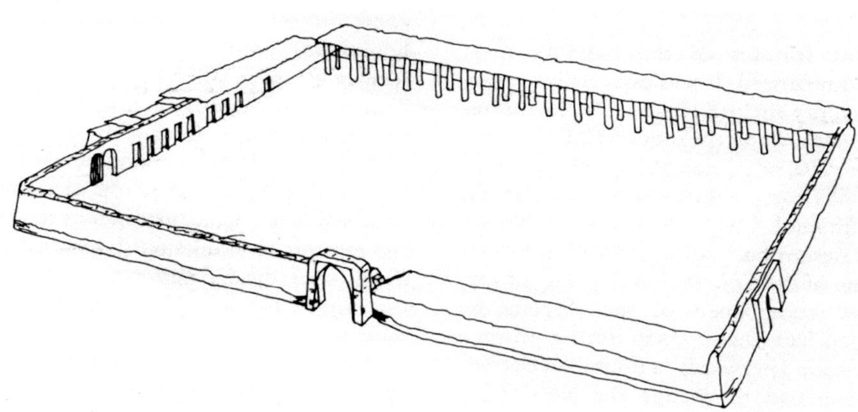

FIGURE 4.4 Medina, House of the Prophet

sanctuaries.[18] This was an early spatial and liturgical hierarchy that came to characterize the organization of the Christian church as it developed.

Eventually the growing faith needed specialized buildings for worship. Even though early house churches established specific liturgical spaces, their influence on church architecture is unclear. J. G. Davies presented a variety of often-competing theories regarding the development of Christian church architecture, concluding that there were actually a number of possible routes to its early dominant type, the Constantinian or Latin basilica. The Roman atrium house may have been an influence, with spaces dedicated to specific functions corresponding to the liturgical spaces of the basilica. Davies cites scholarship that suggested that the *tablinum* of the Roman house, the recess for the hearth and altar for the family gods where the *pater familias* received guests, became the tribunal and bishop's seat, or that the cistern and table in the atrium corresponded to the altar and baptismal, only to dismiss them as unsupported speculation.[19] Alternatively, in a provocative furthering of evolutionary theories regarding the Greek temple, he suggested as more supportable a lineage that begins with the megaron house, transforms into the Greek temple, and eventually informs the Christian basilica.[20]

Perhaps a more plausible correspondence is the incorporation of elements and hierarchies from early house churches into Latin basilican churches, the favored type of the early faith. An early example is Old St. Peter's in Rome, which was built by Constantine and dates from the fourth century CE. It featured an impressive set of steps that ascended to a portico, beyond which was an equally impressive atrium where the catechumens received instruction. The five doors of the aisled basilica fronted this space, marking the boundary between the secular and the sacred, an organization typical of the early church, where sanctuary, sacristy, baptistery, and other liturgical spaces were hierarchically organized.

Just as early church architecture has been attributed to the domestic, the first mosque, at least in some accounts, is traced to the Prophet Muhammad's house in Medina. Islam was founded in the sixth century CE, and it is believed that its founder's house in Medina served as the first sanctuary and even prototypical mosque. Muhammad built it for his family after escaping the increasingly hostile Mecca. The house no longer exists, having been replaced by a successive number of mosques, but it has been dependably described by numerous sources.[21] It was a simple, austere domicile, just nine small rooms for the family located outside the wall of a large courtyard. The size of the walled courtyard exceeded domestic requirements (and the purported austerity of the Prophet), suggesting its use as a congregational space for the religious community. In this case, domestic conventions were adapted to create a house and sanctuary and, according to Robert Hillenbrand, "laid down the norms for the central religious building type of the new community."[22]

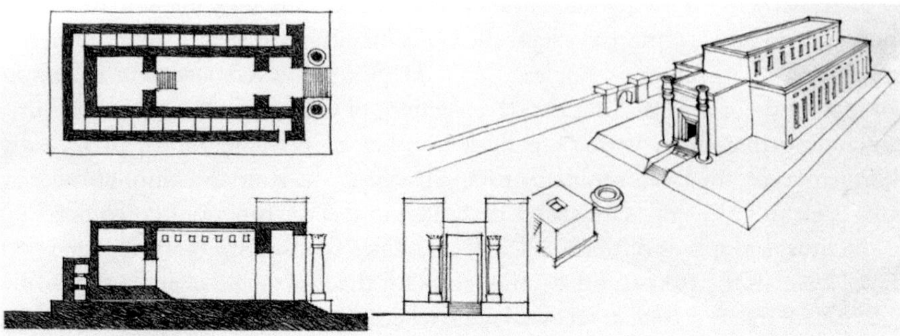

FIGURE 4.5 Reconstruction, Solomon's Temple

FIGURE 4.6 *The Healing of the Lame Man*, Raphael

One of the plain walls of the courtyard was designated the *quibla,* or the wall that originally faced Jerusalem. Inside, the court included a *zulla* ("shaded place"), a double row of palm trunks with a roof of palm leaves affixed with mud plaster, to provide shade for the "companions" when they prayed. When the *quibla* was changed to indicate the direction of Mecca (after Muhammad's revelation to orient prayer to the Kaa'ba), the *zulla* was rebuilt in a new location and was big enough to shelter 100 adherents. In this prototypical Islamic building, there was a particular integration of the domestic and the sacred, and a political center and a sacred place. However, it was not a house for god (Muhammad was not considered divine), but a spiritual and political leader's house adapted for a new faith.

Houses for god

Early religions attributed consciousness, special powers, and divinity to environmental elements and animals. Eventually, these beliefs evolved into deities with human-like qualities. Consequently, the human gods required a home to be able to live among their people, often with very specific locations, organizations, spaces, and materials to serve their needs. When this was the case, specific requirements for housing the divine were outlined in scripture. Solomon's Temple, the *domus dei par excellence*, is presented in *1 Kings* as the "house of the Lord," a specific place for god to "dwell among the children of Israel," (1 Kings 6:1–38) and its location, dimensions, spaces, and materials described in detail. The visions of *Ezekiel* similarly conveyed what the house of the Lord needed to be and, as Ezekiel is guided through the rooms of the temple, each is explicitly described, including the holy of holies: "And he measured the length of the room, twenty cubits, and its breadth, twenty cubits beyond the nave. And he said to me, This is the most holy place" (Ez 41:4).

Both of these passages have provided inspirations and aspirations for church building ever since. In particular, there has been an enduring fascination with Solomon's Temple, and one finds references to it in numerous examples of Christian art and architecture, often as a means to lend authority to lineages from the "first temple."[23] Solomonic columns support the baldachin at St. Peter's in Rome, validating the church as an "original" (e.g. related to origins), Christian edifice. The Abbot Suger, apparently, expressed his admiration for, and aspiration to recall, Solomon's Temple in his building programs at St. Denis, and there is the famous Justinian proclamation, "Solomon, I have outdone thee," on the completion of Saint Sophia in Constantinople. In these cases, the original house of god provides the lineage and justification for positioning the church as the earthly domicile of the divine.

There are also direct references to divine domiciles in the Hindu temple, which is called the "house of God". According to Coomaraswamy, the Hindu temple evolved from early house shrines where Vedic sacrifices were conducted at the central hearth, which housed the fire god Agni.[24] Agni was an interlocutor between humans and the gods and it is not uncommon for him to still be worshipped in Indian homes. According to Coomaraswamy:

> No fundamental distinction can be made between the god-house as such and the dwellings of men, whether huts or palaces, as evident in the case of those cultures, notably the Indian, in which the paterfamilias himself officiates as household priest, daily performing the Agnihotra in the domestic circle.[25]

The site selection, groundbreaking rituals, and design of Hindu temples were specifically outlined and followed to ensure that the deity would "dwell" there. Temples were commonly referred to as "*vamara*" or "well-proportioned," and whether the deity was resident, or not, depending on strict adherence to proportioning systems outlined in detailed texts. The ability of the deities housed in the temple, and the temple itself, to mediate between humans and the world depended on these systems, their authority traced to the *vastu*, a branch of knowledge devoted to architecture, and the *vastu-purusha mandala*, a symbolic representation of the primordial ordering of the cosmos by Brahma.[26] Consequently, in one aspect, the Hindu temple materialized a cosmogony (or formative birth of the universe), and also a cosmology (or form of the universe), and, according to George Michell, a "microscopic image of the universe."[27] Similar to the priests and the gods themselves, the Hindu house for god served as a medium that reflected the order of the world while also maintaining that order.

Domestic sacrality

Just as aspects and elements of the domestic can be identified in religious architecture, sacrality was also found in the domicile. Traditionally, the siting of houses was a quasi-religious ritual where propitious locations were divined to ensure a safe and healthy house and family. Just as the Hindu temple must be correctly sited for the god to dwell there, the best locations for houses were also ritually determined. Similarly, geomantic practices in the East were applied to the siting of palaces, temples, tombs, and cities. [28] Foundation rites worldwide, from sacrificial to benign, were performed to appease, remove, or bar malevolent spirits. Similar to funerary rites and structures, the impetus was often equally fear as reverence. Domestic rituals could also be as choreographed as liturgical rites. Thresholds and doorways, as liminal spaces between the sanctuary of the house and the outside world, often assumed importance, and were marked by a variety of means to protect the house and its inhabitants. Many cultures have prescriptions and prohibitions regarding auspicious ways to enter a house.[29] There are also often specific dictates regarding maintaining the purity of the house, and ritual responses to its pollution by birth, death, or other life events.

Houses often incorporated sacred spaces for worship. Greek houses typically included a shrine for daily devotional practices. The word hearth was synonymous with focus, or center, and the Greek family hearth was perhaps the ultimate sacred space. It was associated with Hestia, the virgin goddess of the house and hearth, and worshipped daily in Greek homes. After a wedding, embers from the bride's home were brought to her new one, and a popular custom was to carry a newborn baby around the hearth as a symbol of their homecoming. In Cicero's words, Hestia's "power extends over all altars and hearths, and therefore all prayers and all sacrifices end with this goddess, because she is the guardian of the innermost things."[30]

In Roman courtyard houses, most dependably illustrated by the Pompeian house, the vestibule, fauces, atrium, tablinum, alae, and peristyle were organized hierarchically from public to private. The outermost vestibule, its name related to Vesta, the Roman equivalent of Hestia, symbolically marked the threshold by recalling the goddess' virginity and resistance to penetration. According to Ovid, the family hearth was located there, establishing the vestibule as the abode of Vesta.[31] The tablinum contained an altar for the penates and lares, the family gods, and was paired with the alae, a space for family portraits – gods and ancestors assuming their rightful place at the center of the house.[32] The house, introverted around its courtyards, constituted a world within itself. Beyond the tablinum was the private peristyle, with a garden that incorporated the natural world as if to invoke its order and regenerative powers.[33] The organization of the Roman courtyard house provided an ontological orientation for living in the world, and according to Clive Knights, was 'the habitat of gods and humans, the material extension of their actions and their gestures as they grapple with the world."[34]

The Roman atrium house also materialized the cultural hierarchy of Roman society with the *pater familias* at its center. The spatial hierarchy of traditional Chinese courtyard houses has been similarly equated with stratified Confucian culture, which defined the family as the primary social unit, and multigenerational families according to rank. Separated from the outside world, it also symbolized the harmonious reconciliation of opposites, centered on its central garden and organized according to a sequence of increasingly private

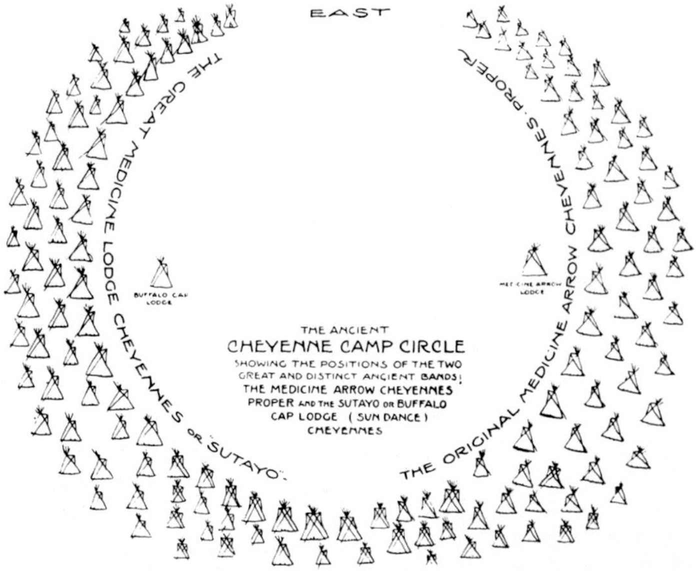

FIGURE 4.7 Cheyenne camp circle

FIGURE 4.8 Taos Pueblo, New Mexico

spaces.[35] Similar to the ancient Greeks and Romans, Chinese daily religion was home centered, and thus many elements of the house were considered sacred.[36]

Home and cosmogram

In the world's major faiths, religious observances on high holy days are conducted at homes and also religious centers. In traditional societies, there was typically no need for both as homes were sacred spaces and served religious needs. The ger is the center of Mongolian domestic and religious life. It is auspiciously oriented to the cardinal directions and centered by a hearth where the fire represents a protective deity. Surrounding the hearth, specific places are designated for particular members of the family, objects, and rituals, and a confluence of Buddhist and animist symbols are accommodated.[37] The Saklava houses of Madagascar are also oriented to the cosmos, but in this case according to the positions of astrological signs. The settlements of the Dogon people of Northern Africa recall the human body, and include anthropomorphically reflective dwellings, especially the *ginuda*, or "big houses," to serve a variety of symbolic and ritual agendas.[38] Each, in particular ways, represent the world of the peoples they shelter.

The human quest to understand the world and their place within it was often reflected in the ordering of the built environment – a potent dialectic in which architecture materialized understandings of the world, while also creating the capacity for furthering them. In this case, architecture was a form of knowledge and also a means of knowledge building. Often the houses of American Indians were cosmograms that symbolized the world and connections with the multiple tiers of the cosmos. As I observed earlier, the origins of the Navaho hogan, or "house place" were positioned at the beginning of time. Their Blessingway Myth was traditionally chanted when a hogan was consecrated (and when periodically re-consecrated), [39] and its cosmic and ceremonial orientations and dispositions communicated and facilitated its roles as an amalgam of the cosmos and the setting for rituals to ensure its continuity.[40]

American Indian architecture was also commonly believed to possess life. Sweat lodges often embodied the animal gods that the rituals sought to connect with, and houses were similarly viewed as animated. But, it was the capacity of the dwelling to represent the cosmos that was perhaps its most meaning-laden and expressive aspect. Just as Mandan earth lodges performed as microcosms of the worlds of their makers,[41] the elements of the Big House of the Eastern Delaware tribe represented the organization of the cosmos. A center wooden post symbolized the support of creation, and was the setting for sacred ceremonies.[42] The conical tents of the Plains Indians also had cosmic symbolizations and ritual uses. For the peoples of the North American plains, the circle was sacred, and thus their dwellings aligned with this formative order of the world. The Sioux word *tipi* means "used to dwell," and they were typically erected with their entrances facing east and around a central hearth. Ceremonial gatherings were likened to a great tipi, and tribes such as the Oglala Sioux and the Cheyenne organized their camps as a series of concentric circles. Like medicine wheels, the circular forms represented the horizon, sun path, time passage, and other environmental conditions in a manner that rendered them accessible, definable, and dependable, and served to represent and even explain the world.[43]

House and settlement as socio-political constructs

The houses and sanctuaries I have presented evidence a diversity of materializations of sacrality and a variety of means to house the divine. They often served to order a people's world and situate them and their gods within it. This may seem benign and affirming, but these were not their only cultural and ontological agendas. The house-sanctuary also served to express and enforce the socio-political conventions of the peoples it housed. The cathedral of the orthodox Christian church was not only the *domus dei* and house for the devout, but the seat of the bishop and center of the diocese he administered. (Cathedral is from *cathedra*, which means "chair" or "seat.") The hierarchy of the orthodox church assigned positions of power relative to Christ – the *pater familias*, or father of the Christian family. Related socio-political power relations are also discernable in the formative mosque and Hindu temple. And, gender roles are often explicit in traditional dwellings such as the ger and hogan. Architecture has often enjoyed a preeminent role in communicating social roles and hierarchies according to gender and kinship, and enforcing them by location, entry, and spatial disposition, aspects of which the following examples were chosen to illustrate.

American Indian houses satisfied multiple cultural and ontological agendas, often in complex and sophisticated ways. They not only symbolized the world and a people's place in it, but also served to organize and communicate their social organizations. According to Nabokov and Easton, the architecture of American Indian dwellings "was a principal tool for socialization – a means by which members of the tribe learned rules of behavior and a particular world view."[44] The mysterious Anasazi of the American Southwest are renowned for their multi-tiered and geometrically organized "cities." The best known is Pueblo Bonito in Chaco Canyon of Northern New Mexico, its cosmically aligned semi-circular plan split between winter and summer people, each centered on their own great *kiva*. Today Pueblo Bonito is a partially restored ruin, but the Taos Pueblo, also in Northern New Mexico, is still an active community. It has been speculated that refugees from Chaco Canyon built the original Taos Pueblo, which has been continuously inhabited for over a thousand years, and its multi-tiered dwelling units recall Anasazi settlements. Like Pueblo Bonito, Taos Pueblo is also physically and symbolically divided, in this case by Red Willow Creek, and between two peoples with specific ritual responsibilities, each of which are served by kivas. The pueblo is centered on an open plaza, which is considered sacred and where ceremonial dances and other communal rituals take place. Its inhabitants characterize the pueblo as "one nest," but within this unity is a complex architectural and social structure.[45]

Iroquois longhouses were described in origin myths and offer another example of the multifarious roles often performed by American Indian domestic architecture. Originally they were rectangular, wooden structures, longitudinally expandable to accommodate additional families over time – domestic structures built at a colossal scale that also served as ritual and spiritual centers. Each family group occupied a section with their own hearth and smoke hole, but all were "people of the longhouse," as they referred to themselves. With the advent of the Iroquois Confederacy, longhouses also came to symbolize the political unity of the League of Five Nations, the creation of which was portrayed as the "building of a longhouse." Their amalgamated territory was also likened to a colossal longhouse, with the Seneca guarding the "western door" and the Mohawk the eastern one.[46]

Domestic symbols in support of socio-political goals are also found in examples of high state sacred architecture. In Egypt, the Third Dynasty Mortuary Complex of King Zoser at Saqqara recalled the nearby capital of Memphis, its crenellated *temenos* walls echoing the walls of the "White Palace." The tomb of the deified Zoser, known as "The Holy," not only symbolized his cosmic status but also served as his eternal domicile. Throughout, domestic forms and materials were immortalized in stone, testament to the importance of domestic symbolism in Egyptian architecture. In the entry hall, engaged stone columns appeared as the bundled reeds of traditional house structures and supported a stone roof carved to imitate the round beams of a timbered roof. The chapels of the Heb-Sed Court similarly reproduced traditional domestic architecture, as did the paired Red and White Palaces that also symbolized the political union of the north and south for which Zoser's reign was known. A periodic renewal and re-birth ritual festival reinforced these themes, where the pharaoh symbolically visited the complex, including the entry hall where the bundled columns symbolized the provinces of a politically-unified Egypt. Centuries later the gateways, courtyards, hypostyle halls, and inner sanctums of New Kingdom pylon temples recalled, at a colossal scale, ruler-palaces. And so the pharaoh,

FIGURE 4.9 Mortuary complex of King Zoser, Saqqara, Egypt

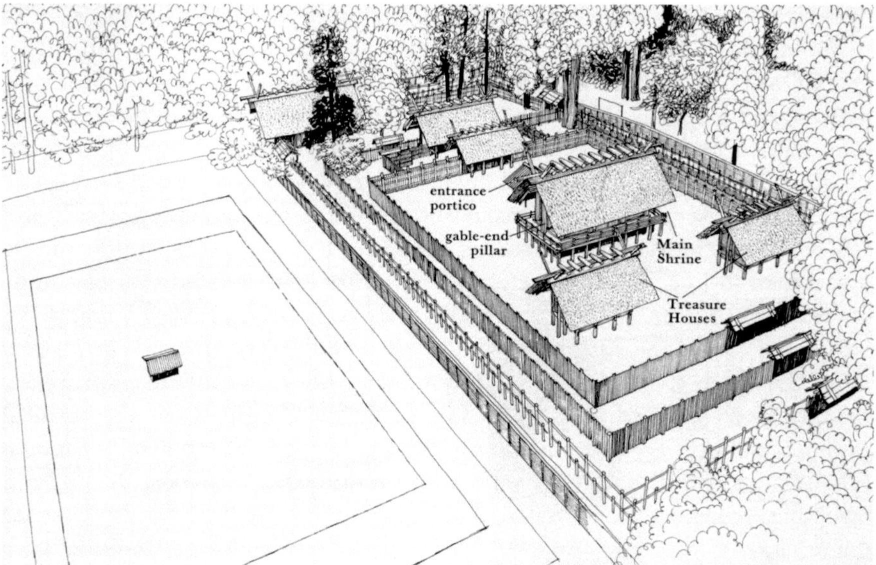

FIGURE 4.10 Inner Shrine of the Grand Shrine of Ise, Japan

a title that meant "great house," represented, and was immortalized by, the multiple roles and meanings of the architecture.

In Classical and Hellenistic Greek cities, the prytaneion housed the city's sacred hearth and fire, and was where official guests were received and entertained, judgments rendered, and citizenship and honors bestowed. In this manner, it reflected many of the functions of the Mycenaean megaron, which it resembled.[47] The prytaneion was typically paired with the bouleuterion where members of the city council met. Together they represented a city's political and social organization, and sacred center. In Athens, these two principal civic buildings were located close to the agora and the acropolis. At the Hellenistic city of Priene, the domestic found eloquent expression in the prytaneion, which was fundamentally a peristyle house with rooms on three sides forming a courtyard, and one room containing the city's sacred hearth. Presumably it was the official residence of the prytanes, a group of city councilors on fixed terms, who ate meals there. The prytaneion was next to the bouleuterion, and also located north of the agora, the plaza, and marketplace, which served in many ways like a civic courtyard. In this aspect, the city itself was representative of the house, recalling Alberti's aphorism, "the city is like some large house and the house is in turn like some small city."[48]

Hestia was the patron goddess of the Greek home, but she also had a civic role as guardian of the sacred hearth of Greek cities, and was closely associated with the prytaneion. Furthermore, she was typically paired with Hermes, whose statues marked Greek roads and the thresholds to houses, and who personified communication, mobility, and openness. Hestia, internal, dark, and stable, and Hermes, external, light, and dynamic, established the prytaneion as equally a center and a threshold. It not only held the sacred fire, but was also a repository for artifacts significant to the city's history.[49] The sacred fire, symbolically significant to both the home and the polis, was often ritually brought to new colonies, symbolizing the continuity of Greek culture and the reciprocity of home and polis. And so Hestia's personified divinity and responsibilities ranged from the family to the polis, house to prytaneion, and symbolized the unity of both.[50]

The appropriation of domestic architecture for socio-political agendas is particularly explicit at the Inner Shrine (Naiku), of the Grand Shrine of Ise (Ise Jingu), Japan's most important Shinto shrine. The sacred structures of the Naiku Shrine offer a compelling example of how domestic architecture expressed and valorized a culture's myths, histories, and socio-political hierarchies. The Naiku Shrine is not the only site of its type in Japan, but it is the one most closely associated with the gods and imperial family. It is located in one of the oldest inhabited areas of Japan and, in many ways, is the symbolic center of the Japanese world, and consequently the preeminent pilgrimage destination for

Japanese. The wooden domestic structures at Naiku have been meticulously rebuilt every twenty years since the seventh century CE. They are constructed according to precise, prescribed site, material, and construction methods in a manner that recreates and represents an ancient architecture associated with the founding of the nation. Naiku means "inner shrine" and is the dwelling of Amaterasu, the sun god and guardian of the nation. [51] The main hall and its flanking east and west treasuries, enclosed by four concentric wooden walls, recall ancient granaries of the early settlements of rice farming peoples, which were similarly enclosed by fences and considered holy.

It is its connection to the imperial family, however, that underscores the conjunction of the domestic and the socio-political. In the late seventh century, Amaterasu became resident and the emperor assumed the responsibility and power to ensure her continued presence. Since then, Naiku has been closely associated with political power, and the imperial family has enjoyed a special relationship with, and access to, its sacred shrines. According to William Coaldrake, at Ise, "There is no apparent distinction between authority imperial and authority spiritual, between the power of the natural world and the powers of imperial governance."[52] The domestic is particularly evoked by the impermanence of the shrines and the necessity of their rebuilding, where the congruence of the orders of the natural world and the political elite are materialized.

★★★

The houses of the Sa'Dan Toraja peoples of northern South Sulawesi, Indonesia were typically oriented to auspicious directions and assigned anthropomorphic elements, and are known for their intricate, decorative carvings. Traditionally, villages were ruled according to kinship, and only nobles could decorate their houses. The ruling noble's house was called *tongkonan layuk*, or "origin house," and was the largest and most completely decorated. In their mythology, the first ancestor built the original house, which was also the first to be decorated and hold rituals. The decorative programs of elite houses communicated the status of village nobles, and their ancestral responsibilities in maintaining the world of their people.[53]

The houses and house symbolism I have presented play important and, at times, preeminent, cultural and ontological roles. The Sa'Dan Toraja houses illustrate many themes explored in this chapter including the congruence of the house and a people's world, and the status and authority of its inhabitants to maintain them. Rulers and gods needed to be housed in a manner that reflected their status and validated their authority. Dwellings were tasked with situating the divine, thus the Solomaic temple was located at the center of the world, and the Hindu temple the axis of the cosmos. Family and kinship groups also required cultural and ontological orientations. Greek, Roman, and traditional Chinese houses evidence the variety of ways houses were created to align with the world, and express family and social hierarchies. Consequently, some houses represented a people's world, or were even believed to create or maintain it. The house's roles in enforcing socio-political hierarchies and power relations were a logical outcome of the diverse and significant roles it was assigned to make sense of the world, render it comprehensible, and maintain its structures.

I began with a cautious appraisal of domestic lineages. Clearly, in traditional cultures, mythological lineages were essential to defining and authenticating the cultural and ontological roles of houses. The value of historical lineages in theoretical postulations is less clear. Logical and defendable historical links are difficult, if not impossible, to establish, and often illustrate the deficiencies of any unified theory or deterministic causes and effects. Moreover, the search for historical continuities distracts from more essential and important considerations of how the domestic and the divine were often associated, coterminous, or congruent. However, that does not discount the value of trying to do so. There are continuities in human history and its material artifacts, and it is through identifying not only the differences but also similarities of preoccupations, themes, means, and goals that valuable consonances between cultures might be revealed. That they are complex, often contradictory, and even inconsistent is actually part of their significance. The recognizable phenomena of the house for the divine or the divinity of the home is a consistent theme, but it plays out in multifarious ways, modified and adapted according to culture and historical setting.

In many of the examples, house and home can be understood as formative types of architecture that served to center the worlds of its creators while simultaneously symbolizing them. The appropriation, creation, or evolution of house and home in sacred architecture is a logical development congruent with the pairings of ruler-god and god-ruler, but evidences a nonetheless surprising lineage in sacred architecture. That is, humankind's quest for meaning and certainty in an uncertain world naturally led to the house of, and for, god, as a means to "solve" the problem of homelessness. It was canny in its multiple agendas for creating stable, dependable places deeply embedded in the continuity of history. The dwellings of American Indians, Mongolian tribesmen, Mycenaeans, Classical Greeks and Romans may have gross and subtle differences, but ultimately they shared themes of valorizing familial and cultural structures and materializing understandings of the worlds they inhabited. They were, in essence, means to connect with the gods in their homes, or invite gods into their own – to come home to, and be at home in, the cosmos.

5

HOUSE TOMBS

Domestic abodes and memorials

The house temple's variety of forms and justifications served to solve the problem of housing god, and rendering divinity material and accessible. Often beginning with simple structures, or recalling them as a means of historical validation, the house temple occupies a particular place in the history of architecture. As such, it illustrates a special type of domesticity. This chapter presents the house tomb as another type of domesticity, but in its case, created to solve the problem of the dead, and accommodate, express, and explain death, a phenomenon equally as ephemeral, indeterminate, and vexing as divinity.

It has often been stated that the only certainty in life is death. The Buddha illustrated this in the *Parable of the Mustard Seed*, where a bereaved mother asks him to revive her dead child. The Buddha responded by asking her to collect a mustard seed from every household that had never known death. She returned empty handed, wiser, and more accepting of this essential truth. If the inevitability of death is part of the human condition, so is the perennial quest to find answers to it. Cicero stated, "Sorrowful weeping and lamentation communicate sadness that is based on our judgment that someone we cherished has been deprived of the good things of life – and senses that very loss."[1] But, when confronted by death do we not also grieve that we are also mortal, and inevitably will also be deprived of life and everything we have always known? And, don't we wish that instead of loss in death, there is gain; and that this gain is eternal life, for others and ourselves? Do we not wish for an enduring home?

Cicero's Stoic pragmatism questioned whether anything endured after death, but the Greco-Romans generally believed in a soul that did.[2] Plato, in *Book X* of the *Republic,* states, the "soul of man is immortal and imperishable," concluding his lengthier considerations of death in the *Phaedo,* and anticipating Christian beliefs in an eternal soul.[3] Christian scripture describes eternal life metaphorically as a house in heaven, a permanent dwelling replacing the corrupted and temporary one of the body. Christ in *The Gospel According to John* asserts, "In my Father's house are many rooms; if it were not so, would I have told you that I go to prepare a place for you?" (Jn 14:2) Paul's domestic metaphor is more explicit: "For we know that if the earthy tent we live in is destroyed, we have a building from God, a house not made with hands, eternal in the heavens" (2 Cor. 5:1). Not content with these assurances alone, beginning in medieval Europe Christians aspired to be buried in the crypts, ambulatories, and family chapels of the "House of the Lord." That they were typically the political, religious, or eventually bourgeois elite was consistent with the memorial function of tombs, though inconsistent with promises by an egalitarian faith of resurrection for all (or, at least all who deserved it). Social hierarchies were even enforced, with the most important afforded locations closest to the altar or relics.[4]

Death and architecture

Beliefs in an enduring soul may have provided comfort to the living with promises of a postmortem existence, but they also presented a problem – what about souls without homes? And, if a homeless soul requires a new and more enduring house, what forms should this house take? Architecture was often enlisted to address these historically ubiquitous questions. Often the responses were direct and homely – sarcophagi and cremation urns that were miniature houses, or home-like tombs furnished for a comfortable and pleasurable afterlife. There were also monumental house tombs that were more cenotaphs to death itself. Many cultures believed death was followed by an interval of transit in a homeless state. Some had concerns and preoccupations regarding ensuring that the dead would reach their destinations – for their happiness, but also so that they would not return to trouble the living. Indeed, funerary architecture was at times as much about protecting the living from wandering malevolent souls, as it was about housing them; thus the importance of specific funerary rites and funerary architecture to ensure both.[5]

The body as a house is a popular metaphor – its structure, skin, machinery, and orifices suggesting its own architecture.[6] But, if the body is a house for the soul, a dead body presents particular problems, and what to do with the body has elicited a range of responses. For some the corpse was preserved as a means to offer, at least in part, a dwelling for the soul. In others, it was destroyed to release the soul so that it might find a new habitation. Disarticulation, cremation, exposure to wild animals, and other means, were employed to this end. In early Hindu traditions, the top of the skull of the deceased was often opened, an oculus of sorts to affect the soul's release.[7]

For many cultures the soul, which needs the architecture of a body, demands another architecture when the body can no longer house it. Many have plausibly suggested that funerary architecture was one of the earliest, and perhaps most symbolically significant, architectural type. It has also been argued that the history of architecture is predominantly one of tombs and monuments.[8] Even the iconoclastic Adolf Loos opined that only the "sepulcher and the monument" truly belong to "art."[9] The prominence of funerary architecture is understandable because the perennial specter of death has begged for reconciliation. According to Lindsay Jones, the history of architecture contains a "fabulous abundance and diversity of extravagant religio-architectural manifestations of the fascination, fear and awe of death – tombs, vaults, sepulchers and sarcophagi, morgues, mausoleums, gallows and graves." [10] The roles of architecture to address the mysteries of death are congruent with its ontological functions. That symbolizations of house and home found particular expression in funerary architecture reflects the ontological plentitude of domesticity. Perhaps nowhere else is the quest for home so poignant, compelling – and futile – as in the house tomb.

House tombs comprise an extensive lineage in the history of architecture. Most surviving examples are elite tombs, which were typically built at a scale that exceeded those for the living, and of enduring materials to outlast them. Tomb palaces often included furnishings, foods, and, in some cases, sacrificed pets, family members, concubines, and servants to provide postmortem sustenance and pleasures. However, the tomb could also be a waystation, a liminal space between life and eternal life, but also where the dead could be accessed.[11] In these contexts, I will present how funerary architecture served a range of goals regarding the housing of the dead, or in some cases, the undead or eternally present ancestors. These considerations include how tombs memorialized the dead, housed the dead to ensure their continued participation in the affairs of the living, appeased the dead to guarantee their beneficence (and avoid their wrath), and represented death and thus rendered it material and even understandable. To do so, I provide a survey of the cultural and ontological roles and traditions of house tombs illustrated by historically significant funerary architecture. Particular attention is paid to the funerary practices and artifacts of American Indian cultures, which, in a variety of ways, had a consistent penchant for house tombs.

There are, of course, many examples where the tomb does not replicate the house, or provide domestic possessions. More often the tomb emulated the temple, which instead of god, gods, or divinity, housed a powerful or divine ruler. Others were modest, and some cultures did not house the dead at all. In other cases, houses of the dead were abandoned and left to decay like their inhabitants. Consequently, this chapter is not a survey of funerary architecture, but a selective discussion of how, in a variety of ways, domesticity found prominence in particular examples. Also, even though there are many examples of tombs replicating or representing the house, this might be because their builders applied the most dependable building conventions they knew. That said, as is often the case, symbolism took on a life of its own and, intentionally or not, the house for the dead often became a symbol of the dead or death itself. I conclude with the position that funerary architecture retains a certain vocality of symbolic content, though often in cipher, which may reveal the significance and meaning, however diverse and diffuse, it holds for us today regarding death – and life.

The symbolic potency of funerary architecture

Death and place are inextricably bound to the human experience, and pose enduring existential questions pertaining to corporality and continuity. Deities first appeared as manifestations of the natural environment, living and dying through days and seasons, but ever-present. The god who dies and is reborn appeared early in the history of religion, and subsequently became an enduring type. In most of their manifestations gods were eternal. Architecture was often tasked with representing their continuity and, by extension, the endurance of a people and their territory. One of the functions of religion has been to bind together the clan, tribe, culture, or nation in support of territorial claims, which is why religion, culture and place were so inextricably connected. Architecture's complex symbol systems often served these diverse agendas. Sometimes rulers – chiefs, pharaohs, kings – became earthly manifestations of deities and when they did their deaths presented an impermanence that needed to be reconciled. Royal tombs typically strived to communicate transcendence over death and the continuity of a ruler's authority. The dead were symbolically materialized and preserved by means of the medium of built forms, spaces, and materials. In the case of deified rulers, mortuary architecture assumed the role of sustaining their power beyond the grave and guaranteeing their dominion over kingdoms and peoples.

Mortuary architecture is arguably the most symbolically potent and diverse building type, which, with inflections in each culture, performed multivalent roles of mediating between life and death, permanence and decay, and humans and their gods. They were built not only to memorialize the dead but as liminal places where contact with the dead, and all they represented, was believed possible. The objectification of the dead consequently produced places of veneration, which took two principal forms – the memorial and the cenotaph.

In the first, the ancestors or rulers were directly memorialized. In the second, the mortuary site represented the dead more abstractly and served more as a cenotaph to death itself. Architecture, of all the art forms, has proven to be the most effective in commemoralizing the dead, and death, and mortuary architecture is one of the earliest and most enduring of building types.[12] This is readily apparent at early civilizations that developed mature building programs – colossal earthwork tombs for important rulers were built in prehistoric Japan and Korea; massive subterranean royal tombs were created during the Shang Dynasty in China; and sophisticated *tholos* tombs distinguished the Bronze Age city of Mycenae.

Traditions of house tombs

Just as temples appropriated forms and symbols of houses and homes, mortuary architecture similarly embodied domesticity. According to Michel Ragon, "From the earliest civilizations… the tomb has appeared as the obverse of the house."[13] The Assyro-Babylonians called graves "houses and residences." Ancient Egyptians referred to tombs as "eternal habitations" or as "residences for eternity." As is well known, their sepulchral domiciles provided many of the accouterments of living, in some cases including wives, servants, concubines, and animals sacrificed according to entombment rites. Their houses of the dead were clearly more important than those for the living.[14] The tombs of the necropolises of Saqqara and Thebes were typically multichambered houses for eternity, and contained massive stores of goods for the afterlife. The fact that signs for houses and tombs were often the same indicates to what degree they were congruent in Egyptian culture.[15]

Egyptian religion, and its ontological preoccupations with the dead and afterlife, has often been called a religion of death. But, their mortuary practices were also cultural, a funerary cult focused on preserving the power of the ruling elite, who aimed to perpetuate their power through tombs that materialized the continued presence of rulers.[16] In dynastic Egypt, significant efforts and resources were dedicated to mortuary houses, and tombs for rulers achieved particular prominence and symbolic depth. As early as the First Dynasty, the cultural and ontological goals and means of funerary practices were established. At Abydos, subterranean brick tombs covered by wooden roofs, and ancillary rooms stocked with everything needed for a comfortable (after)life, created domestic settings for eternally present rulers.[17]

It was the vast and sophisticated necropolises of later dynastic Egypt where the objectification of the dead found mature expressions, and tombs became memorials, places for veneration and state rituals, and cenotaphs to death and rulers. The early funerary complex and step pyramid of the Mortuary Complex of King Zoser at Saqqara, introduced earlier, included a diversity of domestic symbolisms in service of the ontological goals of situating a people in place and time. However, its extensive amalgam of surface and formal symbolizations were also in service of the political hegemony of the ruling class. The deification of Zoser and establishment of his eternal status were made possible through enduring stone, geometry, and symbolism, all of which communicated the continuity of the ruler and the political union of northern and southern Egypt. At Saqqara, the architecture materialized the cultural components embodied by the ruler, while also serving as a medium by which the ruler, and all he represented, could be accessed. In this context, the funerary architecture not only memorialized Zoser but also served as a liminal place where eternal contact with him was believed possible.

Egyptians believed that the endurance of their culture depended on the continuity of the soul, a belief that their funerary architecture was clearly built to serve (and, given the longevity of their culture, seemed to work). The priesthood attended to the dead and eternally present rulers who continued to be influential in death as they were in life. Prayers and offerings to the dead reflected their status as intercessors in the affairs of their people. At Giza, the great pyramids functioned not only as tombs and memorials for the pharaohs they housed, but also as cenotaphs – their abstract geometries communicating the endurance of the culture in a manner that arguably has never been surpassed. In Karsten Harries' words, "The Egyptian pyramids thus present themselves as perfect houses for the dead. As such they have provided funerary architecture with perhaps its most obvious model."[18]

Egyptian monumental necropolises are appropriately recognized for their scale and effusion of symbols, which expressed beliefs in an afterlife and the continued presence of rulers. However, it was the Etruscans who more explicitly created the house tomb.[19] Much of Etruscan civilization is lost – what mostly remains are some of their ambitious necropolises where tomb-lined streets recall the cities of this early urban culture. The tombs, most likely for elite families, were recreations of their houses in stone, and included doors, staircases, servants' quarters, beds, kitchen implements, and pitched roofs. At the necropolis near Cerveteri (in present-day central Italy), thousands of tombs were built on streets like the residential quarters of the living. One of its houses "contained bodies on beds, with gold and silver jewelry, dishes, tripods, a chariot, weapons, vases and shields."[20] One rock-cut tomb at Volumnii (near Perugia), recalls an atrium house with chests containing crematory ashes placed in the tablinum, and a pitched roof carved to represent wooden timbers. Remarkable wall paintings showing scenes of everyday life distinguish many Etruscan tombs. Some depicted erotic

FIGURE 5.1 Tomb of the Leopards, Tarquinia, Italy

FIGURE 5.2 Neolithic longhouses, reconstruction by Peter Dunn

scenes of sensual pleasures to enliven the quiet rooms of the tomb. The so-called Tomb of the Floggings at the necropolis near Tarquinia depicts a series of rather adventurous sexual practices and promised a certain kind of exciting eternal existence. James Stevens Curl argues, "Clearly the Etruscans wanted to make the dead feel as comfortable as possible."[21] They also seemed to want them to be entertained as well.

The Romans adopted some of the funerary practices of the Etruscans with early tombs taking the forms of houses.[22] The Greco-Romans also, at specific places and periods, created house tombs. The rock-cut tombs of Lycia with their entrances recalling house fronts and carvings wooden constructions are best known.[23] However, the Chinese may claim one of the more extensive histories of house tombs. Dating from early historical periods, sarcophagi and crematory urns often replicated houses, and elite tombs assumed domestic forms, organizations, decorations, and furnishings. Some underground tombs included worship spaces above, a pairing of devotional spaces and tombs also found at some early Egyptian examples. Tombs reflected the elite families' status and continued powerful future, and consequently often required more time and resources to build than houses for living.[24] Beliefs that death was as important as life resulted in elaborate palace-like tombs constructed during lifetimes for an imagined postmortem existence. Elite tombs typically included domestic furnishings, and statuary and wall paintings that depicted the deceased as revered ancestors still engaged in everyday acts of the living.[25] Their brick or stone walls and ceilings often imitated wooden construction, including brackets and vaulted ceilings.[26]

The Neolithic peoples of Northern Europe apparently did not furnish their funerary architecture, but their monumental funerary constructions indicate the existence of beliefs and rituals focused on the dead, and death itself, concretized and facilitated through stone architecture.[27] Kong Asker's Høj on the Isle of Møn is the tomb of a local chieftain that dates from 4000 BCE. It was a passage grave, like many found throughout the island, with a massive, corbelled, stone interior reached by a narrow passage that faced due east. Like many tombs, it was built for eternity, as if to symbolize that though the ruler had died, he and his people would endure. Ian Hodder suggests the cultural and ontological goals of Neolithic tombs:

> It was the tomb especially as it began to be used over many generations, which could become the "home" of the dispersed local units. The tomb created continuity and stability in the face of the death and dispersal of community members.[28]

Many Neolithic settlements in Northern Europe comprised wooden longhouses, which also served as charnel houses. Evidence of charnel longhouses, which often were trapezoidal in plan and aligned with the cardinal directions, has been found at various locations. Sometimes they were clustered together like settlements, which poses the question of whether they were for the living first before becoming repositories for the dead.[29] A number of wooden charnel houses have been discovered on the British Isles. At Fussell's Lodge in Wiltshire, archeological evidence indicates the lengthy use of a charnel house, before it was covered in earth, perhaps having been burned beforehand.[30] Aubrey Burl suggests that megalithic barrows replaced and recalled wooden charnel houses. He also argues that the amount of labor required to construct them indicates that they were not merely tombs but places built to "harbour powerful forces," and materialize the "compulsions and dreads that drove people to these efforts."[31]

The West Kennet Long Barrow, located on the highest point of a ridge in the gentle hills of southwest England, stretches over 300 feet along the ridge in an east–west orientation. The east-facing entrance was defined by a transverse row of sarcen stones and led to a series of corbelled chambers that held the remains of multiple generations. Burl suggested that barrows "resembled the rectangular houses of the Neolithic although larger, visualized as dwellings for the dead whose spirits would watch over the living family."[32] Hodder proposed that when funerary longhouses became permanent dwellings for revered ancestors, they served to "create continuity out of discontinuity."[33] However, Rodney Castleden argued that Neolithic tombs served purposes beyond the simple commemoration of the dead, and were not "primarily graves, but cenotaphs. They were not monuments to the dead, but to death itself, and they can be seen as magic gateways through which life could be started anew and where the living and the dead could meet."[34] Clearly Neolithic cultures wanted to house the dead in a manner that reflected a congruence of life and death, and expressed the continued presence of the dead and continuity of their people. It is logical that houses of the living became the abodes of the dead in satisfaction of these compelling and all-too-human desires.

American Indian funerary architecture

As I have observed, some examples of American Indian domestic architecture served, at least in part, as cosmograms, with geometric organizations and celestial orientations providing both replications of, and connections to, the cosmos. American Indian funerary architecture had related ontological goals of establishing connections with larger contexts. Their funerary customs comprised a diverse range of practices, and contemporary understandings of their cultures suggest that their views on death produced culturally distinct rites and artifacts.[35] Dr. H. C. Yarrow conducted a study in the late nineteenth century that was published by the Smithsonian, which documented funerary rites of the native peoples of North America before many were lost. The variety of practices included the Navaho rite of burying the dead in their homes and abandoning the houses afterward, or building small houses for the dead, as certain Pacific Northwest tribes preferred to do.

Charnel house funerary practices were shared throughout the native peoples of eastern North America, and in many instances charnel houses were referred to as "temples."[36] Wooden charnel houses are among the more remarkable examples of house tombs. They served as the settings for multi-stage rituals, which may have included inhumation followed by excarnation, cremation, and deposition.[37] Christopher Carr and Troy Case describe various functions regarding the extensive use of charnel houses by tribes of southeastern North America. They were places for internment, to "process the dead," to connect with the dead through food offerings, to feast "in honor of de-fleshing," to store ritual objects, and to hold the "sacred fire."[38] Carr and Case also outline multi-stage funerary rites, which, similar to the periodic rites of the Huron and Algonquian tribes, may have included participants from diverse geographical locations. All of which is particularly evident in the charnel houses and funerary practices of the Hopewell culture of the American Midwest that date from the first millennium. Even though much has been written about Hopewell social structures, ritual practices, and material artifacts, relatively little attention has been directed to their domestic architecture and, in particular, its appropriation and application in funerary practices that were central to their culture.

The types of rituals performed at Hopewell funerary sites are not definitively known, but there is substantive archeological evidence of their materials and contents. It is known that wooden charnel houses, some with multiple rooms, served as ritual centers and repositories for cremations and talismanic artifacts. Often a sequential number of charnel houses were built in the same location before being burned and covered by an earthen mound, a culminating event that may have been part of important periodic rituals.

Rites of separation and liminality, of spiritually, symbolically, and physically occupying an in-between zone, may have been a characteristic of Hopewellian funerary rites. If so, this would be congruent with shamanistic rituals that aimed to bridge otherwise separate worlds and realities.[39] Hopewell sacred sites materialized a range of symbolic agendas but were primarily positioned as liminal places believed to provide physical and metaphysical connections to the otherwise inaccessible. Just as shamans served as bridges between worlds, Hopewell funerary architecture, which included colossal, geometrically precise, and celestially aligned earthworks, may have served related roles. Similar to the co-joining of worlds symbolized by the Serpent Bridge in Ojibwa mythology,

FIGURE 5.3 Hopewell culture ceremonial house

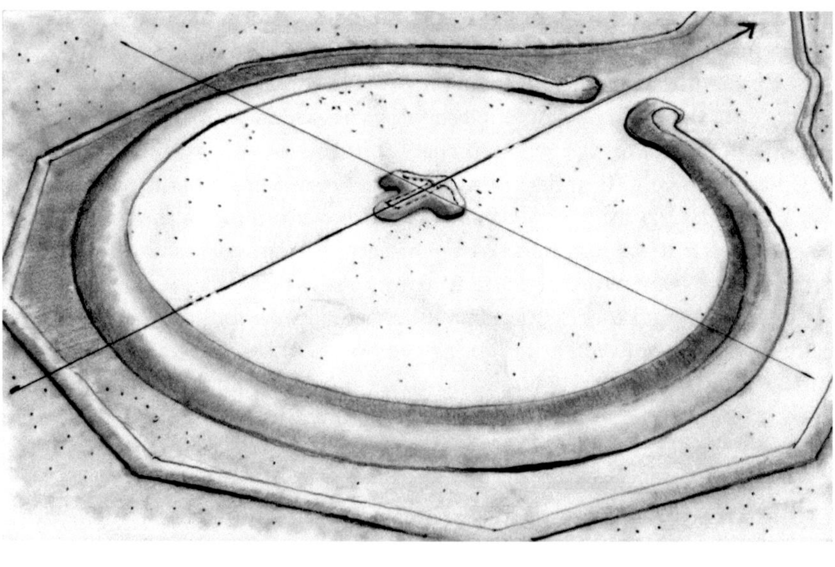

FIGURE 5.4 Reconstruction showing alignment of opening with minimum moonrise, Great Circle, Newark Earthworks, Newark, OH

Hopewell charnel houses, burial mounds, and earthworks can be understood as liminal places that straddled worlds and connected the known with the unknown.

Many American Indian cultures emphasized multi-stage funerary processes rather than one specific event, which often included separation, liminality, and re-incorporation. These rituals, enacted over time and especially during propitious times established by the celestial calendar, were rites of passage that guided the dead to their changed status. In some cases, funerary rites were designed to ensure that the dead would continue to be active participants in the activities of their people. Ancestors may have changed to spirit forms but, like animal spirits, were still present and could be accessed through rituals performed at specific locations. According to Carr and Case:

> Whether spiritual beings are a subtle part of the objective reality or projections of the imaginations of the unconscious mind onto objective reality does not matter. In either case, the person experiencing the spiritual being acts in relation to it and to other humans as though it were real.[40]

Hopewell funerary sites can be understood in this context as liminal places where the spirits of ancestors were accessed by the architecture, and settings to sustain the presence and powers of the dead. The burial mounds and earthworks were not memorials, but places for acts of veneration, in the belief that the blessings and knowledge of the dead and their eternal spirits could be received there. Charnel houses, oriented in the direction of the spirit or "mirror world", were potent transistors with the power to effect these connections and transformations. Domestic symbolism was central to this agenda where house tombs assumed specific roles, symbolizations, and meanings. They served as temporary abodes for the corpses and spirits of the dead, but, once entombed in enduring earthen mounds, performed broader ontological roles. Archeological evidence of Hopewell sites suggest sustained practices centered on the dead and perhaps death itself. It is clear they were places that brought people together through the shared condition of death, and connected them through ritual with the goal of deeper understandings of the dead. The architecture memorialized continuity in a discontinuous world. It created an enduring material place, while simultaneously symbolizing an immaterial threshold that connected the living, the dead, and the cosmos.

Burl has suggested parallels between the mound-building cultures of North America and Neolithic burial rituals and sites. He states, "With such banked rings and with their conical burial mounds they resemble quite closely the middle Neolithic societies of eastern England where round barrows were already being built."[41] Burl's formal comparisons may be of limited relevance, but his four stages of Neolithic burial rituals and artifacts can be fruitfully applied to expand understandings of Hopewell sites. According to Burl, first the dead were buried in their own houses, then in barrows, which then led to the construction of burial mounds. In the fourth stage of stone circles, however, bodies were no longer necessary for the commemoration of the dead. Communion with ancestors was an important component of many of these sites and the ontological goals of many of the Neolithic necropolises were to "transform collective burials into spectacular and indestructible monuments..." where "communication with the ancestors is ritually assured."[42] In particular, some megalithic monuments in Western Europe embodied the dead, the enduring stone symbolizing the continuity of the rulers and their people.[43]

Carr and Case suggested that Hopewell earthworks and burial mounds were ritual centers, with only a small population of priests and caretakers living nearby. Consequently, they can be contextualized as places reserved for episodic gatherings of a more regional character. Archeological evidence suggests that they often served as mortuaries, places for ritual building activities, craft centers, places for feasts, and as initiatory sites. As centers of the Hopewellian world, they materially and ritually appropriated large and even cosmic territories, and ritual gatherings served to concretize the Hopewell culture's religious and ritual hegemony. Moreover, even though singular Hopewell burial mounds and earthworks may have established central ritual precincts, their broad geographic distribution in the Ohio River Basin could also have been a material means to consecrate, or claim, larger territories. Even though it has been argued that the Hopewell culture was more interested in religion than with competing with its neighbors, claimed territories and built artifacts for ritual purposes constitute acts of appropriation.[44] In this context, the houses of the dead marked a sacred precinct but also appropriated the larger territory that it, at least in part, represented.

It is plausible that the wooden charnel houses provided settings for shamanic rituals performed for the benefit of the dead and the living. At the Great Circle of the Newark (Ohio) Earthworks, there is evidence of one or two large charnel houses at its center, over which an effigy figure, named the Eagle Mound, was constructed. Shamanic rituals vary pan-culturally but some share themes of passage from one world (the living) to another (the dead, or "undead" enduring spirits), and depend on the guidance of one who has the ability to mediate between these worlds. At Newark, there may have been rituals to commemorate those who died and ensure the safe passage of their souls to the next world (thus the significance of fire to release their souls), and consequently ensure the health and continuity of their people.

The Great Circle may have performed multiple roles – a place for funerary rituals but also, by means of its celestial alignments, as a ritual calendar, a place of cultural and ontological elucidation, and even as a center of the Hopewellian world. Newark's charnel houses and earthworks would have, in part, served to represent what the Hopewell understood to be their cosmic contexts and their relationship with them. Many have argued that the earthwork's entrance faced in the direction of significant, periodic, moonrise events. The moon was the celestial object most closely associated with death and the mirror world of the land of eternal spirits.[45] And so, in one aspect, the Hopewell houses of the dead were positioned as liminal places with the ability to mediate between worlds – portals to the land of the dead and the spirits of dead ancestors. Similar to ritual itself where the sacred gods and powers of primordial time are recalled, Newark may be conceptualized as a sacred center where timeless powers were believed to be present. Similar to Burl's assessment of Neolithic funerary sites, Newark would have served as a power place and "cult centre(s) for the protection of the living."[46] Just as funerary crematory rites transformed and renewed the soul through fire, smoke, and shamanic rituals, the sacred enclosures themselves may have served as places of periodic individual, communal, and cultural renewal.

★★★

Roman beliefs and conceptualizations about the afterlife were not uniform, ranging from a severance from the pleasures of life, to existence in a diminished wraithlike state, or attainment of a redeemed eternal life. Even though Cicero debated whether there was an afterlife, he did cite "men of old" who believed that death "rather than bringing total and utter destruction, is instead a kind of journey or transformation of life, which leads distinguished men and women to heaven."[47] For some, however, death was merely a continuation of life in which one simply forsook one dwelling for another. The famous epitaph on the Roman "Tomb of a Happy Man" confidently stated, "Ever without tears, my urn knows spring, for I have not died. I have changed my state."[48] For the Romans, the center of religious life was the home, where the family prayed to gods and ancestors at the family shrine in the tablinum. In this context, the house tomb can also be understood as possessing a certain kind of divinity or closeness to the gods, and a dwelling for the dead where they might be accessed.

This recalls another domestic funerary practice – the tomb as a lived space where relatives of the dead come for visits. Couches for this purpose were provided within the sepulchral abodes of some examples of Etruscan tombs. A Greek practice was to sleep in the family tomb so that one's dreams could receive portentous messages from the dead. On designated days during the year, Romans would retire to the family tomb, to offer gifts for the dead and eat family meals. Practices of this type have not entirely died out in the contemporary world. Relatives visit cemeteries in many cultures, and Egyptian families sometimes spend a number of days during the year to live with the dead with rooms provided at tombs for this purpose.[49] And then there is the compelling City of the Dead in Cairo where families, often because it is their best or only option, reside in tombs among the dead.[50]

Provisions for the postmortem world of the dead and the living also continue in some rather bizarre contemporary examples. Cemeteries for the rich of Cairo can resemble palatial houses of the living, with opulent spaces providing comfortable habitations for family visits.[51] Then there are the tombs of the so-called Mexican drug lords in Culiacan, in northwest Mexico. The tombs of Culiacan are multistory grand houses, with richly furnished rooms that often include photos of the dead cartel members. One can presume that the builders of these grandiose "mansions" are largely unaware of the lineage they have joined, but their commemoration of the wars between warring cartels and their "soldiers" are strikingly similar. There are instances where rival warlords are buried close to each other – recalling the treasuries at Delphi that commemorated the changing fortunes of the often-warring city-states and their reciprocal victories.[52]

All of which suggest that the domesticity of death, though not universal, is widespread and diverse. Or, for the most part, used to be. Loos insisted:

> If we were to come across a mound in the woods, six foot long by three foot wide, with the soil piled up in a pyramid, a somber mood would come over us and a voice inside us would say "There is someone buried here." That is architecture.[53]

One may agree with his essentialist assertion, while also recognizing that a mound is a rather inconsequential example in the voluminous history of house tombs, matched only by the diversity of impulses, fears, and hopes that created them. For the most part, the compulsions that produced house tombs as homes for eternally present ancestors are lost. The hopeful beliefs that death was the beginning of life, not the end, or is the transition to a different, or better, state, are diminished in a globalized culture that has little interest in devoting significant time and resources for those who, quite simply, have ceased to exist.

Perhaps this is so because we no longer fear the dead or seek to comfortably house them, but fear death itself.[54] For the most part, the dead are locked away in sealed coffins and secure cemeteries, and have little or no role in the affairs of the living. The West in particular seems to fear the old, shuttering them in a purgatory of nursing homes and senior communities. People often die alone in hospitals, separated from their homes, families, and the comforts they have provided throughout their lives. We may have emancipated ourselves from the cults of the dead that have been essential to the all-too-human desire to reconcile death, and are no longer burdened by fears of postmortem judgments or truncated by the promise of heaven, but we have lost many rituals that provided comfort when confronted by death, and architectural expressions and settings for them.

But, architecture's roles in materializing and explaining life's most disturbing and irreconcilable conditions can still be recognized. Lefebvre reminds us that "monumentality transcends death," and it was the desired and presumed immortality of tombs that endowed them with cultural and ontological significance.[55] That domesticity served an important function is logical. We know home the best, and so through it may come to know death. Home is the most comforting and stable aspect of our lives, and so we wish our dead dear ones a homecoming. But, house tombs, and other monuments to the dead, also materialized death in a manner that invited one to confront, reconsider, and even find some resolution to death, what Lefebvre describes as the "dual aspect of beauty and terrifying content."[56] As such, architecture was assigned the authority to speak of death. It still has that capacity. Otherwise, the building of architecturally significant contemporary mausoleums and crematories would not be so prevalent. Architecture still has a role in providing answers to the inexplicable, comfort for the living, and homecoming for the dead.

6

MATERIALIZING THE IMMATERIAL

The house as a means of self-exploration and expression

In previous chapters, I examined how house and home have served a broad range of cultural and ontological roles – from homely to unhomely, house temples to house tombs. In the latter examples, domestic settings were believed to possess the capacity to co-join worlds and explicate the inexplicable. That is, house and home were engaging, active agents able to materialize the otherwise immaterial. This "affective level," in Lefebvre's words, is not simply signs and symbols to be "read," but actively engages one in a "dialogue," and leads to a "horizon," or diversity of, meanings.[1] This chapter positions domesticity in general, and the house specifically, also as an active agent – a means of self-exploration and expression, and a medium of ontological and spiritual orientations that otherwise would not find full expression.

Chapter 3 "Origins" presented how essential dwellings and formative architecture were typically conflated. Vitruvius' original dwelling house, and those that followed, included only essential elements and materials. However, it was not mere utility, but incorporated a diverse range of cultural, ideological, and ontological capacities. The rustic hut and writer's retreat are particular types of domesticity that have similarly been packed with symbolic content. In particular, for writers and philosophers, the simple or essential dwelling has typically served to materialize their values and facilitate their creative lives. The hermit scholar's retreat in Buddhist literature, introduced earlier, satisfied contemplative requirements of solitude, the values of simplicity and

FIGURE 6.1 *Diogenes*, John William Waterhouse

essential living, intrinsic connections to the natural world, and the potential for enlightenment. These are themes that can also be found in the creation, use, and celebration of rustic huts.

I will briefly present a range of examples to explain these themes, before turning to two case studies: Martin Heidegger's Black Forest hut and Henry David Thoreau's cabin on Walden Pond. Heidegger and Thoreau's writings are particularly expressive examples of how simple dwellings were positioned as a means to materialize, express, and embody important aspects of their philosophies. Subsequently, in their cases, the cultural and ontological roles of the domestic are expanded to include philosophical and spiritual issues.

Diogenes of Sinope's purported domestic barrel outside the temple provocatively illustrates an essential dwelling that represents spiritual priorities and clarity of purpose.[2] The world's religions include many examples of this type – from the hermitages of the Desert Fathers to the cells of anchorites, Muhammad's cave on Mt. Hira to Taoist mountain huts, and Bodhidharma's cave dwelling. The ascetic hut achieved particular prominence in Hinduism and early Buddhism as a collective symbol of tenuous existence and the means of liberation from it.[3] In Western culture, the solitary retreat was more individual, and has enjoyed a privileged position as a productive setting for the personal reflections of writers and philosophers. Bachelard described the "hut dream" as a solitary abode in the country, and its inhabitants occupying a propitious ontological setting.

> The hermit is *alone* before God. His hut, therefore, is just the opposite of the monastery. And there radiates about this centralized solitude a universe of meditation and prayer, a universe outside the universe. The hut can receive none of the riches of this world. It possesses the felicity of intense poverty; indeed it is one of the glories of poverty; as destitution increases it gives us access to absolute refuge.[4]

Goethe's popular poem, "The Wanderer's Nightsong," penned on the wall of a gamekeeper's mountain hut where the Romantic writer spent the night, similarly celebrates the virtues of a thoughtful individual in solitude. These brief examples are complementary contexts for the hopes, presumptions, and experiences of those who have built or occupied rustic huts. The following examples illustrate how, to greater or lesser degrees, the rustic hut served, or was portrayed as, a simple shelter in service of an essential life, an antidote to the deficiencies of contemporary culture, a place deeply embedded in its natural surroundings, a means to realize reflective endeavors, a medium to materialize philosophical positions, and a setting where spiritual insights were possible.[5]

Writers' and philosophers' retreats

The naturalist Henry Beston and the writer Anne Morrow Lindbergh wrote about productive times spent at beach houses. However, they were very different people from different times: Beston, unmarried and a veteran of the First World War; Lindbergh, a privileged woman embedded in post-Second World War suburban culture. Both wrote about the simplicity and restorative capacity of their beach cabins, but conveyed at times different perspectives on their value. Beston spent a year alone in a two-room cabin he built on Eastham Beach on Cape Cod, reflectively documented in his 1928 book *The Outermost House*. Congruent with traditions of essential dwellings, he characterized his house as a remedy for a world that was "sick to its thin blood for lack of elemental things."[6] The house only had "a bedroom and kitchen-living room," with a "brick fireplace with its back to the wall between rooms." It was 16' × 20' and built by a carpenter neighbor according to "home-made plans." A simple hand-pump well provided water.[7] Beston's cabin was a naturalist's laboratory. He explains how the house's "somewhat amateur enthusiasm for windows," ten in all, extended his views outward in all directions to the "four walls of the world." Recalling some of Thoreau's reflections in *Walden*, the house was a pivot point for individual engagements with the natural life of the ocean and dunes of the outer cape, which are depicted in poetic detail.[8]

Beston writes about how his cabin weathered severe storms, juxtaposed with scenes of shipwrecks off the beach. He named it the "Fo'castle," a reference to the storage structure near the bow of sailing ships – a metaphor for the house's exposure to the elements of nature, but also a solitary man weathering life's storms. The house was also a refuge, with an elemental hearth that was "a household god and a friend."[9] He was not always alone; friends visited and the Nauset Coast Guard Station was just two miles north, but it was the solitary times offered by his simple cabin that catalyzed and nurtured his reflective writing.

Similar to Beston's, Anne Morrow Lindbergh's descriptions of her beach house on Captiva Island in Florida, where she spent often-solitary vacations in the late 1940s and early 1950s, are brief, her recounting of, and reflections on, the life it made possible, voluminous. But, whereas Beston's book was focused on relationships with the natural world, Lindbergh's *Gift from the Sea,* a bestseller published in 1955, was primarily concerned with personal relationships. Lindbergh's reflections and positive metaphors describe a woman seeking relief from family obligations. Throughout, she positioned the simple dwelling as an antidote to her complicated life, and a vehicle for one well lived.

She begins with a metaphor of a channeled whelk shell and its former appropriation by a hermit crab to illustrate domestic means to "live a simple life," and to "be at peace with myself."[10] The tiny beach house, where she drafted her best-known and read book, is described as a "cottage as shabby & bare as a deserted seashell – swept with wind & sand & the sound of the casuarina trees & the waves on the beach."[11] Her celebration of a simple dwelling on the beach is distinguished from the conveniences of her home in Connecticut and an antidote for the special conditions of American culture, especially the expected roles of women, which she characterizes as ones of "multiplicity" rather than "simplicity," which "does not bring grace," but "destroys the soul."[12] Instead, the house expresses and facilitates the simplicity necessary for a contemplative life, where she "becomes bare – empty – open as a shell – echoing the sea."[13] Recalling Beston's cabin, the curtainless windows of her beach house provided "a periscope out to the world,"[14] but also a refuge where she could look inward.

Ludwig Wittgenstein and Pablo Neruda also had houses to support their contemplative writing. Wittgenstein's cabin was built in 1914 on the steep slopes of a fjord in Skjolden, Norway. It served as a solitary retreat for the famously peripatetic philosopher, where he often spent extended periods of time and created some of his most important works. Even though he did not characterize his cabin as a remedy for the afflictions of society, it did provide a refuge from his tragic Viennese family and the academic culture of Cambridge University, where he taught. He described the wooden cabin as "Austrian" in style, evoking the alpine architecture that has been mythologized nearly as much as the rustic cabin. It is unclear to what degree Wittgenstein designed it, though friends who visited recalled some of its ingenious details and he was clearly passionate about architecture. He designed and supervised the construction of a house for his sister Gretl in Vienna where its rational organization and obsessive details reflected his training as an engineer and his rigorous philosophy.[15]

The Chilean poet and politician Pablo Neruda had three houses, La Chascona, in Santiago, La Sebastiana, in Valparaiso, and Casa de Isla Negra, that were also sanctuaries for his creative life. But, whereas Wittgenstein's cabin was a spartan retreat for a solitary man, Neruda's houses were social, personal, and effusively furnished. Isla Negra ("Black Island") is not on an island but provided an escape from Neruda's global, political life, and was a sanctuary for his writing. Like his other houses, it was eclectically furnished with collections of items from around the world that represented the poet's interests, but also symbolized the world he endeavored to capture with poetry. When he purchased the original house in 1939, he had started a new direction for his poetry, and reflected that its "wild coastal strip, with its turbulent ocean, was the place to give myself passionately to the writing of my new song."[16] Neruda worked with architects to enlarge the house several times, often participating in its design. Eventually it stretched along the coast with most rooms, including his study, giving broad

FIGURE 6.2 Isla Negra, Chile

FIGURE 6.3 Carl Jung's house, Bollingen, Switzerland

views of the Pacific and the rocky shoreline. Eventually, among many items, it was filled with Neruda's collections of art, masks, shells, glass, ship models, and ship figureheads. Here, he and his third wife, Matilde Urrutia, entertained friends and politicians, and Neruda wrote.

Neruda's *100 Love Sonnets*, first published in 1959, is filled with love for his wife and their home – and house metaphors. The dedication to Matilde describes the sonnets as made "out of wood," and "little houses, so that your eyes, which I adore and sing to, might live in them."[17] Outside the house, "waves shatter on restless rocks," but inside:

> Here are the bread – the wine – the table – the house:
> a man's needs, and a woman's, and a life's
> Peace whirled through and settled in this place:
> the common fire burned, to make this light.[18]

In one of the last sonnets, Neruda tells his wife that if he dies before her:

> I don't want your laugh or your footsteps to waver;
> I don't want my legacy of happiness to die;
> don't call to my breast: I'm not there.
> Live in my absence as if in a house.[19]

He died at Isla Negra in 1972, shortly after the Chilean military coup.

Carl Jung built a solitary retreat on the shore of Lake Zurich in Bollingen, which was also a family vacation house and a place to entertain friends. Similar to the previous examples, Jung intended it as an essential dwelling for authentic living in harmony with his surroundings. He often spent extended periods alone there. However, it is different because its construction, some of which was done by Jung, served as a medium for his psychological and spiritual explorations. Begun in 1923 and built in stages over thirty years, Jung employed the house to advance and materialize his self-explorations and analysis begun a decade earlier during the formative time he characterized as his "confrontation with the unconscious."[20] He began with a cylindrical, quartered, stone building, a primitive hut and "maternal hearth" of archetypal family dwellings, and his writings on the house celebrate the simple and essential life it provided:[21]

> I have done without electricity, and tend the fireplace and stove myself. Evenings I light the old lamps. There is no running water, and I pump the water from the well. I chop the wood and cook the food. These simple acts make man simple: and how difficult it is to be simple![22]

The house was completed, following the death of his wife, with a final upper story, which signified for Jung "the extension of consciousness achieved in old age" and materialized a "symbol of psychic wholeness."The building of his house was a means of reconciliation and connection, and a medium through which he carved out "rough answers" to life's questions.[23] And so for Jung, the essential dwelling served as a means to not only withdraw from his busy family and professional life and live a simple and earthy existence, but also to confront, and seek reconciliation with, life's most vexing psychological, philosophical, and spiritual questions.[24]

Two houses – different perspectives

Predominant interpretations of Thoreau's cabin on Walden Pond and Heidegger's Black Forest hut portray them as solitary hermitages. But, reflections by their creators convey broader and more generalized functions. In *Walden*, Thoreau's best-known and influential work, his self-built cabin on Walden Pond served as means to realize and illustrate his philosophy. Chapters such as "Economy" and "Where I Lived and What I Lived For" reveal the cabin as a demonstration project for how to live an essential, spiritual life in harmony with the world. Heidegger wrote little directly about *die Hütte*, though his reflections on Black Forest farmhouses in *Building, Dwelling, Thinking* (1951),[25] and the earlier essay "Why Do I Stay in The Provinces?" (1934), illustrate its virtues. Heidegger's and Thoreau's writings have been profusely and diversely interpreted, but, for all that has been written about these two thinkers, little has been posited regarding the implications of the architecture of their huts, or their spiritual motivations in creating them. In particular, the spiritual life or spiritual aspects of their work remain largely unexplored: Thoreau is typically studied according to the literary, social, and political aspects of his work; Heidegger largely through the meaning and impact of his often dense and challenging philosophy, his contributions to the phenomenological school of thought, and his compromising association with National Socialism. Contributing to the difficulty of the subject is that neither Thoreau nor Heidegger wrote much directly about their respective houses. That said, there is more architecture to work with in Thoreau, and it is surprising how much has been written about the architectural significance of Heidegger's writings, and how little about Thoreau's.

Even though the following does not focus on comparing or contrasting these two houses, there are obvious similarities and differences between them that contribute to understandings of their meaning and significance. On one hand, Thoreau and Heidegger present the potency of their retreats to authentically engage the world – in "Sounds," Thoreau describes the multi-sensual experiences engendered by its natural setting; in a section of "Why Do I Stay in the Provinces?" Heidegger reflects on the reciprocal relationship between his philosophical explorations and the pastoral world that surrounds him. On the other hand, the relationship between Thoreau's cabin and his philosophical investigations are often direct in ways that Heidegger's are not. Thoreau routinely positions his cabin and the perspectives it facilitates as a counterproject to the predominant culture of his time; Heidegger in "Why Do I Stay in the Provinces?" does also, but in a more limited fashion. Heidegger also presented his hut as historically and culturally connected to the vernacular farm buildings it overlooked. Thoreau had no interest in redemptive notions of this type.[26] In both cases, there are allusions to the capacity of architecture, and in particular the simple rustic hut, albeit indirectly, to mediate between, and access, broader ontological and metaphysical orientations and understandings.

Heidegger's Black Forest hut

Many architectural attributions have been credited to Heidegger's writings, even though he actually wrote very little directly about architecture. His terms "to build" and "to dwell" have been equated with the creation and inhabitation of architecture, but can be more substantively understood as referring to acts of experiencing and creating a place in the world; of living authentically as a means to disclose some truths about existence, and existence itself. To "dwell," as outlined in *Building, Dwelling, Thinking*, is to be joined with the "fourfold" of the earth, sky, divinities, and mortals. In this essay, the reciprocity of "dwelling" and the "fourfold" are illustrated by the example of a bridge over a river. The bridge, as evoked by Heidegger, is a real, material presence, a "thing" like the jug in the essay "The Thing" (1950), but is not merely that. In a typical Heideggerian reversal, the legibility of the place depends on the bridge, not the other way around. By "bridging," it "gathers" the river and its banks in a manner that shapes peoples' experiences, and "discloses" broader ontological understandings of space, place, and the world.

The small vacation house he built in Todtnauberg near Freiburg in the Black Forest Region of Germany can be understood similarly, as an authentic dwelling that, for Heidegger, facilitated life lived in unity with the "fourfold," but also disclosed it. In this context, architecture served to satisfy the two schools of phenomenological thought I outlined in the Prologue – a means to deeply engage and experience the world, and a portentous setting for ontological understandings of the world and one's place in it.[27] For Heidegger, it was where he could live naturally while also thinking philosophically.

In 1922, Heidegger, then 33, was appointed Chair of Philosophy at Marburg University. In the same year, he built *die Hütte* as a family vacation cottage. In

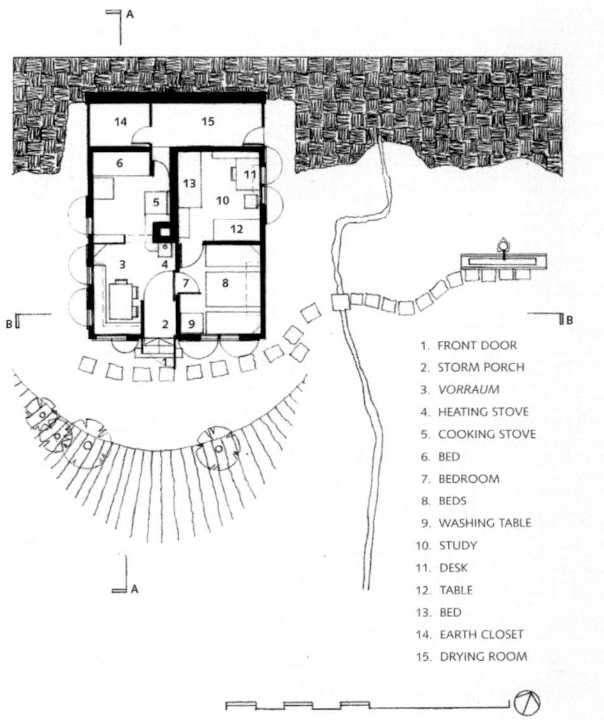

FIGURE 6.4 Plan, Heidegger's Black Forest hut

FIGURE 6.5 Martin and Elfride Heidegger in front of the hut

time, it also served as a private retreat where he wrote many of his major works. The small house, set into the slope of the land, faced almost exactly south and overlooked a farming valley. It is a small house, 6 by 7 meters, comprising three rooms, a kitchen and dining area, bedroom, and an east-facing study where Heidegger worked. There was no running water, or plumbing, only a simple well and an "earth closet." Heidegger did not design the house and in fact his wife Elfride initiated the project, found the property and carpenter, and paid for it with an inheritance. Consequently, it is difficult to tell how much he actually participated, if at all, in its design and construction.[28] It is for the most part a practical house, built of wood siding inside and out according to local building traditions. But once inhabited, Heidegger clearly appropriated it as a place that accommodated and expressed his philosophical values.

He was often there alone and it provided a setting to live a life he considered most essential, while writing some of his most probing works regarding the nature of existence. In 1934, after Heidegger had resigned as Chair at Freiburg University, he was offered the Chair of Philosophy in distant Berlin, which he declined. Subsequently he wrote "Why Do I Stay in The Provinces?" where *die Hütte* is portrayed as a "ski hut," and its overhanging roofs compared to neighboring farmhouses.[29] He recalls the natural setting of "dark fir-trees," and the "radiant expanse" of the "summer sky," where two hawks circle overhead. In this brief passage, he economically describes an authentic dwelling enmeshed with its natural and cultural settings. This, he states, "is my work world."

He goes on to insist that he does not observe his surroundings in a distanced, aesthetic manner, but is "embedded" in them and participates in their "hourly changes."[30] In this regard, his simple dwelling serves as a setting where "questions become simple and essential" and the "resistance of the towering firs" as they sway in a snowstorm mirror the challenges of philosophy.[31] He goes on to equate his philosophical work to the simple labors of the peasant, arguing that it is not "like the aloof studies of some eccentric," but "belongs right in the midst of the peasant's work."[32] Consequently, the house, set in harmony with its cultural and environmental setting, facilitates Heidegger's desire for connection with his environmental and cultural surroundings, and living an authentic and philosophically productive life.

In his short essay, Heidegger also describes friendships with local farmers where, "We smoke our pipes in silence," and "mostly say nothing at all," but, as pure and romantic as Heidegger portrayed *die Hütte*, it turns out to be a more complicated matter.[33] He invited close friends to visit and conducted summer seminars there for graduate students, including one in 1933 for members of the National Socialist Party to discuss changes to the university under their regime. It was also a refuge for Heidegger after he resigned from Freiburg University,

FIGURE 6.6 The well at Heidegger's Black Forest hut

FIGURE 6.7 Martin Heidegger at the well

apparently because by then he had become disillusioned with the Nazis, though because of his association he spent many years following the Second World War as a discredited thinker and shunned academic.[34]

A more complete, though analogical, description of *die Hütte* appears in the section of *Building, Dwelling, Thinking* devoted to "a farmhouse in the Black Forest." Heidegger describes the farmhouse as sited, "on the wind-sheltered slope looking south among the meadows close to the spring," and where the act of dwelling "gave it the wide overhanging shingle roof whose proper slope bears up under the burden of snow, and which, reaching deep down, shields the chambers against the storms of the long winter nights."[35]

The farmhouse embodies the "raising of locations by the joining of their spaces" in a manner similar to how the Greek Temple, presented in the earlier *Origin of the Work of Art*, "makes visible the invisible space of air."[36] The Black Forest farmhouse and the Greek Temple embody dwelling, but more importantly, in a typical rhetorical reversal, results from one's ability to "dwell."[37] The farmhouse, in particular, discloses the life it shapes and is shaped by,[38] and reveals the capabilities Heidegger attributes to *die Hütte*. In all, Heidegger expressed himself through the inhabitation of his hut, and can be understood, at least in part, through it.[39]

Thoreau's cabin at Walden Pond

Henry David Thoreau's simple dwelling on Walden Pond is perhaps the most famous house ever built, and *Walden* the most famous book ever written about a house. However, in many ways, Thoreau's philosophical discussions regarding the building and inhabitation of his simple hut, similar to the metaphysical digressions of the earlier *A Week on the Concord and Merrimack Rivers* (1849), are not about a house at all, but occupy a broad territory, encompassing practical, economic, social, political, psychic, spiritual, sensual, quotidian, metaphysical, and cosmic realms. Thoreau argues that "every man is tasked to make his life, even in its details, worthy of the contemplation of his most elevated and critical hour,"[40] and systematically portrays the virtues of an authentic life, and the means to achieve it. Throughout his extended essay, even though anchored to a specific place and the direct experiences it offers, he looks inward and outward.

In the building and inhabitation of his cabin Thoreau aspired to shed the superfluous encumbrances of material life and consequently access a broader, more authentic consciousness.[41] He built the cabin himself in the spring of 1845, on land a mile from Concord, MA owned by his friend and mentor Ralph Waldo Emerson. Thoreau had learned carpentry skills by assisting in the construction of his parents' house in Concord, and apparently the most help

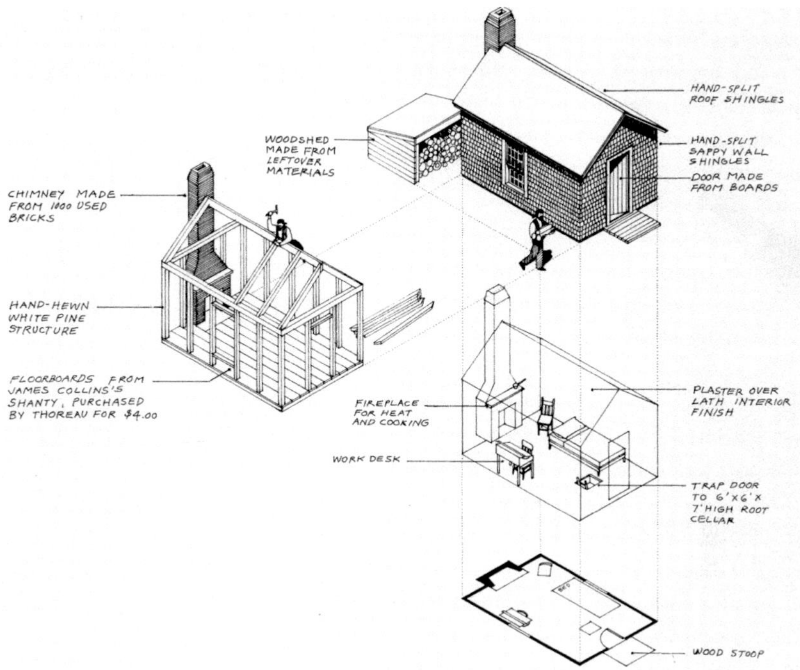

FIGURE 6.8 Thoreau's cabin at Walden Pond

FIGURE 6.9 Thoreau's cabin at Walden Pond

he received was in raising his cabin's modest timber frame and roof, an event attended by, among others, Emerson, Bronson Alcott, and Ellery Channing. It was a simple, wooden, gable-roofed, one room cabin, 10' × 15', set over a basement he excavated on a south-facing slope. It had two windows, a fireplace, and a single, wooden entry door, and was sparsely furnished with furniture he mostly made himself.

He moved in on July 4, before it was completed, in what was perhaps a deliberate eschewing of an important national holiday, and wrote in his journal the next day, "I came here to live,"[42] and a version of perhaps his most famous passage from *Walden*:

> I went to the woods because I wanted to live deliberately, to front only the essential facts of life, and see if I could not learn what it had to teach, and not, when I came to die, discover that I had not lived.[43]

He lived there for two years and two months, and while there wrote his first book, *A Week on the Concord and Merrimack Rivers*, and completed a draft of *Walden*. He was not solitary, but it was the solitary moments of realization, connection, and ecstasy that distinguish the narrative of *Walden*. Many have argued that this was the most philosophically productive period of his life.[44]

Each chapter addressed different aspects of his philosophy, framed through the lens of his self-constructed house. In the first chapter, "Economy," Thoreau described the bare essentials for a simple dwelling, and their minimal costs, in a manner that suggested that the important tasks of life can be focused on once this basic need is met.[45] Subsequent chapters addressed those areas of life he deemed essential, now accessible through the means of a dwelling that does not encumber one, and the ways of living it affords. In "Reading," he discussed the value of knowledge; in "Solitude," the virtues of a solitary existence in harmony with nature; in "Visitors," the depth of social interaction and discourse provided by his house that "had only three chairs… one for solitude, two for friendship, three for society"; and in "Higher Laws," the reconciliation of a sensual life with spiritual aspirations, which he found to be of equal value.[46] Thoreau believed that the world was elucidative and transcendent, not sinful and corrupting as in Protestant beliefs. He writes in a typical Thoreauvian dichotomy, "I have found in myself, and still find, an instinct toward a higher, or, as it is named, spiritual life, as do most men, and another toward a primitive rank and savage one, and I reverence them both."[47]

It was also the setting for ecstatic moments that defined his early life (recorded in the journals he began in 1837), that were most often accessed by solitary sojourns in nature. In the chapter "Solitude," he describes a synesthesia of sensory experiences engendered by his surroundings. "This is a delicious evening, when the whole body is one sense, and imbibes delight through every pore. I go and come with a strange liberty in Nature, a part of herself."[48] In "Sounds," his hut, and the life it affords, creates contemplative opportunities:

> Sometimes, in a summer morning, having taken my accustomed bath, I sat in my sunny doorway from sunrise till noon, rapt in a revery, amidst the pines and hickories and sumachs, in undisturbed solitude and stillness, while the birds sang around or flitted noiseless through the house, until by the sun falling in at my west window, or the noise of some traveller's wagon on the distant highway, I was reminded of the lapse of time. I grew in those seasons like corn in the night, and they were far better than any work of the hands would have been. They were not subtracted from my life, but so much over and above my usual allowance, I realized what the Orientals mean by contemplation and the forsaking of works.[49]

Thoreau's cabin was a means to shed the encumbrances of material life, while also providing the means to do so. His dwelling and the essentially solitary life of the spiritual seeker, it appears, were congruent. But, even though the narrative of *Walden* prejudices solitary experiences, reflections, and epiphanies, it is also peopled by neighbors and visits by friends. Thoreau may have written "I love to be alone. I never found a companion that was so companionable as solitude,"[50] but also that he was not "naturally a hermit."[51] In "Visitors," Thoreau recounts how, when all three of his chairs were occupied, others "generally economized the room by standing up." He continues by asserting that even when "twenty-five or thirty souls" were in the room it did not feel crowded.[52] His only complaint – his cabin's small space at times felt insufficient to hold "the big thoughts" of the conversations it housed.

Social, political, and religious criticism find regular voice in *Walden*, and Thoreau earned a deserved reputation of being a Yankee Diogenes.[53] His cabin is positioned as an antidote to the extravagance of most dwellings and buildings, including voluminous cellars fit only for the "vermin which infest them." He insists that most men work for their houses, which are more than they need and do not own, and consequently are "poor all their days because they think they must have such a one as their neighbors."[54] In "Economy," he writes, "We have built for this world a family mansion, and for the next a family tomb." For Thoreau, most houses were prisons to escape from, or tombs to avoid.[55]

Like Heidegger, he also appropriates the farmers who at times visit him, to illustrate the embodiment of an unencumbered life, but one in Thoreau's estimation with limits. One, simply described as "a Canadian, a woodchopper and postmaker," who, though literate, responds to a passage from Homer read by Thoreau by saying "That's good," and when asked if he thought some aspects of society might be reformed, replied, "No, I like it well enough."[56] Thoreau characterizes his visitor to make a point: an essential "animal man" is paradoxically insufficient to confront "the essential facts of life." Thoreau may have built his hut where "a woodchuck had formerly built his burrow," but this was in service of transgressing the limits of what he saw as his culture's still-largely animal, or spiritually undeveloped, nature.[57]

Thoreau may celebrate and, in many ways, embodied the natural and authentic life, but this was in service of higher ideals, perhaps illustrated by the enigmatic parable of "The Artist of Kouroo" that appears in the "Conclusion." This short mythical account, constructed by Thoreau from a number of Eastern sources with direct allusions to the Hindu *Bhagavad Gita*, illustrates how devotion to contemplative practices and art are the highest of ideals. It begins:

> Why should we be in such desperate haste to succeed in such desperate enterprises? If a man does not keep pace with his companions, perhaps it is because he hears a different drummer. Let him step to the music which he hears, however measured or far away.[58]

He goes on to describe an artist who "strives for perfection," through the making of a staff, and as he does so, time and space are transcended, ages come and pass away, and vast cosmologies are revealed. Through the creative act of the fashioning of a staff, he creates a new perspective on the world. Thoreau concludes, "The material was pure, and his art was pure; how could the result be other than wonderful?"[59] One can plausibly argue that Thoreau's cabin on Walden Pond, the life it supported, and the perspectives it produced, can be similarly described.

★★★

Mahatma Gandhi and his simple dwelling at Sevagram Ashram, in Wardha, Nagpur, are eloquent expressions of a life of simplicity and the personal and societal benefits this can bring. However, his dwelling was not so much a personal expression of beneficent austerities, but a symbol of them and consequently has elicited diverse interpretations. Heidegger's and Thoreau's huts have also become symbols that point to, and disclose broader cultural and ontological interpretations, revealing what they represent more than what they might have meant to their builders. Heidegger's hut has been the locus of a variety of interpretations regarding its significance and relationship to his work. As Adam Sharr proposes, the hut has been presented as:

> The site of heroic confrontation between philosopher and existence, as the petit bourgeois escape of a misguided romantic, as a place with fascist overtones that remains suspicious, or as an entirely unremarkable little building.[60]

Thoreau's hut has also been subject to multiple interpretations, as a solitary refuge of a societal outlier, a noble experiment in self-determination and reliance, a model for environmental responsibility, and an exemplar of cultural resistance.[61] Both houses are pilgrimage sites for devotees whose opinions regarding their relevance and meaning vary as widely as the scholars who have dissected Heidegger's and Thoreau's philosophies.[62]

Wittgenstein, referencing the house he designed for his sister stated, "Working in philosophy... like work in architecture in many respects... is really more a working on oneself,"[63] and the design of her house can be understood as an embodiment of aspects of his uncompromising philosophy. Jung's retreat at Bollingen specifically served as a means to materially explore and articulate the deep inner work he engaged during its stages of construction. Neruda eloquently expressed his poetic sensibilities through his houses. They became extensions, or even embodiments, of the poet. The poem "La Sebastiana," first published in 1962, is an ode to the five-story, tower-like house he built on one of the hills of Valparaiso.[64] The house comes alive as it is constructed: "The tower dances, the doors and staircases sing," and when completed:

> The house grows and speaks:
> stands on its own feet:
> has clothes wrapped round its skeleton:
> and as from seaward the spring:
> swimming like a water nymph:
> kisses the sand of Valparaiso.[65]

Heidegger's hut was not a medium for the philosopher to access inner understandings, but a place set in surroundings that represented his values and supported his work. Heidegger's conjunction of his work and that of the peasant, and his hut's emulation of local dwellings, reveal his valorization of a culturally distinct, and separate, place. Similar to the special agency of the Greek temple, his hut did not so much represent, or stand in for, something else, but embodied it. He writes, "A building, a Greek temple portrays nothing," and later, "The temple, in its standing there, first gives to things their look and to men their outlook on themselves."[66] Thoreau can also be direct regarding the values his hut embodied, albeit from a characteristic contrary position.

> When I think of acquiring for myself one of our luxurious dwellings, I am deterred, for so to speak, the country is not yet adapted to *human* culture, and we are still forced to cut our *spiritual* bread far thinner than our forebears did their wheaten. Not that all architectural ornament is to be neglected even in the rudest periods; but let our houses first be lined with beauty.[67]

However, Thoreau had larger ontological goals than improved dwellings. His cabin was more ephemeral – a precise utility that freed him to "solve some of the problems of life, not only theoretically, but practically."[68] He insisted, as recalled by Emerson, that "The other world is all my art; my pencils will draw no other; my jack-knife will cut nothing else; I do not use it as a means."[69] Thus when his cabin had done its job in assisting and expressing his spiritual and moral maturation, it was abandoned.

Walden also reveals Thoreau's social reform aspirations, which were more explicitly expressed in the essay "Civil Disobedience" (1849), and his participation in the New England anti-slavery movement. His direct engagement with the design, realization, and inhabitation of the Walden Pond hut served as a means to attend to higher spiritual and social ideals and purposes. Heidegger had no such aspirations, beyond philosophy's generalized goals of explicating aspects of human consciousness and existence.[70] His hut was predominantly a setting for the focused pursuit of his individual, philosophical investigations, and a refuge from his otherwise conventional, complicated life.

Beston and Lindbergh described their cabins as frames for the worlds they sought to understand. Thoreau and Heidegger celebrated the contemplative, individual experiences their simple dwellings provided, the importance of place, and the ultimate value of unmediated experience. Thoreau may have regretted the loss of his youthful experiences of ecstasy, but as he matured those experiences were perhaps more embedded in the mundane events and activities of his life.[71] Heidegger, in a letter to his wife from *die Hütte* in 1932, conveys how his "cabin existence has acquired its proper form," and he is "making progress with the wood & as I go along I think of the lines from Goethe: 'Dragging wood with rapture be it done, 'Tis the seed of many an earthly sun.'[72] Emerson wrote, "Every spirit builds itself a house; and beyond its house a world; and beyond its world a heaven. Know then that the world exists for you.... Build therefore your own world."[73] In a variety of ways and means, the houses I have discussed served as means for writers and philosophers to build their worlds. The domestic was also a medium to understand the world and their place in it, and suggests ways we might better understand them, and perhaps ourselves.

7

DOMESTIC IDEOLOGIES

Modernism, postmodernism, and the house

The previous chapter presented house and home as a means of self-exploration and expression, and a medium for disclosing and making sense of the world. However, the examples were singular and personal, and their builders had little interest in envisioning improved houses, and homes, for others. This chapter will present twentieth-century modernist architects who set out to do just that. To do so, I will discuss how the house in modernism often served as a preeminent platform to explore new and better ways of living. Moreover, for some architect-theoreticians of this time, the house represented the larger tasks of architecture. When this was the case, a type of secular spirituality was assigned the house, and it was positioned as redemptive to architecture and society. Theoretical tracts of prominent modernists were typically declarative, often moralistic, and at times deployed spiritual language to lend authority to their largely secular and idiosyncratic positions. Postmodernism provides a counterpoint but, whereas its adherents stridently reappraised modernist positions and programs, they also retained vestiges of their ideals. In all, the house was often deployed to develop, apply, validate, and promulgate particular theories.

Modernist polemics redefined

Modernism is difficult, if not impossible, to define. Marshall Berman aptly stated, "If we think of modernism as a struggle to make ourselves at home in a constantly changing world, we will realize that no mode of modernism can ever be definitive."[1] Architectural modernism is equally challenging, and its historiography includes a diversity of attributions regarding its rational, functional, formal, technological, visionary, autonomous, ahistorical, secular, international, and socio-political goals. Influential modernist architects were often presented, or presented themselves, as aspiring to create an architecture that reflected a dramatically changed world, or sought to effect said changes. This is all true, to a certain extent, but the literature often characterizes modernist polemics, in their broadest definitions, as a secular phenomenon and misses its spiritual undertones. Renata Hejduk and Jim Williamson name this the "apocryphal project of modern architecture," where the "deep religiosity of, in particular, the masters of Modernism is missing in the historiography of architecture, and more often than not, relegated to footnotes or a special issue of a journal or magazine."[2]

Even though the rationalist sheen of modernism may have suggested otherwise, twentieth-century manifestos did not so much diminish the sacred dimensions of architecture but created more heterodox expressions of it. These included pronouncements regarding societal deficiencies, and redemptive means for their improvement, eschatological prophesies, historical validations, and essentialized values. During this period, secular buildings, and even architecture itself, became sacraments of a new future. Colin Rowe argues in his influential *The Architecture of Good Intentions: Towards a Possible Retrospect*, "It can scarcely be an exaggeration to propose that the modern movement typically conceived of itself as a church," and in doing so became "an elaborate icon," which excited adherents with its promise of overcoming the past and creating a more hopeful, and morally superior future.[3] Adolf Loos exhorted like a nineteenth-century reformer, Walter Gropius warned like a biblical prophet, Frank Lloyd Wright sounded like a missionary for a new American religion, and the moralizing tone of Le Corbusier rivaled any Evangelical minister.

A proliferation of theoretical tracts and manifestos defines, at least in part, twentieth-century architectural modernism, especially during the interwar period. Its principal proponents typically relied on rhetorical polarities and the demonizing of the past to construct a progressive vision of the future. To this end, some appropriated Christian millennialism – the fall, paradise lost, and judgment, followed by redemption – to insist that time was short, change was needed immediately, and architecture was the savior. Eschatological pleas underlined the urgency to act, though their religious undertones were often occluded by the rationalism of the time. Charles Jencks argued that modernist jeremiads adopted Old Testament tropes of identifying enemies, constructing binary *shoulds* and *should-nots*, and establishing consequences to enforce compliance.[4] For Rowe, modern architecture became a "dynamic faith" for those who would hear the call, including dire consequences if they did not.[5]

Michael Benedikt suggests, "Modernism itself was, arguably, a religious movement from the start."[6] The totalizing polemics of Le Corbusier and Wright, and the strident manifestos of their contemporaries, described architecture itself in terms reminiscent of religion. Walter Gropius answered the question, "What is architecture?" by insisting it was "The crystalline expression of man's noblest thoughts, his ardour, his humanity, his faith, his religion!" and, in the same essay, prophesied a second coming of sorts of the true architect, the "Lord of Art."[7] Others were equally prophetic. Adolf Loos in *Ornament and Crime* set out to reform decadent architecture with a missionary zeal; De Stijl manifestos called for a spiritual crusade of sorts to establish an "international unity of life, art, and culture";[8] and Bruno Taut insisted that "only a complete revolution in the spiritual realm will establish a "paradise on earth" (or at least once there was glass architecture "everywhere").[9] Louis Sullivan, in his brief essay of 1902, "Education," imagined a redemptive era emerging from a dissolute past when he stated, "After a long night and a longer twilight, we envision a dawn-era: an era in which the minor law of tradition shall yield to the greater law of creation," where "man at last is become emancipated" – all for the "moral and mental vigor of the race," where "true art may flourish."[10] Wright, who I will turn to later, was even more prognostic, insisting that the end was near, and only the architect could lead society to a new Eden.[11]

The oft-cited roster of modernist architects, while preoccupied at times with leading or responding to the zeitgeist of their times, could be surprisingly atemporal in their championing of timeless fundamentals. They may have talked a good game about a new, timely, and progressive architecture, but they also drew liberally from historical sources. Le Corbusier's and Mies van der Rohe's classical influences have often been cited, but it is not so much classical forms that informed their work but classical ideals. Le Corbusier's visionary idealism recalls the Platonic idea of the potential of pure form to reveal an otherwise hidden world. How else to explain his self-constructed origin myth cited earlier and its presentation as a means to validate transcendent, ideal proportions for architecture, and the benefits they promised? Mies van der Rohe waxed poetic about the virtues of process over form, positioning the architect as an anonymous channeler of a new, universal architecture.[12]

The purity and value of original forms of unpedigreed architecture also appears in numerous modernist tracts and reveal the Romantic impulses of the time. Even Loos, the theoretician most closely associated with the anti-style, ornament-condemning side of modernism, poetically described the virtues of alpine houses and, in the words of Theodor Adorno, could display "some remarkably bourgeois traces."[13] However, it was the Romantic notion of the interrelationship of society and its artifacts that was more prevalent and influential.[14] When Gropius and others complain about the deficiencies of their contemporary culture, they insist that architecture is the problem and therefore architecture is the solution.

What does all of this have to do with the house and home? The house in many cases was the predominant modernist project where houses designed by influential modernists advanced and broadcast their theories. There were particular preoccupations with the presentation of ideals related to purity and original sources, the anonymous application of rationality and science, a deterministic process of design, production and engineering, and the improvement of society through architecture. The early modernists were radical, but not in the way the word is reflexively defined. Instead, they were radical according to its Latin root, *radix*, in their aspiration to rediscover and establish fundamentals or essentials. Their industrial, mechanistic, evangelical, and millennial emphases were heir to a combination of eighteenth- and nineteenth-century progressive positions, which also led to significant proposals for mass housing. But it was the house, and all that it represented, that dominated. And it was the house, even though many insisted modernism was devoid of symbolism, that performed as an iconic billboard for their theories.[15]

The valorization of the house in modernism

Architects have used single-family houses as laboratories to carve rough answers out of materials and space, a means to apply and test new ideas and theories, and a media to announce what they discovered. Perhaps the most recognized and early example is John Soane's house in Lincoln's Inn Fields, London, a typical London row house that, beginning in 1812, Soane transformed over time in a manner that anticipates the experimentation of modernism.[16] The house as an experimental laboratory, however, found particular resonance in modernism, especially during the 1920s and 1930s when the modernist polemic was most influentially formulated and communicated, and the house employed to advance, test, and broadcast ideas.

The house preoccupied many of the most influential early modernist architects, and the loudest promulgators of modernism had much to say about it.[17] Their work has been routinely characterized as inventive formal, material, and spatial responses to modernity, but their theories and pronouncements often had more universal, emancipatory, goals. The following focus on these well-known architects, and their ubiquitously referenced theoretical and built works, is not to insist that they created superior expressions of the modern house, but to question why they were often credited with doing so. And, it is because their profuse postulations were, and still are, influential that they are the most appropriate sources to understand what modernism was meant to be, and came to mean.[18]

Frank Lloyd Wright, as one might expect, had quite a lot to say about the house. He began *The Natural House* of 1954 by negatively characterizing the typical American house as one that "lied about everything," and whose builders were "criminals." Wright's "dark age" of the house can only be transcended by means of "the qualities in all things," a rather oblique statement that suggests universal truths. He predictably disparages academics, and states that his "textbook" is "the book of creation," which has saved him from "the hell of tradition."[19] However, Wright's means for accomplishing a "new house" that expressed "the human spirit" were often rather prosaic – form, materials, details, and building and environmental technologies. Often the new house is more about what it should not include – attics and basements for example – as what it should.

Often with Wright, there are Unitarian-infused insistences on unity and validations of his "organic" architecture through religious references, all delivered in lofty rhetoric that recalls Walt Whitman. He insists the house should be *on* the ground, not *in* it, alluding to the disturbing troglodyte–nomad characterization that appears in *The Living City*.[20] In this short parable, knowingly or not, he recasts the *Genesis* story of Cain and Abel, where Cain is a murderous proto-urbanist, and subsequently deploys it in service of the dispersed, individual settlement patterns he advocated.[21] He goes on to state that in time, "disciples and friends" gathered around him to achieve an organic domestic architecture, which he insists, without irony, "dates back to Laotse (sic) 500 B.C., and later to Jesus himself."[22]

Given his output of houses, Wright certainly had the authority to offer his opinions. Like Soane, he also experimented on his own houses, beginning in 1889 with his house, and eventually studio, in Oak Park, Illinois. Establishing an architectural practice in one's own house in the suburbs, though not without precedent, was very unusual,[23] and it is readily apparent that Wright's insistence on the unity of life and work were an *a priori* condition for a home where he could "live as I'll work as I am!"[24] Oak Park was an early suburban residential development where the self-reliant and family-focused, single-family house found influential expressions, thanks, in part, to all of the houses Wright built there. Wright's house displayed his preoccupations with Romantic infused pastoralism and essential shelter, hearth, and vistas where, like New England transcendentalist utopian visions, family, industry, and intellect were all sheltered. Similar to the influential modernist houses that followed, it broadcast its ideals, though arguably less stridently.

However, Wright was not so much interested in reforming society, as in reforming architecture to preserve the individualism, autonomy, and freedom he saw as defining American characteristics, which were challenged in his time by rapid urbanization.[25] But, for his early modern European contemporaries, the house served to instruct regarding not only better ways to build but also to live. Modernism, as it is commonly understood, can be said to have coalesced

FIGURE 7.1 Entry fireplace, Frank Lloyd Wright's house and studio, Oak Park, IL

FIGURE 7.2 Schröder House, Utrecht, Netherlands, Gerrit Rietveld with Truus Schröder

in the pivotal 1920s and 1930s. It was during this time that the most influential manifestos were issued, theoretical tracts published, and schools and groups formed. The De Stijl group, founded in 1917 in Holland by Gerrit Rietveld, Piet Mondrian, Theo van Doesburg, and others, had a robust publication program, with manifestos that included declarative statements regarding new problems and solutions for architecture, and special interests in the domestic. The group's manifestos promoted a unity of the arts and architecture, and the value of order, clarity, and objectivity. Van Doesburg, in particular, insisted on a pure architecture, unmoored from tradition, context, and in some cases even gravity. He envisioned an architecture that would transcend its earthbound limits, rising to the spiritual purity of the abstract.

Rather than provide mere domesticity, the modern house often aimed to instruct regarding new formal and material means, and the capacity of the house to improve society. The Schröder House in Utrecht, designed by Gerrit Rietveld in collaboration with the owner and interior designer, Truus Schröder, and completed in 1924, can be understood as a built manifesto.[26] Located at the end of a block of brick row houses on a site that originally faced open land, its size and scale respected its context. But that is where any similarity with neighboring houses ended. Congruent with Rietveld's theoretical interests, the house's composition of planar elements expressed dynamic, formal, and spatial organizations, and its rationalism suggested reciprocity with universal orders. Its didactic formal qualities are well known – what is less discussed are its domestic agendas. Truus Schröder was interested in progressive ideas of her time regarding women's roles, domesticity, and the raising of children. In her house a relatively conventional ground floor led to the dynamic upper one, its fluidity epitomized by movable walls presumably for a variety of spatial configurations and uses. Retracted, the entire living area became one space where children were included, and domestic hierarchies subverted.[27] The freedom of adaptability spoke about the transgression of static designations of domestic rooms, and, by extension, static lives, and an autonomous architectural idea to improve one's life.

In *The Natural House*, Wright obliquely dismissed Le Corbusier as a latecomer, a "Swiss discoverer"[28] (presumably of Wright's unique ideas). Their enmity is well known, and understandable as they spoke in similar voices. In *Towards a New Architecture*, Le Corbusier provided prescriptive dictates regarding appropriate sources, methods, materials, and expressions of architecture, with particular attention given to the domestic. He opens his discussion of the ideal house by citing "a question of morality," and the need for "truth." Referencing the primordial nature of the house as the "first tool that [man] forged for himself," he argues that the current "out of date tool" should be relegated to the "scrap heap."[29] To make his case, Le Corbusier first outlines the deficiencies of contemporary tastes and houses, in a manner similar to Loos' earlier *Ornament and Crime*, to argue, in unambiguous terms, that they reveal vestigial and outmoded notions of the house.

> Men live in old houses and they have not yet thought of building houses adapted to themselves. The lair has been dear to their hearts since all time. To such a degree and so strongly that they have established the cult of the home. A *roof!* and other household gods. Religions have established themselves on dogmas, the dogmas do not change; but civilizations change and religions tumble to dust. Houses have not changed. But the cult of the house has remained the same for centuries. The house will also fall to dust.

He then presents the type of moralizing argument many modernists of his era were prone to.

> A man who practices a religion and does not believe in it is a wretch; he is to be pitied. We are to be pitied for living in unworthy houses, since they ruin our health and our *morale*. It is our lot to have become sedentary creatures; our houses gnaw at us in our sluggishness, like consumption. We shall soon need far too many sanatoriums. We are to be pitied. Our houses disgust us; we fly from them and frequent restaurants and nightclubs; or we gather together in our houses gloomily and secretly like wretched animals; we are becoming demoralized.[30]

Because the house is the cause of the moral degeneracy he describes, then naturally the house is the solution. For Le Corbusier, "the problem of the house is the problem of the epoch,"[31] and the redemption of architecture and society, requires the "pure" and the "abstract," as epitomized by the eponymous engineer – and Le Corbusier's Purism. In doing so, Le Corbusier routinely presented two otherwise unrelated sentiments: the beauty of formal aesthetics, and the instrumentality of precise, mass-produced architecture. In the same manner that the automobile evidenced aesthetic and practical virtues, the house, in Le Corbusier's opinion, "will be a tool as the motor-car is becoming a tool."[32] Consequently, his counterproject, which is presented apocryphally as part of a "new epoch" and a "new spirit," valorized machine aesthetics and a Fordist production of houses.[33] His proposals for multi-family housing illustrated the virtues he extolled. However, in his 1922 proposal for mass-production workman's houses, the units may have repeated like so many automobiles, but their site-crafted "cement-gun walls" bore little relationship with the "industrial production" he proposed, revealing perhaps that theory, and language, at least in this case, superseded built form. As Matthew Nowicki complained in 1951, "in the overwhelming majority of modern design, form follows form, not function."[34]

This disparity is conveniently illustrated by his most famous house, the Villa Savoye located in the suburbs of Paris, which came to epitomize his dictum, "The house is a machine for living in."[35] At first glance, mechanistic and mass-production imagery formally define the house: the ground floor derived from the driveway to the garage; the ramp that conveys its inhabitants without interruption; the ocean liner imagery of railings and roof forms; and the suggestion of assembled building components. But, Villa Savoye is not a mass-production house, but a one-off, custom-built one. And, even though it may have been formally inventive, mechanically it was not. For example, it did not include a shower, the American invention that at the time was revolutionizing bathing.

But, in spite of what he said, Le Corbusier had other agendas. Indeed, this small house was tasked with doing quite a lot. His *animal rationale* needed a dwelling that sheltered his needs and also his spirit.[36] Like the classical temples it recalled, it embodied ideal qualities in a self-possessed, geometrically derived, and autonomous manner. It was placed in opposition to the nature around it, a pavilion of Apollonian rationality, similar to eighteenth-century English country houses that had similar motivations. Le Corbusier described the formal qualities of the house as a complement to the "rural landscape of Poissy," with no front, back, or side of the house, a "box in the middle of the meadows, dominating the orchard."[37] Like a Palladian villa, it surveyed its surroundings with a cool and rational eye from the *piano nobile*, but in this case through panoramic banded windows.

Inside, however, the plan abandoned the ordered rationality of the exterior in favor of the dynamic movement insisted by its ramp. The first clue, of course, is the rear curve calibrated to the turning radius of a car. The entry foyer displayed a nervous domesticity with a table uneasily cantilevered from a column, presumably to drop one's car keys. There was also an industrial wall-hung sink, but its purpose is unclear, other than to suggest a type of ritual ablution before rising away from the servants' quarters to the living level above. To do so, there was not only a ramp but also a stylized spiral stair, at the top of which a phone, an icon of modernity in its own right, was displayed. Past the second floor, the ramp rose up to the roof, an unambiguous path to the sky, light, and, one might infer, enlightenment.[38]

The kitchen, living room, bedroom, and bath evoked essential, healthy living, presumably for body and spirit, including Victorian notions regarding the benefits of fresh air and sunshine in the roof garden. All of which were mixed up with symbols of modernity – a ship, a car, industrial fittings, and furniture – to produce a mélange of images, but more importantly, assertions regarding how one might live better and the essential role the house plays to do so. Reyner Banham argued that Le Corbusier, because of his preeminent position in twentieth-century architecture and the confident prescriptions and promises of

FIGURE 7.3 Villa Savoye, Poissy, France, Le Corbusier

FIGURE 7.4 Schindler-Chace House, Los Angeles, CA, Rudolph Schindler

his writings, made an easy target, and that "he was probably no worse than the rest of his generation."[39] As such his writings and houses are more illustrative of the reconsiderations of the house, and home, in his time, and the written and iconic language deployed to do so, than an indictment of them.

Despite the Villa Savoye's assertions regarding improved domesticity, it was actually more about disembodied ideals. Le Corbusier's acerbic and prolonged polemic regarding "home" had actually very little to say about domesticity, and was emblematic of modernism where according to one scholar, "The domestic, perpetually invoked in order to be denied, remains throughout the course of modernism a crucial site of anxiety and subversion."[40] The same might be said about the Schröder house but obviously not about all modernist houses of this period. For example, the Schindler-Chace House, King's Road, in Los Angeles, designed by Rudolph Schindler and completed around the same time as the Villa Savoye aimed, at least in part, to improve the family by reconfiguring it through the house.

Schindler designed the house for his wife Sophie Pauline Gibling, and their friends Clyde and Marian (de Camera) Chace, so that both couples – and four individuals – could live separately and communally. Its domestic and architectural arrangements recalled William Morris' plans to add a wing to The Red House so that Edward Burne-Jones' family and his own could live together.[41] Morris' plans were never realized, but the Schindler-Chace house was in 1922. There were separate wings for the two families with workrooms for each individual, but they shared a communal kitchen and presumably other aspects of their lives around the common hearth of the courtyard fireplace. Named by Schindler "A Cooperative Dwelling," it was imagined as a new and improved way of living, and a critique of the constraints of conventional houses and marriages.[42] Gibling's interests in communism and social reform were instrumental in the conceptualization of the house. She and Marian de Camera were classmates at Smith and worked together on social projects, including residency at Hull House in Chicago.[43] Similar to Wright's Oak Park house and studio, where Schindler and Gibling lived for a while, the Schindler-Chace house co-joined home, work, and public affairs. For a number of years, it served as a salon for regular gatherings of the Los Angeles artistic community and in this role, positioned as an agent of social change. Their domestic utopia was short-lived, however; the Chaces left in 1924, Pauline in 1927.[44]

Postmodern counterpositions

Did all of these packed agendas for the house end with the "end of modernism?" Hardly, but they did change. Clearly a fatigue sets in during the 1960s regarding the capacity of architecture to explore new forms and materials, embody ideals,

FIGURE 7.5 Glass House, New Canaan, CT, Phillip Johnson

FIGURE 7.6 Mother's House, Chestnut Hill, PA, Robert Venturi

and effect societal change. Instead, what was more often the case were deliberate rejections of the modernist progressive mission in favor of more autonomous, aesthetic, and intellectual considerations. Phillip Johnson became a strange champion of these new "values." He began as a cheerleader for modernism, but as early as 1954, in a talk at the Harvard University School of Architecture, dismissed what he called the "seven crutches of modernism." Instead he insisted, "Architecture is the sum of inescapable artistic decisions that you have to make."[45] The series of buildings and pavilions he built on his property in New Canaan, Connecticut, described by Johnson as a "diary of an eccentric architect,"[46] reflected his diffuse, eclectic positions.

The Glass House, completed in 1949, was a glass and steel pavilion that formally and materially recalled Mies van der Rohe's work, only to deny it in details.[47] The Glass House's transparency allowed unobstructed views inside and out (the house was visible from a distant road but the extensive grounds were very private); the juxtaposed Brick House, completed at the same time, was almost completely enclosed and served as a guest house.[48] When the Brick House was later renovated, Soane's house was cited as a source, and subsequent structures Johnson added to the extensive grounds expressed his eclectic tastes.[49] He was essentially a classicist, but in a formal not philosophical sense. Unlike some of the modernist personages he admired, he eschewed aspirational, spiritual-infused language to explain his work. Instead, the Glass House, gardens, and other buildings broadcast the intellectual pedigree of their erudite, connoisseur architect.

However, in other postmodernists, one finds familiar invocations that recall modernist polemics – the selective demonizing of the past, descriptions of a time of crisis, the anointing of prophets to lead from sin to salvation, and the exhortation of others to convert and follow. Robert Venturi arguably came to define the postmodern project and its anti-modern stances and theories. But like the modernists he found so objectionable, he supported his positions by characterizing his contemporary setting as distinct from what preceded and demanding new architectural responses. Whereas Le Corbusier was a self-appointed prophet for a new age, Venturi's project is emancipatory, a Protestant Reformation to free the architect from, in his strangely ecclesiastical terms, the "puritanically moral language of orthodox modern architecture."[50] In the game-changing *Complexity and Contradiction in Architecture* of 1966, he argued that modern architecture needed to be supplanted by "a complex and contradictory architecture based on the richness and ambiguity" of contemporary culture. [51]

Venturi was certainly not the only theoretician to challenge, criticize, and upend the tenets and artifacts of orthodox, style-based modernism. However, he was one of the better known, in part because of an early work, a house for his mother in Chestnut Hill, Philadelphia, Pennsylvania, completed in 1962, which

Vincent Scully described as the "biggest small building of the second half of the twentieth century."[52] Like *Complexity and Contradiction*, which was written at the same time he designed the house, Mother's House (as it came to be known) was a "gentle manifesto," where the functionalist "easy unity of a few or many motival parts," is replaced by "a difficult unity of a medium number of diverse parts." [53] Even though the nautical motifs of the Villa Savoye were presented without irony, in the case of Venturi's Mother's House, much of it *was* ironic. The exterior was a metaphor for a gabled-roof house in a manner that is equally suspicious and supportive of its cultural content – from its chimney image, to the broken pediment and its stage-front presentation. Inside it wasn't any clearer, with familiar domestic elements such as stairs and fireplaces upending expectations. For Venturi, the house served to rehabilitate metaphor and symbolism, and deny progressive goals for architecture, while also expressing the taste of its erudite architect.

Peter Eisenman was even more direct in disassociating architecture from technological, social, and cultural obligations, congruent with what became known as deconstructivist architecture, with which he was closely associated.[54] Deconstructivist architects were as loosely formed as the "Five Architects" of the early 1970s (of which Eisenman was one of the "whites," as they came to be known), and shared iconoclastic sentiments that not only rejected progressive ideologies but also questioned their very rationale. However, some adopted stances similar to their predecessors – only a new architecture, led by visionaries with the clairvoyance to see the future, could lead architecture from its current inadequate state to a new vision. Its tenets, albeit loosely defined, were most stridently articulated by the writings of Eisenman (and his major influence, the French philosopher Jacques Derrida),[55] who was primarily interested in deconstructing social constructs and conventions expressed through works that deconstructed normative architecture. Early in his career, Eisenman constructed a persona of a renegade visionary and iconoclast of conventions, all delivered through dense and, at times, eschatological prose. In his influential "The End of the Classical," he prophetically intoned that classicism and modernism were more similar than not, and that both were equally irrelevant. It is a time of "the end of the beginning, the end of the end" – an endgame of sorts that demanded new ideas.

Similar to Le Corbusier, Venturi, and others, the house for Eisenman proved to be a particularly potent type to explore and express his theoretical interests. He is perhaps most known for his Ten Houses Project, cryptically titled by number as if to deny their domesticity, where binary oppositions, language, syntax, and formal operations, and the bifurcation of design and program, were explored.[56] Indeed, House IV, designed for himself and illustrated in *Houses of Cards*, was described as "NOT A HOUSE in a traditional sense,"[57] (Eisenman capitalized

FIGURE 7.7 House VI, Cornwall, CT, Peter Eisenman

FIGURE 7.8 The Cabanon, Roquebrune-Cap-Martin, France, Le Corbusier

the first three words, in case one didn't get his un-domestic positions). Of all of the houses, however, House VI in Cornwall, Connecticut for Suzanne and Dick Frank and completed in 1975, is perhaps the best known and analyzed. Robert Stern predictably dismissed it as "a mathematical abstraction in a Copernican world," a "dream of pure structure" where the role of the client seemed to be nil, and even as a nonplace and "the opposite of home sweet home."[58] Others assigned it a preeminent position in the history of architecture. John Hejduk described it as the "second canonical De Stijl house."[59] Kenneth Frampton compared it to the Schröder house and other works of the European *avant-garde*, and wrote that it was a "self-conscious effort to cap" modernism and move to a "more formalist, post-humanist attitude."[60]

Throughout the design of the house, Eisenman questioned notions and preconceptions of domesticity, and even denied them. He rejected Dick Frank's request for a fireplace because, as recounted by Suzanne Frank, "it smacked of nostalgia."[61] It is most famous for the couple's bedroom and its bed split into separate halves, perhaps an insightful – or insensitive – commentary on marriage, but one that was eliminated when the house was renovated in 1990. (The clients had never previously slept in separate beds.) Elsewhere, an inaccessible stair leads nowhere and a column awkwardly divides the dining table seating. As if to modify or deny any direct references to alternative architecture or domesticity, the architect explained that "in House VI, the experience of the physical environment does not lead to any mental structure – the experience is, in fact, quite the reverse. Once the conceptual structure is understood, it detaches itself from the initial physical experience,"[62] and that these experiences "can only take place in the mind."[63] This cyclical argument has much in common with psychoanalytical theory, arguably one of the secular religions of the twentieth century. However, in spite of Eisenman's pronouncements regarding the dominance of formal elements, intellectual organizations, and the disembodied experiences of the house, an accidental spirituality results. Suzanne Frank recalled her initial experiences in almost revelatory terms, where "light filtered in and for a moment life seemed a careless spiritual existence,"[64] and where she and her husband felt a "quiet and dynamic spirituality," and "found only a source of spiritual satisfaction in the distribution of forms in space, the subtle neutral colors, and warm and diaphanous lighting."[65]

★★★

It is well known that many of the most assertive domestic reformers had, at least at times, sad, challenging, or chaotic home lives. Perhaps equally known are the failures of their domestic experiments – the leaky roofs, the rotting walls, and the sagging structures. Corbusier may have dismissed the "household god" of the roof, but the one at the Villa Savoye leaked spectacularly to the extent that his clients threatened legal action. House VI had serious functional, water, and rot problems, which eventually required an almost complete rebuilding. And then there were the unintended consequences. Shortly after the publication of *Towards a New Architecture*, Le Corbusier was commissioned to design workman's housing at Pessac, near Bordeaux. When completed its repetitive blocks and concrete walls were an image of the mass-produced housing he advocated. However, the tenants who worked in a nearby factory apparently wanted homes that spoke not to an idealized future but to them, so over the years pitched roofs, shutters, and picket fences were added.[66]

Some architects reserve the homey, familiar, and the personable for themselves. Peter Eisenman has no interest in living in one of his own designs. In fact, he stridently makes the distinction between houses, which are his means for architectural experimentation, and homes, in which he lives, including a cozy nineteenth-century townhouse in New York City and a charming mill house in Connecticut. Le Corbusier, however, lived in two homes of his own design – a quirky apartment in Paris and a strange one-room retreat in Roquebrune-Cap-Martin on the Mediterranean coast. Located relatively close to the brutalist Unité d'Habitation tower block in Marseilles, the twelve-foot-square, self-titled "cabanon" was sheathed in rustic siding on the outside, and was as sparse as a monk's cell inside. Cabanon has a number of definitions, the most common is a rustic shepherd's hut, a symbol of unschooled, practical design. There was no kitchen, nor a need for one as there was a restaurant, owned by a friend, next door. There was just enough space to sleep, read, and wash. (There was a small bed for his wife, but she complained that it placed her head in the toilet, so she often slept elsewhere.) And so, the champion of rational, anonymous, international, machine-like homes built himself one that was personal, sensual, and very private, and in doing so created a home that, perhaps more than any of his others, symbolized the pure and original ideals he promoted. He died there, swimming in the ocean, shortly after mentioning to a friend that it would be a glorious way, and presumably place, to die.

The visionary nature characteristic of architectural theory often pairs otherwise incompatible elements – a quest for the new and a return to the Eden of fundamentals. Modernism was the most strident regarding the necessity of returning to, or advancing towards, immutable fundamentals, and insisting that the spiritual health of a culture was determined and revealed by its architecture. However, postmodernism, and its deconstructivist iterations, could at times be equally judgmental and didactic. One could also argue that it simply replaced the instrumental functionalism and technology of modernism with an instrumental aesthetics – and was equally divorced from conventional domesticity. As I have observed, the house often stood in for ideological agendas where theory trumps, and even denies, the ontological and quotidian functions of home. Never the less, in the cases I have presented, the house plays starring roles in materializing the theories that produced it, and illustrating the future its architects imagined.

As the next chapter illustrates, the house, even the most ubiquitous, is often primarily about an idea, or ideas, rather than conventional domesticity. It is ideas that are perhaps the most significant virtues of the modernist house – ideas, in and of themselves, and in some cases, the tangible results they produced. Wright's Usonian houses featured technological innovations that continue to have influence, and created humanly scaled and detailed environments that still can prove elusive in contemporary homes. The Schröder house also included technologies advanced for its time, but, more significantly, its spatial adaptability embodied a fluidity of conventional gender roles that were popular in Holland at this time, and found particular expressions later. The postmodern elevated theory and text to equal standing with built artifacts. House VI is strangely unmoored to its site as if it were more at home as a model, drawing, or text, which perhaps it actually is. Le Corbusier, Venturi, and Eisenman, in their own ways and in their own periods, demonstrate that architecture without ideas, and an incisive intellect to formulate and apply them, is, to propose an alternate Ruskinian dyad, mere building.

8

DOMESTIC CULTURES

The twentieth-century house and suburb

In modernism, architecture was often positioned as a socially progressive means to improve society and the house assigned special roles to do so. This chapter will examine the twentieth-century house and home and, in particular, the American single-family house (hereafter referred to as the suburban house), and its suburban settings, as cultural artifacts that reveal and are also disclosed by the predominant cultural values and beliefs of their time. It is not a critique *per se* of its subject – there is no shortage of others who have compellingly done so – but an explanation of the primary reasons, and their significance, why it achieved such a prominent position. Suburban houses and their settings are, of course, found worldwide, but they have played the most potent cultural and ontological roles in Anglo-American contexts. Consequently, particular attention will be directed to the class, religious, and economic forces coterminous with the early suburbs of England and their North American counterparts. I will also present how predominant attitudes regarding the suburban house were often deeply embedded in national psyches, but revealed through didactic and assertive popular books and media.

It is an obvious point that the suburban house has occupied a preeminent position in Anglo-American and, particularly, twentieth-century American cultures. What is less obvious are the multitudinous reasons why this is so. Further challenging cogent and dependable analyses are the difficulties of understanding the recent past, or worse, a still developing present, where the volume of information does not naturally lead to the mature understandings more distant histories can sometimes afford. But, it can be confidently stated that house and home as central to people's lives and identities is a modern, Anglo-American invention. For Greco-Romans home may have been important, but it was secondary to the virtues of public life; aspects of which are recognizable in the histories of European and Latin American cities.[1] This has not been the case in Anglo-American contexts, dating from eighteenth-century England and nineteenth- and twentieth-century America. Temples, civic buildings, markets, and plazas centered the public realm of the Greek and Roman city – but the centers of the suburbanized city are autonomous residential units.[2]

There are, of course, many reasons for the values ascribed to the twentieth-century house and home. As I will discuss some beliefs and attributions that support its hegemony found early expressions in Imperial Rome, Renaissance Italy, and Georgian England. However, what follows is not a history of the suburban house and its suburban settings, but an explication of its predominant symbolizations and materializations. Like many symbols, it is a shape-shifter, adapting to changing contexts without losing potency. But throughout, as recognizable in other house forms and functions, it embodied and expressed the values of self and society that produced it. Initially the suburban villa was presented as providing settings for health and leisure in pastoral settings, and expressed the taste and status of its inhabitants. Later, the suburban house was positioned as the best place for family and children, a means of spiritual and social progress, and a reflection of freedom, privacy, individuality, and self-identity. It also became a symbol of personal autonomy, development, and achievement, as Alain de Botton transparently illustrates when he states that to be considered home the house needs to "embody moods," provide a "helpful vision of ourselves," remind us of what "we need," and aid in the construction of identity.[3]

Classical precedents

As presented in Chapter 2, the English country house was a particularly potent cultural symbol. It was often depicted in literature as organically emerging from the countryside and as a uniquely English foundation of civil society.[4] Ben Jonson's poem "To Penshurst," ostensibly an ode to an aristocratic estate, portrays an Edenic world where the house symbolizes health, repose, culture, and the virtues of a stable, hierarchical society.[5] Until Jonson's time, country estates were the exclusive privilege of the aristocracy who expressed their taste, privilege, beneficence, and power through their houses. Typically, the Classical language was employed, and architectural texts often valorized the virtues of country estates by citing Roman and Italian Renaissance precedents.

The first suburban villas were arguably Roman, the *villa suburbanae* of the aristocrats of the late republic and early empire. During this time, it was expected that aristocrats would maintain country estates, typically located within a twenty-mile radius of Rome in the Apennine foothills or on the coast. Eventually many villas dotted the areas surrounding Rome including, most famously, Hadrian's Villa in Tivoli.[6] Pliny the Younger's celebrated accounts of his Laurentian and Tuscan villas described places of retreat from the affairs of Rome by a worldly man, where the villa served as a setting for individual development, contemplation, and study.[7] In his letter to Gallus, Pliny described his seaside, Laurentian villa as just seventeen miles from Rome, but worlds away from its affairs. The Roman poet Martial portrayed the pleasures of the country house as follows:

> You tell me, friend, you much desire to know:
> What in my villa can I find to do?
> I eat, drink, sing, play, bathe, sleep, eat again:
> Or read, or wanton in the Muses train.

Architects of the Italian Renaissance drew from classical writers in formulating analogous attitudes and traditions regarding the virtues, benefits, and architectural expressions of country estates.[8] Alberti, in *The Art of Building in Ten Books* of 1485, cited Martial to present country houses as places of repose, recreation, and rest. Even though a city house was deemed necessary for conducting business, the country house was required for health and wellbeing. He states, "The physicians advise us to dwell in the clearest and openest air that we can find; and there is no room to doubt that a country house seated upon an eminence, must of course be the best," and concludes that there are none "so commodious or so healthy as the villa."[9]

Andrea Palladio furthered Alberti's sentiments in *The Four Books of Architecture*, first published in 1570. He also mentioned the conveniences of city houses, but described country houses as healthier and more restorative. Recalling Pliny's reflection that his Tuscan villa promotes "health of body and mind,"[10] he stated that in the country "the body more easily preserves its strength and health," and "the mind, fatigued by the agitations of the city will be greatly restored and comforted, and be able quietly to attend the studies of letters, and contemplation."[11]

Palladio designed the Villa Capra (Rotonda)[12] as a country retreat for the Venetian Canon Paolo Almerico. The house and grounds, located outside of Vicenza, typified the bucolic estates also built outside Venice, Rome, and Florence by the landed gentry of this time, and the practice of *villeggiatura*, or withdrawing to the country.[13] The surrounding land was not a working farm but a cultivated landscape, surveyed from raised columned loggias on each side

FIGURE 8.1 Villa Capra, Vicenza, Italy, Andrea Palladio

FIGURE 8.2 Chiswick House, London, England, Lord Burlington

of the symmetrically composed house.[14] It was actually more a pavilion for entertainment than an extensive villa,[15] fulfilling Alberti's validation of "pleasure-houses just without the town."[16] Palladio was one of the more prominent architects in Renaissance Italy but mostly known for his churches. The Villa Capra communicated the rationality of Italian Renaissance architecture while also incorporating recognizable church organizations and forms. Its conflation of the ecclesiastical and the domestic was perhaps a matter of the formal prejudices of the architect, but it signaled the quasi-sacred status of the house that was to influence its progeny. Palladio wrote:

> The ancient sages used to retire to such places where being oftentimes visited by virtuous friends and relations, having houses, gardens, and such like pleasant places, and above all their virtues, they could easily attain to as much happiness as could be attained here below.[17]

That the Renaissance villa came to have profound formal and stylistic influence is well known; what is less explicit is its contribution to the ideal of the cultured house in nature and its promises of a superior way of life. It was in Georgian England that Palladian villas came to represent the model of aristocratic country estates, and Georgian aristocratic houses were studiously dependent on them. Lord Burlington's Chiswick House, built between 1726 and 1729 in suburban London, overtly deployed these recognizable motifs and symbols of status. House styles and symbols have a long history as expressions of status, and in England it was Palladianism that was tasked with this ennobling role. But, perhaps more importantly, similar to the subtle connotation of the sacred to the domestic in Palladio's villas, Chiswick House's form and organization, which drew liberally from the Villa Capra, expressed a setting for retreat and contemplation. In fact, it was not a house at all, but a two-story pavilion built to display Richard Boyle, Third Earl of Burlington's, art and library, and solely dedicated to his private affairs and public gatherings. It was characterized as more of a house of the muses, of the Lord's individual inspirations and, as such, communicated these through the architecture and its setting.[18]

Palladio's villas, idealized through *The Four Books of Architecture*, distilled Classical notions of ideal dwellings in cultivated landscapes in a manner profoundly influential in Georgian England.[19] Similar to the Villa Capra, Chiswick House overlooked its surrounding countryside from the porch and windows of its *piano nobile*, including extensive cultivated gardens of walks, bridges, sculptures, and pavilions. Expressions of aristocratic good taste found particular expression in picturesque gardens, which recalled Roman and Renaissance *villa suburbanae*. Stourhead, in the Wiltshire countryside, is perhaps the consummate

FIGURE 8.3 Stourhead Gardens, Wiltshire, England

example of a remarkably naturalistic cultivated landscape. Along miles of trails, some of which circled a created lake, pavilions that recalled Classical themes appeared – the Pantheon art gallery; the hilltop Temple of Apollo; the Lakeside Temple of Flora; and the Grotto with statues of nymphs and a river god. There was also a "Palladian Bridge" and the rustic counterpoint of a "Gothic Cottage." The house, set on a hill, with its predictable three-part Palladian façade, serenely surveyed its surroundings. The exact Classical or literary sources of Stourhead's gardens have been much debated, but they clearly expressed pedigreed erudition and taste.[20] The Palladian house, with its grand halls, library, and picture galleries performed similar communicative roles. Throughout the estate, classical sources were recalled and expressed, nodes of repose and contemplation provided, and walks and grounds for restorative recreation available. The juxtaposition of the ideal and the natural – the cultured house in cultivated nature – was a common theme of Georgian villas, which subsequently found expression in the modern suburb's attempts to reconcile country and city with the suburb.

English suburbs

Country estates traditionally were the privilege of the aristocracy. However, with the rise of a new mercantile and business middle class in the late seventeenth and early eighteenth centuries, for the first time in British society there were wealthy families who had achieved positions of economic and political power through their own entrepreneurship. Eventually the ability to own properties and houses was not limited to the landed gentry, but instead increasingly open to the emerging middle class who exercised their prerogative to build homes that responded to their needs and reflected their new status. The notion of the "self-made man" resulted in a building type to serve it – the suburban single-family house. This, in many ways, a radical reconsideration of home, can be understood according to specific historical precedents, some of which the new English middle class were keenly aware of, some they were not.

Arguably the first suburbs were built outside of London, where notions regarding the benefits of healthy, pastoral living, the primacy of the family, the suburbs as a means of spiritual and social improvement, and the house as reflecting one's social and economic status, coalesced. The Thames River Valley outside of London had long been a setting for the country estates of kings and the aristocracy. In Richmond, Henry VIII built a palace surrounded by hunting grounds, and nobles such as Lord Burlington built villas not far away. Henry VIII's palace is gone, but many of the aristocratic estates remain such as Ham House and the Gothic Revival Strawberry Hill. Richmond and its environs were also where the new, bourgeois middle class (who some pejoratively called *nouveau riche* or *parvenu*), came to build their own suburban villas and where the confluence of political reforms, available land, and a clientele with the means to purchase homes, coalesced. St. Margaret's Estate near Richmond, named for the aristocratic owner of a country house and begun in 1854, featured curvilinear streets lined with houses interspersed with private parks. It was built on the banks of the Thames like its aristocratic predecessors, but it was not an estate but an assemblage of modest houses, close to Richmond Green, and convenient to rail travel to London.[21]

The new suburbs conveyed the political and monetary gains achieved by this new class by appropriating images of power of the country estates of the aristocracy, while also maintaining the necessary connections to the city – a reconciliation of sorts between country and city. Like St. Margaret's Estate, early subdivisions often adopted aristocratic names. Victoria Park in Manchester, named for Queen Victoria, was planned by a group of wealthy businessmen as a model suburb.[22] It was not a park, but instead featured large houses on curvilinear streets, with a surrounding fence and "toll gates" recalling the country estates of the aristocracy. Opened on July 31, 1837, it was described as providing:

> The advantage of close proximity to the town with the privacy and advantage of a country residence which, in the rapid conversion of all the former private residences of the town into warehouses, has long been deemed to be a deseratum.[23]

Essential to expressions of the achievement of social status equal to the aristocracy was domestic separation from the "lower classes," and the dirt, noise, and disease of the industrial city. The early suburbs signaled a gradual but significant change. Previously, one's social position depended only on title or peerage, as the classes freely intermingled in cities such as London and Manchester, now it demanded the physical separation only the new suburbs could provide.

The growing means and influence of the bourgeois precipitated the creation of the first English suburbs. However, ascendant religious beliefs of the Anglican Evangelical movement of this time significantly influenced the values associated with the new suburbs. The Victorians have been credited with defining family, and the home, as an autonomous center of religious and cultural life – the Evangelicals with influencing attitudes regarding new and, presumably improved, domestic settings for families. This moralizing, prescriptive movement was ambitious regarding reforming what they viewed as a shallow Anglican Church and morally corrupt society, with house and home playing predominant roles in affecting the envisioned reforms.

Evangelicals effectively promulgated their strictures through influential publications, which presented home and family as preeminent, leisure activities outside home sinful, and religious devotion, self-denial, hard work, and focus on the family virtuous. Evangelicals had specific ideas regarding what constituted a devout Christian home, and the roles women should play in nurturing it.[24] Contrary to the heterogeneous social and business relationships of the city, they insisted that the nuclear family was the most important social unit. Women were elevated to the head of the Christian home and appointed the leader of religious life, while simultaneously separated from opportunities for social discourse and power offered by the city.[25] One of the Evangelicals' most prominent spokesmen was William Wilberforce who, in *Practical Christianity* (1797), argued that women were naturally led to religion, which made them ideal for domestic and nurturing roles.[26] He wrote:

> [The female] sex seems, by the very constitution of its nature, to be more favourably disposed than ours to the feelings and offices of Religion; being thus fitted by the bounty of Providence, the better to execute the important task which devolves on it, of the education of our earliest youth. Doubtless, this more favourable disposition to Religion in the female sex, was graciously designed also to make women doubly valuable in the wedded state: and it seems to afford to the married man the means of rendering an active share in the business of life more compatible than it would otherwise be with the liveliest devotional feelings: that when the husband should return to his family, worn and harassed by worldly cares or professional labours, the wife, habitually preserving a warmer and more unimpaired spirit of devotion, than is perhaps consistent with being immersed in the bustle of life, might revive his languid (lacking vigor) piety, and that the religious impressions of both might derive new force and tenderness from the animating sympathies of conjugal affection.[27]

Proclamations regarding the corrupting influence of the city were also crucial to their proscriptions. John Newton, a prominent Evangelical, asserted, "Sin overspreads the earth; but in London the number and impunity of offenders, joined with the infidelity and dissipation of the times, makes it a hot-bed or nursery of wickedness."[28] Cities such as London may have been characterized as degenerate but the new suburbs were promoted as settings where women and children could live morally superior Christian lives. Of course, the men still had to work in the city, hard work was still a virtue, but family and work now became geographically, socially, and spiritually separated. According to Robert Fishman, the early English suburbs constituted a "radical re-thinking of the relation between the residence and the city," one in which "exclusion" was its central position – separation from work, commerce, entertainment, lower classes, and

FIGURE 8.4 Clapham Common, London, England in the nineteenth century

FIGURE 8.5 Monticello, Charlottesville, VA, Thomas Jefferson

other intrinsic elements of the city.[29] The men still had access to the diversity offered by the city, including the temptations of its morally compromising elements, but presumably were more able to resist them. Their faith, one can presume, fortified them, but so did the refuge of their religiously consecrated homes. Making use of improved roads and carriages, they commuted to the city, but when their work was done returned to the sanctuary – in all its meanings – of their ideal houses.[30]

Clapham, a London suburb adopted by prominent Evangelicals, epitomized the virtues of untainted family life achieved by the relatively separate location and natural setting of a farming village. Houses ringed a common with a church to serve the Clapham Sect, representing the devout family and child-centered environment they desired. Here, Evangelicals could live by example – women could perform their duties to family, children, and society, and men could work hard, worship together, and devote themselves to their families. At Clapham, a model emerges of exclusive residential enclaves, set in ex-urban settings, and connected to work and commerce by new transportation technologies, which satisfied and expressed religious, cultural, and social imperatives. Even though the twentieth-century suburb that followed was very different, it did reflect some of the priorities of Clapham and its houses.[31] These included the benefits of living with socially and religiously compatible neighbors, house and home as the foundations of a moral society, the suburb as an antidote to the spiritual and physical dangers of the city, and the reconciliation of the private realm of the house and the public through its common setting.[32]

American counterparts

The American suburban house reflected many of the ideals of its English contemporaries, but found unique expressions in a culture that oscillated between class distinctions and egalitarian self-determination. Its founding fathers built country villas that may have expressed class prestige, but also became national icons of individual achievement. In both cases pastoralism, self-identity, and status found distinct American expressions. George Washington's Mount Vernon, located on a bluff overlooking the Potomac River and within commuting distance of the capital, and Monticello, Thomas Jefferson's rural hilltop villa, came to represent preferred ways of living promised to those who embraced the country's humanist, progressive democracy. At Monticello, Jefferson adopted Palladian planning and style that recalled its aristocratic predecessors (including Chiswick House), without insisting on its exclusivity. Deferring to Palladio's dictum, his house was "elevated on a cheerful" hilltop in the countryside near Charlottesville, Virginia. Like English estates, the offices, or support spaces, were suppressed in deference to the main house. However, it was not a pleasure pavilion or an aristocratic estate, but a working farm that depended on the labor of enslaved people.[33]

The symbolic content and impact of American houses and homes depended on English precedents and their continental influences. The English had a long history of promoting particular types and styles of domestic architecture. Robert Morris' *Lectures on Architecture* (1734–36) popularized the classical style, and his widely disseminated books included specific plans and proportions for houses. However, he also presented the capacity of houses to induce states of contemplation, repose, and insight.[34] In the seventeenth century, Henry Wotton's benediction of house and home distilled this personal function:

> Every man's proper mansion house and home, being the theatre of his hospitality, and seat of self-fruition, the comfortablest part of his own life, the noblest of his son's inheritance, a kind of private princedom; nay, to the possessors thereof, an epitome of the whole world.[35]

John Ruskin in *The Seven Lamps of Architecture* of 1849 insisted that private houses should reflect one's character, occupation, and position in society. Not only that, but the correct house was an instrument for self-improvement, necessary for self-fulfillment, and even a lasting memorial to one's life.[36] Ruskin also had a bit to say about the home as a refuge and a wife's role in making it so:

> This is the true nature of home – it is a place of Peace; the shelter, not only from all injury, but from all terror, doubt, and division… it is a sacred place, a vestal temple, a temple of the hearth watched over by the Household Gods [where the] woman's true place [is that she never sets] herself above her husband, but that she may never fail from his side.[37]

Similar to the motivations of their English counterparts, some American books on houses and homes also had religious overtones. The influential books of Catherine Beecher, whose father, Lyman Beecher, was a member of the Evangelical clergy, not only provided innovations for the single-family house, but also promoted it as a Christian ideal. Women were declared to be in charge of the home and the religious life of the family – echoing the English Evangelicals of a century before.[38] However, Beecher's positions were also the product of American religious movements of the time where, according to Claudia Stokes, the home was positioned "as a kind of heaven on earth, a perception that imputes sacred authority to women in creating an environment of happiness that portends that of the millennium and the afterlife."[39] American idealism was also at play here – a positivist position regarding the potential of individuals to craft their own destiny. Enlightenment sentiments incorporated into the Constitution regarding the equality of all men and their right to pursue their own destiny are illustrative. Horatio Alger's novels of the mid nineteenth century and their rags-to-riches themes overtly expressed these attitudes. The crafting of an individual destiny, but also the virtues of bucolic settings, were central to the writings of Transcendentalists such as Ralph Waldo Emerson.[40] Andrew Downing's popular pattern books on single-family houses, while providing specific plans and styles, insisted on the potential of the house to build and also express one's character.[41]

Suburbs composed primarily of single-family houses have proven to be a ubiquitous American development pattern and potent individual and collective symbol. Early American suburban residential developments borrowed freely from their English counterparts with single-family houses arranged on curvilinear streets and set in the countryside. Llewellyn Park in West Orange, New Jersey, completed in 1857, has often been referred to as the first planned community in the US. Like St. Margaret's Estate in Richmond, it featured serpentine streets fronted by individual houses and lawns, interspersed with common greens. Like Victoria Park in Manchester, it had a gatehouse. However, unlike its early English predecessors, it was located distant from any civic or commercial areas, an early, single-use subdivision that came to distinguish the American suburbs.[42] But, it was also connected to New York City, one hour distant by rail, and thus while this early, gated residential enclave promised a restorative natural setting, it was also connected to the work and commerce upon which the status of its inhabitants depended.

There are certain elements of nostalgia and utopia that define Llewellyn. This could also be said about the planned communities that followed, such as Riverside, located outside of Chicago and designed by Frederick Law Olmsted in 1868.[43] Broadacre City, first designed by Frank Lloyd Wright in 1932 and expanded throughout his career, owes much to Olmsted in its agrarian, naturalistic planning. It also reflects Wright's philosophy of self-autonomy and self-determination that was informed by his interpretations of American Transcendentalism. Broadacre City was never realized, but Wright's Usonian houses, designed beginning in the 1930s, came to represent a certain kind of model of American suburban houses.

American utopian communities comprise a tangential but relevant context regarding notions of self and community improvement realized through housing and the built environment. They had their genesis in the philosophies and proposals by Charles Fourier who envisioned ideal, communal settlements away from the corrupting influences of the city.[44] From Brook Farm, founded by

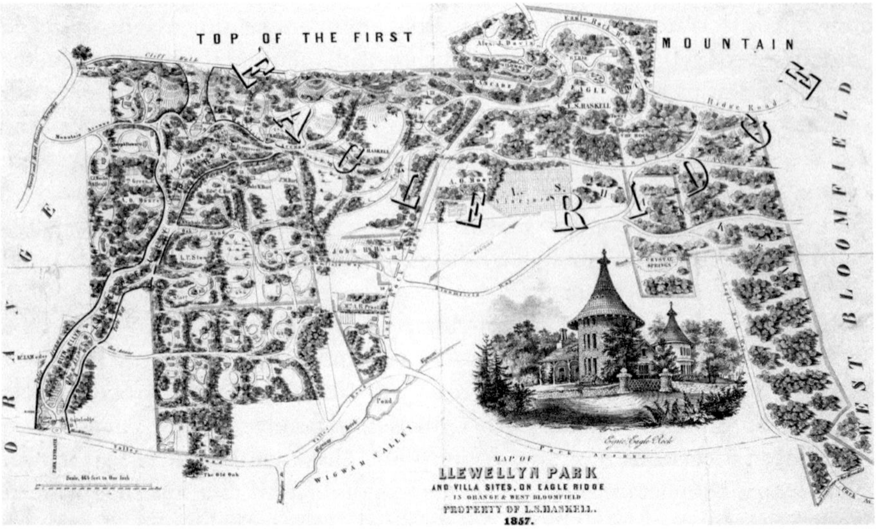

FIGURE 8.6 Llewellyn Park, West Orange, NJ

FIGURE 8.7 Levittown, Long Island, NY

Transcendentalists outside of Boston, to New Harmony, set in the countryside of Indiana, settlements reflected beliefs that the quality and organization of the built environment could improve behavior and society, and support religious life.[45] Most utopian communities were short-lived. This was not the case with the first Levittown. Built beginning in 1946 by Abraham Levitt and his sons, on farmland in the innocent and bucolic-sounding Hicksville, Long Island, New York, within commuting distance of New York City, it became the most substantial, and perhaps influential, of the post-war developments. Even though it was far from utopian, it did make its own promises for a better life and superior community. Like housing of this time in general, it also had political undertones, insisting that home ownership was the foundation of democracy and a bulwark against communism. In the words of William Levitt, "No man who owns his own house and lot can be a communist. He has too much to do."[46]

Eventually, over 17,000 houses were built, the first bought exclusively by veterans, who soon began raising families. It was planned to maximize the number of houses per acre, built efficiently and consistently by employing Fordist standardization and specialization of trades, and sold at competitive prices. Levittown and its progeny achieved what many of the early suburbs promised, albeit in a truncated, distinctly American manner – houses in planned developments, separate from the city and close to nature, which expressed individuality but with a homogeneity of residents that promised a peaceful community and bucolic life ideal for families and children. Its explicit restrictions regarding excluding Jews and African Americans have often been criticized, but they can be understood (though not excused) as a product of the homogeneity suburbs sought to achieve. This was not new – Andrew Downing, an early American proponent of suburban enclaves, penned religiously-imbued bromides regarding their redemptive capacity, while also proclaiming that suburban houses were for those who were "largely descended from Anglo-Saxon stock."[47]

Cultural priorities and expressions

Cultures tend to devote resources to what they consider important, either in the form of public support or private enterprises. According to Kenneth Jackson, the suburbanization of America was "as much governmental as a natural process," and a number of key twentieth-century federal laws and programs proved instrumental to the suburbanization of the country. The National Housing Act of 1934 created the amortized mortgage, which made home ownership much more accessible, and after the Second World War, federal programs increased mortgage guarantees that enabled and encouraged returning veterans to purchase new single-family houses. Tax benefits supported home ownership and eventually became the nation's largest federal housing subsidy. Just as new transportation technologies enabled the early English suburb, the late nineteenth-century streetcar in America catalyzed suburban housing developments.[48] Streetcar suburbs were more an outcome of private entrepreneurship than government policy. However, the Interstate Highway System was a remarkable national commitment of resources that had the most profound impact on the American built environment.[49] Though its goals were diverse, the result was an economic and transportation infrastructure that supported an unprecedented effusion, and diffusion, of the suburban house and suburbia.[50]

Another effective infrastructure of suburbia was popular culture and especially television, which articulated and enforced the predominant social norms of the time. From its beginnings in England, suburban domesticity was exclusive – suppressing those elements seen as compromising or corrupting to the imagined untainted life it promised. This legacy produced much iteration, with particular inflections in America, where the exclusionary goals of the suburbs took on a particular specificity during the post-World War II period. Suburbia's dual goals of autonomy and community, epitomized by individual houses linked by shared lawns, proved to have little tolerance for deviations to its scripts of the good life. Television, in particular, was presented as an effective means to establish a common cultural ground, while suppressing discordant voices.[51]

When it came to domesticity, the script was predictable and consistent regarding the virtues of the suburban house. The subject was perhaps first introduced by the 1948 film *Mr. Blandings Builds His Dream House*, starring Cary Grant, where comedy of errors challenges in building a suburban dream house led to a predictably redemptive and socially affirming ending.[52] *Leave it to Beaver* was one of many serialized popular television programs of the late 1950s and early 1960s that presented the virtues of suburban domesticity in an uncomplicated, uncompromising, and, one might add, unapologetic manner. The child-centered culture it promoted was appropriately presented by its main character, Beaver Cleaver, and told from "the Beaver's" point of view. Set in the fictitious town of Mayfield, it presented ideals of the suburban house and a white, middle-class world, where the father, Ward, is the breadwinner and mother, June, a nurturing stay-at-home mom.[53] In many ways, popular programs of this type illustrated how the social mores and conventions of the post-war period were explicitly delivered through nascent television sitcoms with the suburban house playing a supporting role.[54]

Criticisms of suburbia have, of course, been around for almost as long as it has. Indeed, it did not take long for popular culture, otherwise an unapologetic cheerleader for suburbia, to present complementary perspectives.[55] The suburban sitcom presented masculine-infused elements of self-determination, individuality, and social improvement, but also ceded this power to a feminized, child-centered domesticity where men are paradoxically absent. Not that this was emancipatory for women, whose choreographed roles were little expanded from the procreative, nurturing, and religious assignments that preceded it. Throughout, the suburban house, like its classical and English predecessors, presented an idealized or, one might say, fictionalized story about the good life and the domestic means to achieve it. In James Ackerman's words, "The villa accommodates a fantasy which is impervious to reality."[56] Similar to the idealized villa in domesticated nature, the suburban house was the means to control one's destiny and realize one's dreams. Like attributes regarding the English aristocratic estate encapsulated by Jonson's ode to Penshurst, the twentieth-century suburban house was regularly positioned as a foundational and stabilizing component of society. Even though these beliefs were often at variance with their social and economic contexts, and the suburban house eventually deemed to affect just the opposite, the acceptance of these fictions has not substantively diminished.

★★★

Unlike modernist architects and their polemics regarding the house, architects are largely absent in suburban domesticity. But that doesn't mean ideologies regarding the redemptive capacity of home are any less present or potent – they are simply subtler and ubiquitous, and forwarded by more diffuse sources.[57] I have argued that cultural proclivities shaped the first English suburbs, the suburbanization of America, and the valorization of the suburban house. The first English suburbs reflected emerging values of its time – for the middle class they satisfied pastoral ideals and class aspirations, for Evangelicals the primacy of the family and the benefits of homogeneous community. These aspects were also present in America but the association of the suburban house with individual freedom, autonomy, and identity assumed particular importance. It is also clear that American suburbanization enjoyed significant federal support, and was pursued with, at times, an evangelical zeal that rivaled the devout builders of the Gothic cathedrals. America has often been labeled the most religious country in the world. Yes, it may be institutionally religious, but at times it also displays a remarkably religious fervor about issues that matter to it and, like religion, are just as culturally embedded. Of these, the owner-occupied suburban house holds a privileged position. Today, the suburban house promises qualities uncannily similar to its Classical and English predecessors. As James Ackerman insightfully observes about the villa generally:

> The villa inevitably expresses the mythology that causes it to be built: the attraction to nature, whether stated in engagement or in cool distance, the dialectic of nature and culture or artifice, the prerogatives of privilege and/or power, and national, regional or class pride.[58]

Of course, it is a long and discontinuous path from Rome to the American suburb, but there are also recurring themes of health, pleasure, and family, spiritual and societal progress, status, taste, and the construction and expression of self that have, to greater or lesser degrees, been associated with the suburban house. The ideal of the "self-made man,"[59] who is able to "hold and transmit property" as a basic right, are enduring American ideals. Home ownership of a house typically serves to represent one's social and economic class, supported by imagery that bears a remarkable affinity with its English predecessors. The layouts of planned unit developments assiduously adopt symbols of pastoral settings, with curvilinear roads that recall country lanes, and gated entrances reminiscent of aristocratic estates. House models and subdivisions often use English names, paired or portmanteau titles that not only suggest upper-class pedigree, but also directly refer to country estates. Names typically conjure images of country farms, hunting estates (park and reserve), or English town or country nomenclature. It is a model that has proved to be highly adaptable to changing demographics and gender hierarchies, with each formally disenfranchised group aspiring to own a "home" in a "prestige community."[60]

Over time, American culture came to prejudice the suburban house at the expense of other housing models. What is euphemistically called the "American Dream" typically means living in a suburban house, and those who own them tend to hold the view that any other housing type will adversely affect the character and value of their community, and those that don't tend to aspire to own one. Indeed, one's identity is often conflated with their house to the degree that any perceived threats to the house are viewed as personal attacks.[61] It is hard not to see religious undertones in these contexts. As I have recognized, religion often informed beliefs regarding the centrality of the family and the capacity of the home to house the self, provide happiness, and express one's social, economic, and moral status. Indeed, one could argue that not only is a "man's" home "his castle," it is also "his" temple, and, as such, the center of "his" world.[62] An ontological function of the suburban house, especially its early iterations, was to situate self and society. Americans may require self-autonomy and self-determination, but they also desire connection to others who reflect and support their values. There is also a reassuring hierarchical order in the typical American suburb, where family is the foundation of a stable society and the house reflects status resulting from self-achievements, while its setting evinces a reconciliation of rural autonomy and urban community. These are some of the features that continue to influence and buttress, though often unrecognized, the dominance of the American suburban house, in spite of the dramatic demographic shifts in family make-up, structure, gender equality, and work habits that one might expect would more substantively call it into question than it has to date.

It is clear there are many congruent and conflicting cultural assignations regarding suburban domesticity. The variety of positions of promulgators and critics comprises a broad reception history of the promises and contradictions of the suburban house. All give voice to what the predominant culture values or diminishes: prejudices or dismisses. Similar to other areas of domesticity, the house, once again, plays a starring role. Its cultural and ontological roles are a potent mix of appropriations of aristocratic mores, emblems of individual achievement, symbols of religious superiority, and icons of national character. No wonder it has achieved the hegemony it enjoys, despite the fact that it inadequately supplies most of the things it promises. No matter, what is perhaps most important is the phenomenon of the power of the domestic to materialize and communicate a range of class, religious, and cultural beliefs in a manner that has proved to be resistant to the mitigations of the facts of its deficiencies.

EPILOGUE

Making a home in the world

House and home at first seem familiar and easily defined, but under scrutiny are shape-shifters, assuming diffuse guises and meanings. Consequently, I have addressed the subject from multiple positions, not as a reductive method to establish discrete definitions, but instead to encircle a center where perhaps more dependable understandings may lie. As such, the core of my investigations has been the variety of ways house and home served the human quest to make sense of the world and create places they could call their own. The multiplicity of reasons and ways this was done outlines a diverse reception history of the subject – a distillation of its themes, a horizon of understanding.

In this spirit, I would like to suggest three fundamental aspects of house and home. First, there is the house of the body – the home of the inner realms of psyche and soul and their mysterious territories of memories, dreams, and self-definitions. Second, there is the house for living – the place of comfort, rest, and ease, of family meals, and intimacy, the setting for the dramas, passages, pains, and joys of life – which is called home. And last, there is the house of the world, the condition of interconnection with others and the built and natural environment – of being at home in the universe. Bachelard wrote, "A house… allows the poet to inhabit the universe, to put it differently, the universe comes to inhabit his house."[1] Houses and homes are not only refuges from the world, but also places that connect with the world. Home satisfies phenomenological and psychological needs for comfort and security, while also providing an ontological threshold to the broader world. It is a place that looks inward and outward. Consequently, home may be understood in more diverse and multifarious ways, from inner psychic realms to vast cosmic perspectives, which may serve to inform the housing of the psyche and the incorporation of sacrality into the places we create. In this manner, the broader tasks of architecture serve the enduring human need to come home to the universe, others, and ourselves.

★★★

The words house and home conjure images of one's own home, separate and serving only individual and family needs. But, the scales of domesticity can be expanded to include one's hometown, homeland, and even home planet. As cited earlier, a reciprocity between house and city was suggested by Alberti who stated, "The city is like some large house and the house is in turn like some small city."[2] This was poetically expanded five centuries later by Aldo van Eyck as:

> Tree is leaf and leaf is tree – house is city and city is house – a tree is a tree but it is also a huge leaf – a leaf is a leaf but it is also a tiny tree – a city is not a city unless it is also a huge house – a house is a house only if it is also a tiny city.[3]

What do these theoreticians mean by these assertions? Alberti stated that architecture requires "compartition," its success depends on the harmonious relationships between its parts in service of a Vitruvian inspired goal of a "single, harmonious work that respects utility, dignity and delight."[4] Houses should fulfill these requirements, but the city should also: "It should be extremely healthy, it should offer every facility and every convenience to contribute to a peaceful, tranquil, and refined life."[5]

Alberti's principal interest was how ordered architecture reinforced an ordered society.[6] Aldo van Eyck, though clearly aware of Alberti's model, had a broader, more humanistic agenda. In *Place and Occasion* (1962) he wrote:

> Start with this: make a welcome of each door and a countenance of each window. Make of each a place; a bunch of places of each house and each city, for a house is a tiny city, and a city a huge house.[7]

Even though this recalls Alberti's analogy, a further examination of van Eyck's theory reveals that he meant something very different. For example, van Eyck's rebuttal to Christopher Alexander's 1966 article, "A City is Not a Tree," challenged the part to whole hierarchy of Alexander's "semi-lattice" theory as overly systemic, "oversimplified," and ultimately "unpoetic."[8] Van Eyck was suspicious of any system that suggested a structured or formal autonomy divorced from how humans interact with the each other and with the built environment.[9] Instead, van Eyck simply argued that house and city are "both a bunch of places for human beings,"[10] with all of the complexity and ambiguity that comes with human existence. He states:

> To proceed from the idea of dwelling in the sense of living in a house in order to arrive at the idea of living in the sense of living in the city, implies simultaneously that you proceed from the idea of living in the sense of dwelling in the city in order to arrive at the idea of dwelling in the sense of living in a house.[11]

In a talk in 1963, van Eyck clearly articulated his humanist position: "The job of the planner is to provide built homecoming for all, to sustain a feeling of belonging. I would go so far to say that architecture is built homecoming."[12] What van Eyck meant is that the same ontological roles of home can also be extended to broader considerations of the built environment. The interrelationship of house and city recalls the duties of Hestia, illustrated earlier, who was the goddess of the house and the hearth, but who also had a civic role as guardian of the sacred hearth of Greek cities and was closely associated with the prytaneion.[13] For Greek male citizens, the public realm was preeminent, but deeply connected to the domestic, where, according to Lefebvre, "A unity was achieved… between the order of the world, the order of the city and the order of the house."[14] However, the Greek city is not an ideal, but an aspect of a civic home. After all, for the most part it was an exclusive extension of the *pater familias* of the Greek house.[15] Also, as a theoretical construct, the city–house, house–city analogy risks oversimplifying a complex subject. Van Eyck's colleague Herman Hertzberger had little patience for it, declaiming that van Eyck's theory was "too limited, too narrow," and that he would "prefer to forget the city as a house."[16] Of course, he is right, an analogy in and of itself does not explicate. However, in this case, the city–house construct serves to broaden the inquiry into the multitudinous aspects of home. It reveals how the values and roles of domesticity might be productively considered at larger scales.

In a scene from the Woody Allen film *Midnight in Paris*, where themes of ontological anxiety permeate and the city is positioned as redemptive, the lead character wonders:

> How is anyone ever going to come up with a book, or a painting, or a symphony, or a sculpture that can compete with a great city? You can't because if you look around every street, every boulevard is its own special art form.[17]

He goes on to ponder how "in a cold, violent, mean universe that Paris exists," and that "way out in space you can see these lights, the cafes, people singing. For all we know Paris is the hottest spot in the universe." In this film, Paris, and by extension the city generally, is an oasis amidst the homogeneity and enormity of an uncaring, incomprehensible universe. The city is a meaningful home on a planet that is our only home.

We are still homeless. The more we learn about the universe, the more we recognize the preciousness of human life on earth and how alone we are in the cosmos. As I introduced earlier, for many years, scientists have sought intelligent neighbors or future homes beyond the earth, but so far, only silence and barrenness have been found and we remain lonely. We also increasingly recognize the possibility of becoming homeless – of losing our home planet. Of course, at some point in the distant future, our sun will turn into a red dwarf and then flame out, but not before rendering earth uninhabitable long before its demise. But, there are more timely issues of global climate change's effects on inhabitation, and as its impacts become apparent, we feel estranged from our home planet as it adapts to our careless indifference with an indifference of its own.

★★★

These broadened contexts suggest reconsiderations of predominant cultural beliefs regarding domesticity. House and home have become the center of our cultural and ontological worlds, especially in the West and particularly in the twentieth century. As I have observed, this is a relatively recent phenomenon that dates from Victorian England. Families, and the houses that house them, have largely replaced cultural and religious institutions as the means by which self and society are defined and valued. There is an obsession with family, homes, and houses, supported by diverse myths and beliefs, and they have achieved a remarkable preeminent position. Houses are lived in, but people also live through them, striving to achieve, and measuring themselves by, the societal standards set for them.[18] Jonathan Franzen writes about clearing out his childhood home, and reflects about how his mother defined herself through it:

> In the days after the memorial service, as my brothers and I went from room to room and handled things, I came to feel that the house had been my mother's novel, the concrete story she told about herself. She'd started with the cheap, homely department-store boilerplate she'd bought in 1944. She'd added and replaced various passages as funds permitted, reupholstering sofas and armchairs, accumulating artwork ever less awful than the prints she'd picked up as a twenty-three-year-old, abandoning

> her original arbitrary color schemes as she discovered and refined the true interior colors that she carried within her like a destiny. She pondered the arrangement of paintings on a wall like a writer pondering commas. She sat in the rooms year after year and asked herself what might suit her even better. What she wanted was for you to come inside and feel embraced and delighted by what she's made; she was showing you herself, by way of hospitality; she wanted you to want to stay.[19]

The cultural valorization of house and home is often contrasted by its deficiencies. Humans build houses and make homes in the world the best they can, but imperfectly and incompletely. The suburban house has typically occupied a social space of conventions, expectations, and cultural hierarchies. Here, as I have observed, the home "stands in" for a range of cultural expectations. However, it does not "stand with" much of anything. Most commonly, it is preoccupied with control, largely autonomous in its societal contexts, and isolated from its environmental settings, conveniently illustrated by ubiquitous subdivisions, gated communities, and environmentally sealed houses – all at the expense of a culturally and environmentally sustainable future. In the words of Juhani Pallasmaa, "we have become homeless in our culture of abundance."[20]

Concepts of house and home, in all of their cultural and ontological diversity, reveal clear limits of understanding. Literary and philosophical homelessness may express aspects of the human condition, but also belie a particular lack of maturity regarding enmeshed relationships between people and the cosmos. Theories on the origins of architecture ignore intuitive environmental responses when they ascribe human agency to them, and many origin stories were more interested in lending authority to cultural or theoretical positions than in providing dependable histories. Houses for god illustrate the desire to situate and claim the divine, but also territorial claims and cultural hegemonies that excluded the multifaceted divinity embedded in a world beyond comprehension. The artifacts of dominant civilizations often reveal agendas to control, suppress, convince, and coerce. House tombs are no exception, but also express rather primitive notions of death and naiveté about eternal life. The bucolic retreat was often an idealized, individualistic version of home – the modernist house an idiosyncratic expression of the preoccupations and ambitions of architect-theoreticians.

However, the diversity of domesticity across history, and its shortcomings, also provides valuable perspectives and lessons. House and home, with all of its attributions and manifestations, evidence humans as meaning and security-seeking creatures striving to situate themselves in the world. Western and Eastern concepts of homelessness and homecoming provide complementary positions – the first emphasizing the importance of constructing specific places to satisfy one's individual ontological needs – the second the necessity of coming home to broader, interpersonal and interconnected ways of being. The literature on home reveals the capacity of artifice to communicate what is valued, desired, or feared. Philosophical and theoretical constructs of the origins of the house communicate that the relationship between architecture, culture, and ontology is deeply embedded in history. Houses for god describe the quest to situate the divine in place and time, and imbue a people's lives with sacrality. House tombs express the mystery and fear of death and material means to render it comprehensible. The rustic retreat represents each individual's responsibility to know themselves and discover personal reconciliations with the world. Modernist and twentieth-century aspirations for house and home speak about the desire to create an improved world, and the promise of architecture to do so.

Culture is constructed to define a people and their place in the world, and house and home often tasked with materializing its beliefs and values. As I have observed, from the earliest examples to contemporary iterations, house and home have served to materialize, express, and enforce predominant cultural values. In this context, what house and home were asked to do is often more revealing than what they actually did. Just as important is what ancient and contemporary houses and homes say to us today. Recognizing what they mean, and the values still ascribed to them, is a way to more substantively understand them, and ourselves.

★★★

Alberti and van Eyck illustrate complementary approaches to the problem of house and home and their larger contexts. Alberti provides universal, abstract solutions from a specific cultural position – van Eyck particular, tangible remedies for his own culture. Both are valuable in illuminating particular aspects of the problem. However, a third strategy lies in-between these two, what I term congruities, where clusters of related elements reveal commonalities that transcend the universal and the particular. This book's larger project has been to suggest some broader tasks of architecture as viewed through the lens of the domestic. Architecture and the home can be understood as cultural and ontological constructs that reveal specific attributes of their historical settings. From this ground, a diversity of interpretations can emerge, which may suggest congruities, however nuanced and complex they may be. When viewed comparatively, alignments of aspirations, attributions, and materializations of habitation may serve to situate investigations beyond contemporary limitations and exigencies. In this manner, cultural and historical differences are recognized while also incorporating commonalities of the human condition – what joins in addition to what divides.

I have suggested that humans have sought to humanize their worlds through artifice, and that house and home were preeminent means to do so. The quest for meaning and certainty – ontological orientation and environmental control – are themes that have appeared in a diversity of examples. The communicative capacity of architecture, and house and homes' ability to articulate a diversity of proclamations and approbations – to their creators and history – has been routinely recognized. These are congruencies that describe the special cultural and ontological roles of the domestic, and the larger tasks of architecture. It is what architecture, and the house and home, in their most enduring, significant materializations, do.

Proust described literature as the ultimate intellectual construct of reality: "Real life, life finally discovered and explained, and thus the only life worth living, is literature."[21] Wallace Stevens positioned poetry as a reconciliation of thought and reality. However, the special power of the built environment is that it is not only an intellectual enterprise, but also a material one. It conceptualizes the world while also creating settings where the world might be more substantively considered. Emmanuel Levinas states that the house evidences an "outpouring of consciousness," and thus "consciousness of a world is already consciousness through that world."[22]

In the first chapter, I suggested that, historically, architecture performed roles of materializing the human condition, positioning it more meaningfully in the world, and assisting in collective homecoming. I also presented the variety of cultural and ontological tasks assigned architecture, and house and home. However, this poses a fundamental question: is architecture, and house and home, up to the task now? G.W.F. Hegel in *Aesthetics: Lectures on Fine Art* influentially pronounced the end of art's "highest vocation," its ability to coalesce, condense, and communicate communal beliefs.[23] The diffusion and diminishment of art since then seem to confirm his assertion. As Karsten Harries aptly stated, "Modern art is much too often found disappointingly empty, at times fun, often annoying, too frequently boring."[24] Much faith has been placed in science and reason, but they have proven insufficient to substantively address ontological questions. One could also argue that architecture doesn't have any special providence to help humans explicate the world and facilitate homecoming. The enormity of the task alone limits its capacity to articulate the human condition and render it comprehensible and meaningful. But, similar to Winston Churchill's statement that "democracy is the worst form of government, except for all those other forms that have been tried from time to time,"[25] architecture is perhaps one of the better means available – even our best hope.

Because it is a human construct, architecture will always be imperfect and inadequate. The teahouses of the Japanese medieval period seem to embody this imperfection in their rustic incompleteness as if to suggest the necessity of looking beyond mere artifice. At best, built works point to what is sought. But, as in the Zen adage that the finger that points to the moon is not the moon, architecture is only a means not an end. In recognition of the limits of human understanding, it should not be asked to do more than it has the capacity to do. Otherwise, notions, assignments, and aspirations can become overly ideological or instrumental – proscriptive and prescriptive means to achieve goals dislocated from the larger cultural and ontological tasks of the built environment. At best, architecture, and house and home, is a synecdoche, or a locus to apprehend the more complete.

This is our only home. We know this practically – it is embodied in us ontologically. It is imperative that we continue to collectively learn to care for our home – our home planet, megalopolises, cities, towns, homes, fellow inhabitants, other beings, our bodies, and souls. We begin by caring for our embodied spirits and psyches, as a means to seek the strands that connect us to others and the world. Pascal reflected:

> Let man, returning to himself, consider what he is in comparison with what exists; let him regard himself as lost and from this little dungeon, in which he finds himself lodged, I mean the universe, let him learn to take the earth, its realms, its cities, its houses and himself at their proper value.[26]

We can only work with what we truly know – self-understanding, the wisdom of others, and the intellectual and material record of architecture. In this realization, we build as best we can with the highest of intentions. We build to advance human consciousness, to care for our home in reverence, care, and wonder. We build a home in the world. That is all we can do.

NOTES

Prologue – The problem of house and home – topics, themes, and analytical methods

1 As Smyth and Croft have pointed out, studies on the house and home differ from other cultural studies in one crucial way – everyone has had experience of home, unlike studies on film, literature, or other areas of the humanities, where they may not have. Gerry Smyth and Jo Croft, eds, *Our House: The Representation of Domestic Space in Modern Culture* (Amsterdam: Rodopi, 2006), p. 12.

2 As Rapoport points out, the psychological and sociological aspects of house and home are predominant with a dearth of discussion concerning the physical environment of the house. Amos Rapoport, "A Critical Look at the Concept 'Home,'" in David N. Benjamin, ed., *The Home: Words, Interpretations, Meanings, and Environments* (Aldershot: Avebury, 1995), p. 42.

3 Joseph Rykwert, "House and Home," *Social Research,* Vol. 58, No. 1, Spring 1991, p. 52.

4 Paul Oliver, *Dwellings: The Vernacular House Worldwide* (London: Phaidon, 2003), p. 15.

5 Chiara Briganti and Kathy Mezei, eds, *The Domestic Space Reader* (Toronto: The University of Toronto Press, 2012), p. 5.

6 Rykwert, "House and Home," p. 54.

7 Rapoport, "A Critical Look at the Concept 'Home,'" pp. 30–45.

8 Tim Ingold, "Shifting Contexts: Transformations in Anthropological Knowledge," in Briganti and Mezei, eds, *The Domestic Space Reader*, p. 32.

9 "Capital: A Critique of Political Economy, Volume 1" (1867), quoted in Michael Parker Pearson and Colin Richards, eds, *Architecture and Order: Approaches to Social Space* (London: Routledge, 1994), p. 2.

10 Paul Oliver states, "The dwelling is more than the structure, as the soul is more than the body that envelopes it." Oliver, *The Vernacular House Worldwide*, p. 15.

11 Maurice Merleau-Ponty, *Phenomenology of Perception,* translated by Donald A. Landes (London and New York: Routledge, 2012), p. xiii.
12 From *Four Quartets*, "East Coker," T.S. Eliot, *The Complete Poems and Plays, 1909–1950* (New York: Harcourt, Brace & World, Inc., 1971), p. 129.
13 Ruth McElroy, "Labouring at Leisure: Aspects of Lifestyle and the Rise of Home Improvement," in Smyth and Croft, *Our House*, p. 87.
14 Oliver, *The Vernacular House Worldwide*, pp. 17–18.
15 Claire Cooper Marcus, *The House as Symbol of Self: Exploring the Deeper Meaning of Home* (Berkeley, CA: Conari Press, 1995), p. 4.
16 John R. Gillis, *A World of Their Making: Myth, Ritual, and the Quest for Family Values* (New York: Basic Books, 1996), p. 13.
17 Hannah Arendt, "The Human Condition," in Peter Baehr, ed., *The Portable Hannah Arendt* (New York: Penguin Books, 2000), p. 203.
18 Rowan Moore, *Why We Build: Power and Desire in Architecture* (New York: Harper Design, 2013), p. 65.
19 Hans-Georg Gadamer, *The Relevance of the Beautiful and Other Essays*, Robert Bernasconi, ed., translated by Nicholas Walker (Cambridge: Cambridge University Press, 1986), pp. 66–7.
20 Henri Lefebvre, "The Production of Space," in Briganti and Mezei, eds, *The Domestic Space Reader*, p. 27.
21 Jonathan Z. Smith, *Map is Not Territory: Studies in the History of Religions* (Leiden: E.J. Brill, 1978), pp. 144–8.
22 A term used by Emanuel Levinas. Emmanuel Levinas, *Totality and Infinity: An Essay on Exteriority*, translated by Alphonso Lingis (Pittsburg, PA: Duquesne University Press, 1969), p. 17.
23 A term used by Adam Hardy. Adam Hardy, *The Temple Architecture of India* (Hoboken, NJ: John Wiley & Sons, 2007), p. 19.
24 See Levinas, *Totality and Infinity,* p. 152.
25 Diana Fuss, "The Sense of an Interior: Four Writers and the Rooms that Shaped Them," in Briganti and Mezei, eds, *The Domestic Space Reader*, p. 346.
26 Gadamer states, "I should simply like to use my own craft of philosophical thinking to help people to see what they can all come to understand themselves." Gadamer, *The Relevance of the Beautiful,* pp. 66–7.

Chapter 1 – Homelessness and homecoming: cultural contexts, ontological roles, and the task of architecture

1 Wallace Stevens, "Notes Towards a Supreme Fiction," in Holly Stevens, ed., *The Palm at the End of the Mind: Selected Poems and a Play* (New York: Vintage Books, 1972), pp. 2–10.
2 Brenden O'Donoghue, *A Poetics of Homecoming: Heidegger, Homelessness and the Homecoming Venture* (Newcastle-upon-Tyne: Cambridge Scholars Publishing, 2011), pp. 26–9.
3 Karsten Harries, "Building and the Terror of Time," *Perspecta: The Yale Architectural Journal*, Vol. 19, 1982, pp. 59–69.
4 Blaise Pascal, *Thoughts*, translated by A.J. Krailsheimer (London: Penguin Books, 1995), p. 95.
5 For a cogent summary of the search for other life or habitable planets in the universe, see Lee Billings, *Five Billion Years of Solitude: The Search for Life Among the Stars* (New York: Current/The Penguin Group, 2013).

6 Wallace Stevens, *The Palm at the End of the Mind*, Holly Stevens, ed., p. 207.
7 The poetry of the German Romantic poet Friedrich Holderlin (1770-1843) has often been characterized as mourning the loss of the presence of the gods of antiquity in the modern world.
8 Sigmund Freud, *The Uncanny*, translated by David McLintock (New York: Penguin Books, 2003), p. 147.
9 Robert Mugerauer explains Heidegger's position: "Insofar as a displacement would be metaphysical, collapsing our grounding and orientation in the world/cosmos, it would be seen that a recovery would require, or even amount to, an ontological homecoming." Robert Mugerauer, *Heidegger and Homecoming: The Leitmotif in the Later Writings* (Toronto: University of Toronto Press, 2008), p. 24.
10 *The Dhammapada*, translated by Juan Mascaro (London: Penguin Books, 1973), p. 47.
11 The "hero's journey" is a term created by the religious scholar Joseph Campbell and comprehensively presented in Joseph Campbell, *The Hero with a Thousand Faces* (Princeton, NJ: Princeton University Press, 1949).
12 See Kazi K. Ashraf, *The Hermit's Hut: Architecture and Asceticism in India* (Honolulu: University of Hawaii Press, 2013), pp. 1–10.
13 *The Dhammapada: The Sayings of the Buddha*, translated by Thomas Byron (New York: Vintage Books, 1976), p. 56.
14 Jonathan Z. Smith, *Map is Not Territory*, p. 101.
15 Yi-Fu Tuan, *Space and Place: The Perspective of Experience* (Minneapolis: University of Minnesota Press, 1977), p. 152.
16 O'Donoghue, *A Poetics of Homecoming*, p. 3.
17 "The Noble Rider and the Sound of Words," in Harold Bloom, *Wallace Stevens: The Poems of Our Climate* (Ithaca, NY: Cornell University Press, 1976), p. 172.
18 *Vitruvius: The Ten Books On Architecture*, translated by Morris Hicky Morgan (New York: Dover Publications, Inc., 1960), Book II, Chapter 1, p. 38. Vitruvius goes on to equate the birth of architecture with the creation of language and the founding of culture. Ovid wrote in Metamorphoses, "All other creatures look down toward the earth, but man was given a face so that he might turn his eyes toward the stars and his gaze upon the sky."
19 For Harries, architecture has a particular function of embodying the timeless and consequently ameliorating the reality of the passage of time and its implications regarding mortality. Harries, "Building and the Terror of Time."
20 Karsten Harries, *The Ethical Function of Architecture* (Cambridge, MA: The MIT Press, 1998), p. 136.
21 Harries, *The Ethical Function of Architecture*, p. 149.
22 Wallace Stevens, *The Palm at the End of the Mind*, Holly Stevens, ed., p. 46.
23 Cicero, *De Natura Deorum*, from *De Natura Deorum, Academica*, translated by H. Rackham (Cambridge, MA: Harvard University Press, 1933), p. 271.
24 Norman Crowe, *Nature and the Idea of a Man-made World: An Investigation into the Evolutionary Roots of Form and Order in the Built Environment* (Cambridge, MA: The MIT Press, 1995), p. 30.
25 Karsten Harries suggests that acts of building serve as a "domestication of space," and "every house may be considered an attempted recovery of some paradise." Harries, "Building and the Terror of Time," p. 59.
26 Oliver, *The Vernacular House Worldwide*, p. 178.
27 Paul Oliver, *Built to Meet Needs: Cultural Issues in Vernacular Architecture* (Amsterdam: Elsevier, 2006), pp. 59–60.

28 Kim Dovey, "The Silent Complicity of Architecture," in Jean Hillier and Emma Rooksby, *Habitus: A Sense of Place, Second Edition* (Aldershot: Ashgate, 2005), p. 291.
29 See Oliver, *The Vernacular House Worldwide*, pp. 154–6, and Peter Nabakov and Robert Easton, *Native American Architecture* (New York: Oxford University Press, 1989), pp. 325–30.
30 See Gary Witherspoon, *Language and Art in the Navaho Universe* (Ann Arbor: The University of Michigan Press, 1977), pp. 13–46.
31 Amos Rapoport, *House Form and Culture* (Englewood Cliffs, NJ: Prentice-Hall, Inc., 1969), p. 50.
32 While also recognizing that pattern finding in architecture is often about pattern seeking with contradictory elements at times excised. And, as Oliver points out, there are examples that possess a complexity that does not align them easily with the binary systems he employs, as in the case of the Berber house. Oliver, *The Vernacular House Worldwide*, p. 179.
33 See Oliver, *The Vernacular House Worldwide*, pp. 170–89.
34 Hans-Georg Gadamer, *Truth and Method*, second revised edition, Joel Weinsheimer and Donald G. Marshall, eds (London: Continuum, 1989), p. 151.
35 For example, Georg Trakl's poem, "A Winter Evening," is discussed at length to illustrate Heidegger's positioning of phenomenology as a "return to things" and the ontological significance of home and domestic rituals. Christian Norberg-Schulz, *Genius Loci: Towards a Phenomenology of Architecture* (New York: Rizzoli, 1980), pp. 8–11.
36 Gaston Bachelard, *The Poetics of Space*, translated by Maria Jolas (Boston: Beacon Press, 1969), p. 6.
37 Joe Moran points out that the physical attributes of home Bachelard promotes are Western-centric and even close to the house where he was raised in rural Champagne. Smyth and Croft, eds, *Our House*, pp. 28–9.
38 From "Heidegger, Gagarin and Us," in Emmanuel Levinas, *Difficult Freedom: Essays on Judaism,* translated by Séan Hand (Baltimore, MD: The Johns Hopkins University Press, 1990), p. 232 (italics in original).
39 Rowan Moore, *Why We Build,* p. 61.
40 Bachelard, *The Poetics of Space*, pp. 18–19.
41 Claire Cooper Marcus, *The House as Symbol of Self*, pp. 4 and 40.
42 "IV, Down There (for Irving Weiss)," and "V, Up There (for Annie Weiss)," in W.H. Auden, *About the House* (New York: Random House, 1965), pp. 14–15.
43 See Thomas Barrie, *The Sacred In-between: The Mediating Roles of Architecture* (London: Routledge, 2010), pp. 64–79.
44 Thomas Moore, *The Re-Enchantment of Everyday Life* (New York: Harper Collins, 1996), p. 77. Moore also states "The need for home lies deep in the human heart: when our homeland is threatened we go into action to defend it, and when our family house is violated we are profoundly offended. We spend our lives trying to "make a home" – building, buying, renting, borrowing houses, staying in the old family homestead or moving from house to house according to the winds of fate. Few things are more important than finding a home and working at it constantly to make it resonate with deep memories and fulfill deep longings." Moore, *The Re-Enchantment of Everyday Life*, p. 42.
45 Moore argues, "nothing is more intimate than home, and therefore nothing more proper to the soul. Whatever it takes to call forth the spirits of home, our own lares and penates – ancient Roman household spirits – are worth our effort and expense." Moore, *The Re-Enchantment of Everyday Life,* p. 85.

46 Crowe, *Nature and the Idea of a Man-made World*, p. 34.
47 As recounted in *The Vimalakirti Sutra*, an important Mahayana text first translated into Chinese in the second century CE. See Burton Watson (trans.), *The Vimalakirti Sutra* (New York: Columbia University Press, 1997).
48 Herman Hertzberger, *Space and the Architect: Lessons in Architecture 2* (Rotterdam: 010 Publishers, 1991), p. 19.
49 See the Introduction by Robert Bernasconi to Hans-Georg Gadamer, *The Relevance of the Beautiful and Other Essays*, p. xiv.
50 Robert Mugerauer, *Interpreting Environments: Tradition, Deconstruction, Hermeneutics* (Austin: The University of Texas Press, 1995) p. xxi. According to Lindsay Jones, architecture can serve as a primary means of deciphering a culture, its assigned meanings revealing a culture's histories, values, and self-awareness.

> Architecture is a particular sort of cultural production, but it need not, as the disparaging assignation "mute text" implies, be judged as inherently lower, weaker, or crippled documentary resource to which one retreats only in the absence of the certainty that written texts can provide.
>
> Lindsay Jones, *The Hermeneutics of Sacred Architecture: Experience, Interpretation, Comparison. Volume 1: Monumental Occasions, Reflections on the Eventfulness of Religious Architecture* (Cambridge, MA: Harvard University Press, 2000), p. xxv.

51 But, as I have also argued, their packed agendas included a panoply of elements – from the declarative, didactic, and coercive, to the nurturing, instructive and transcendent. See Barrie, *The Sacred In-between: The Mediating Roles of Architecture*.
52 Jones, *The Hermeneutics of Sacred Architecture*, volume 1, pp. 29 and 36.
53 According to Pérez-Gómez, "The fundamental thrust of architecture… [is] a poetic representation of significant human action." Alberto Pérez-Gómez, *Built Upon Love: Architectural Longing after Ethics and Aesthetics* (Cambridge, MA: The MIT Press, 2006), p. 125.
54 *The Odyssey of Homer*, translated by Samuel Butler, Louise Ropes Loomis, ed., (Roslyn, NY: Walter J. Black, Inc., 1944), pp. 74–75.
55 The song "A House is Not a Home," written by Burt Bacharach and sung by Diane Warwick, was recorded in 1964.
56 As Claire Cooper Marcus states, "A home fulfills many needs: a place of self expression, a vessel of memories, a refuge from the outside world, a cocoon where we can feel nurtured and let down our guard." Marcus, *The House as Symbol of Self*, p. 4.
57 Quoted in Anatxu Zabalbeascoa, *The House of the Architect* (New York: Rizzoli, 1995), p. 6.
58 Peter Matthiessen, *The Snow Leopard* (Toronto: Bantam Books, 1978), p. 45.
59 Harries, *The Ethical Function of Architecture*, p. 213.

Chapter 2 – A home in the world: house and home in literature

1 Herman Melville, *Moby Dick or the Whale* (New York: Modern Library, 1982), p. 1.
2 "Poem 609," Emily Dickinson, *Collected Poems* (Philadelphia, PA: Running Press Book Publishers, 1991), p. 128.
3 Robert Frost, *The Poetry of Robert Frost: The Collected Poems, Complete and Unabridged*, Edward Connery Lathem, ed. (New York: Holt, Rinehart and Winston, 1969), p. 38.

4 Carol Ingalls Johnson, *Of Time and the Artist: Thomas Wolfe, His Novels, and the Critics* (Columbia, SC: Camden House, Inc., 1996), pp. 11–12.
5 Thomas Wolfe, *Look Homeward Angel: A Story of a Buried Life* (New York: Charles Scribner's Sons, 1929), unnumbered prologue.
6 Thomas Wolfe, *You Can't Go Home Again* (New York: Harper & Brothers, 1940), unnumbered prologue.
7 Wolfe, *You Can't Go Home Again*, p. 103.
8 Wolfe, op. cit., p. 56.
9 Wolfe, op. cit., p. 706.
10 Wolfe, op. cit., p. 499.
11 Marshall Berman, *Modernity: Yesterday, Today, and Tomorrow* (New York: Penguin Books, 1982), p. 6.
12 Rainer Maria Rilke, *The Notebooks of Malte Laurids Brigge*, translated by Michael Hulse (New York: Penguin Books, 2009), pp. 30–1. Heidegger quoted this passage in its entirety in *Die Grundprobleme der Phänomologie* to argue that the scene disclosed deeper essences of the world. See Hulse (trans.), n. 7, p. 169.
13 James Salter, *Light Years* (San Francisco, CA: North Point Press, 1982), p. 34.
14 William Dowie states, that the novel "is imbued from its opening lines with a nostalgic tone." William Dowie, *James Salter* (New York: Twayne Publishers, 1998), p. 62.
15 Salter, *Light Years*, p. 12.
16 Salter, op. cit., pp. 7–8.
17 Salter, op. cit., p. 205.
18 Maya Angelou, *The Complete Collected Poems of Maya Angelou* (New York: Random House, 1994), p. 252.
19 Angelou, *The Complete Collected Poems of Maya Angelou*, p. 252.
20 Marcel Proust, *Swann's Way*, translated by C.K. Scott Moncrieff (New York: Random House, 1970), p. 22.
21 Proust, *Swann's Way*, p. 22.
22 Proust, op. cit., p. 10.
23 Proust, op. cit., p. 11.
24 Harper Lee, *To Kill a Mockingbird* (New York: Warner Books, 1960), p. 8.
25 Lee, *To Kill a Mockingbird*, p. 8.
26 Lee, op. cit., p. 9.
27 Lee, op. cit., p. 15.
28 Anthony Vidler, *The Architectural Uncanny: Essays in the Modern Unhomely* (Cambridge, MA: The MIT Press, 1992), p. 3.
29 Edgar Allen Poe, *The Fall of the House of Usher*, in George McMichael, ed., *Anthology of American Literature, Volume I, Colonial Through Romantic* (New York: Macmillan Publishing Co., Inc., 1974), pp. 783–99.
30 Nathaniel Hawthorne, *The House of the Seven Gables: A Romance* (Pleasantville, NY: The Reader's Digest Association, Inc., 1985), pp. 14–15.
31 Hawthorne, *The House of the Seven Gables*, pp. 21–2.
32 Hawthorne, op. cit., p. 27.
33 Hawthorne, op. cit., p. 14.
34 Hawthorne, op. cit., p. 225.
35 Hawthorne, op. cit., p. 240.
36 Hawthorne, op. cit., p. 274.
37 Hans Biedermann, *Dictionary of Symbolism: Cultural Icons and the Meanings Behind Them,* translated by James Hulbert (New York: Meridian, 1989), p. 245. See also W.C. Ferry, "The Wisdom of Odysseus," *Parabola*, Spring 2014, pp. 28–37.

38 A stringed instrument and lute respectively.

39 Translated by Burton Watson, *Four Huts: Asian Writings on the Simple Life* (Boston: Shambhala Publications, 1994), pp. 88–9.

40 Po Chü-i was a government official in the T'ang capital city of Ch'ang-an, and an outspoken critic of the government, and eventually was demoted to a post in a remote area. Here he began visiting the nearby Mt. Lu, eventually building a retreat there to be used when he was free of official duties.

41 Watson, *Four Huts*, p. 5.

42 A stringed instrument. Watson, op. cit., n. 2, p. 21.

43 Watson, op. cit., pp. 8–9.

44 Watson, op. cit., p. 98.

45 Watson, op. cit., p. 9. A poem purportedly written at a gathering after completion of the house makes explicit its essential nature.

> A new thatched hall, five spans by three;
> stone steps, cassia pillars, fence of plaited bamboo.
> the south eaves catch the sun, warm on winter days;
> a door to the north lets in breezes, cool in summer moonlight.
> Cascades from the spring that drip on the paving splatter it with dots;
> the slanting bamboo that brushes the window isn't planted in rows.
> Next spring I'll thatch the side room to the east:
> fit with paper panels and reed blinds for my *Meng Kuang*.
>
> Watson, op. cit., pp. 18–19.

46 The narrator recalls in detail how his mother had:

> sent out for one of those short, plump little cakes called "petites madeleines," which look as though they had been moulded in the fluted scallop of a pilgrim's shell. And soon, mechanically, weary after a dull day with the prospect of a depressing tomorrow, I raised to my lips a spoonful of tea in which I had soaked a morsel of the cake. No sooner had the warm liquid, and the crumbs with it, touched my palate than a shudder ran through my whole body, and I stopped intent upon the extraordinary changes that were taking place. An exquisite pleasure had invaded my senses, but individual, detached, with no suggestions of its origin. And at once the vicissitudes of life had become indifferent to me, its disasters innocuous, its brevity illusory – this new sensation having had on me the effect which love has of filling me with a precious essence; or rather this essence was not in me, it was myself.
>
> Proust, *Swann's Way*, pp. 34–5.

47 *Petite maison*, or "little house," also colloquially referred to retreats for sexual liaisons and houses of prostitution.

48 Jean-François de Bastide, *The Little House*, translated by Rodolphe el-Khoury (New York: Princeton Architectural Press, 1996), pp. 66–7.

49 de Bastide, *The Little House*, from the *Introduction* by Rodolphe el-Khoury, p. 33.

50 V.S. Naipaul, *A House for Mr. Biswas* (New York: Alfred A. Knoft, Inc., 1961), p. 201.

51 Richard Gill, *Happy Rural Seat: The English Country House and the Literary Imagination* (New Haven, CT: Yale University Press, 1972), pp. 3–7.

52 Josh Silvers and Toby D. Olsen, "Pride and Prejudice: Establishing Historical Connections among the Arts," in Rumiko Handa and James Potter, eds, *Conjuring the Real: The Role of Architecture in Eighteenth- and Nineteenth-Century Fiction* (Lincoln: University of Nebraska Press, 2011), p. 192.

53 Gill, *Happy Rural Seat*, p. 20.
54 Gill op. cit., p. 21.
55 Malcolm Kelsall, *The Great Good Place: The Country House and English Literature* (New York: Columbia University Press, 1993), p. 169.
56 Jane Austen, *Pride and Prejudice* (New York: Pocket Books, 2004), p. 17.
57 Austen, *Pride and Prejudice*, p. 183.
58 Austen, op. cit., p. 273.
59 Austen, op. cit., p. 274.
60 Austen, op. cit., p. 418.
61 Calvin Trilling, *The Opposing Self: Nine Essays in Criticism* (New York: Viking Press, 1955), p. 210.
62 Malcolm Kelsall suggested that *Mansfield Park* "is structured upon the fundamental binary opposition between good and evil houses." Kelsall, *The Great Good Place*, p. 107.
63 Austen, *Mansfield Park* (New York: Hyperion, first published 1814), p. 342.
64 Austen, *Mansfield Park*, p. 345 (italics in the original). See also Gill, *Happy Rural Seat*, pp. 245–6.
65 Austen, op. cit., p. 380.
66 Austen, op. cit., p. 382.
67 Vidler, *The Architectural Uncanny*, pp. 3–4.
68 William Maxwell, *So Long, See You Tomorrow* (New York: Knoft, 1980), p. 25.

Chapter 3 – Origins: stories and theories about the first house

1 Wayfarers and travelers were under Jupiter's protection.
2 As recounted by Ovid in the Eighth Book of *Metamorphoses.* (It also famously appears in Goethe's *Faust Part Two.*)
3 According to Robert Mugerauer, "The 'arche' in 'arche-tecture' originally meant 'first principle' or 'first element.' 'Tecton,' today echoed in 'techne' and 'technology,' means 'making or setting into work.' 'Arche-tecton,' then, refers to the first skill, primary craft or chief work." Robert Mugerauer, "Toward an Architectural Vocabulary: The Porch as a Between," in David Seamon, ed., *Dwelling, Seeing, and Designing: Towards a Phenomenological Ecology* (Albany, NY: State University of New York Press, 1993), p. 103. See also Karsten Harries, *The Ethical Function of Architecture*, p. 113.
4 According to Norman Crowe, "The idea of a house as the origin of architecture pervades the myths of societies everywhere." Norman Crowe, *Nature and the Idea of a Man-made World*, p. 34.
5 Joseph Rykwert, *On Adam's House in Paradise: The Idea of the Primitive Hut in Architectural History* (Cambridge, MA: The MIT Press, 1972), p. 183.
6 Quoted in Marie-Louise von Franz, *Projection and Re-collection in Jungian Psychology: Reflections of the Soul,* translated by William H. Kennedy (LaSalle, IL: Open Court Publishing Company, 1980), p. 6.
7 According to Alberto Pérez-Gómez, "For many architects, myth and poetry are generally considered synonymous with dreams and lunacy." Alberto Pérez-Gómez, *Architecture and the Crisis of Modern Science* (Cambridge, MA: The MIT Press, 1983), p. 6.
8 Peter Nabakov and Robert Easton, *Native American Architecture*, p. 38.
9 Oliver quotes Margaret M. Wheat, "Patched and repaired from year to year, abandoned when not needed, or burned when death occurred in them, Paiute shelters were mainly protection from the elements. They were never 'home.'" Paul Oliver, *Built to Meet Needs*, p. 57.

10 This myth is perhaps embedded in the distant histories of the Navaho of the American Southwest, who are descendants of peoples from western Canada that migrated from there around the eleventh century, and brought with them traditions of building round, pit-house type domiciles.

11 Nabakov and Easton, *Native American Architecture*, pp. 325–33.

12 See Crowe, *Nature and the Idea of a Man-made World*, p. 34.

13 Harries, *The Ethical Function of Architecture*, p. 204.

14 Gaston Bachelard, *The Poetics of Space*, p. 15.

15 Peter Zumthor, *Thinking Architecture* (Basel: Birkhauser, 1998), pp. 7–8.

16 This was especially the case in the eighteenth and nineteenth centuries where Enlightenment ideals, industrialization, and advancing knowledge of other building traditions threatened the aesthetic foundations of architecture. See Jonathan A. Hale, "Gottfried Semper's Primitive Hut: Duration, Construction and Self-Creation," in Jo Odgers, Fiona Samuel and Adam Sharr, eds, *Primitive: Original Matters in Architecture* (London: Routledge, 2006), p. 57.

17 Rykwert, *On Adam's House in Paradise*, p. 183.

18 According to Rykwert, Vitruvius' account shows "all of the characteristics of a myth – a myth reflecting ritual usage and harnessed to changing religious demands." Joseph Rykwert, *The Dancing Column* (Cambridge, MA: The MIT Press, 1996), p. 320.

19 Vitruvius, *The Ten Books On Architecture*, p. 40.

20 Rykwert argues that his positions are essentially Stoic. Rykwert, *On Adam's House in Paradise,* p. 110.

21 Robin Dripps, *The First House* (Cambridge, MA: The MIT Press, 1997), p. 4.

22 Leon Battista Alberti, *On the Art of Building in Ten Books*, translated by Joseph Rykwert, Neil Leach, and Robert Tavernor (Cambridge, MA: The MIT Press, 1988), p. 8.

23 A note by the editors states his source for this account was Pliny and that it includes a number of inaccuracies. *On the Art of Building in Ten Books*, translated by Rykwert, Leach, and Tavernor, p. 368.

24 Excerpted in Harry Francis Mallgrave, *Architectural Theory: Volume I, An Anthology from Vitruvius to 1870* (Malden, MA: Blackwell Publishing, 2006), pp. 536–7.

25 Mari Hvattum, "Origins Redefined: A Tale of Pigs and Primitive Huts," in Odgers, Samuel and Sharr, eds, *Primitive: Original Matters in Architecture*, p. 37.

26 See Mari Hvattum, *Gottfried Semper and the Problem of Historicism* (Cambridge: Cambridge University Press, 2004), p. 35.

27 See Hvattum, *Gottfried Semper and the Problem of Historicism*, pp. 35–7.

28 Le Corbusier, *Towards a New Architecture* (New York: Holt, Reinhart and Winston, 1927), pp. 65–6.

29 Le Corbusier, *Towards a New Architecture*, p. 66.

30 Hvattum, *Gottfried Semper and the Problem of Historicism*, pp. 30–1. See also, Pérez-Gómez, *Architecture and the Crisis of Modern Science*, p. 61.

31 Lorems Holm, "The Primitive Hut: Fantasies of Survival in an All-White World," in Odgers, Samuel and Sharr, eds, *Primitive: Original Matters in Architecture*, p. 49.

32 Harries, *The Ethical Function of Architecture*, p. 7. According to Mari Hvattum, "Laugier's 'origin' then, is a highly abstract idea, dressed up in the metaphorical guise of the primitive hut." Hvattum, *Gottfried Semper and the Problem of Historicism*, p. 34.

33 Marc-Antoine Laugier, *An Essay on Architecture*, translated by Wolfgang and Anni Herrmann (Los Angeles, CA: Hennessey & Ingalls, Inc., 1977), p. 13.

34 As Karsten Harries points out, "It was of course not so much the Greek Temple that was constructed in the image of the primitive hut, as the hut that was constructed in the image of the Greek temple." Harries, *The Ethical Function of Architecture*, p. 115.

35 Frank Lloyd Wright, *The Living City* (New York: New American Library, 1958), pp. 23–5.
36 Adolf Loos, *On Architecture*, Adolf and Daniel Opel, eds, translated by Michael Mitchell (Riverside, CA: Ariadne Press, 2002), pp. 73–4. See also, Rykwert, *On Adam's House in Paradise*, p. 27.
37 Frank Lloyd Wright, *The Natural House* (New York: New American Library, 1954), p. 15.
38 Dripps states, "What is being offered is the hope that the apparently bewildering condition of the present might be traced back to a common beginning more stable and more powerful." Dripps, *The First House*, p. 10.
39 Ananda K. Coomaraswamy argued that the first monasteries in India were groupings of single-cell huts. Ananda K. Coomaraswamy, *Essays in Early Indian Architecture* (New Delhi: Indira Ghandi National Centre for the Arts/Oxford University Press, 1992), pp. 105–6.
40 Kamo no Chomei, "Record of the Ten-Foot-Square Hut," in Burton Watson, trans., *Four Huts: Asian Writings on the Simple Life*, pp. 89–91.
41 Okakura Kakuzo, *The Book of Tea* (Rutland, VT: Charles E. Tuttle Company, 1956), p. 62.
42 Thomas Barrie, *Spiritual Path – Sacred Place: Myth, Ritual, and Meaning in Architecture* (Boston: Shambhala Publications, 1997), pp. 180–213.
43 Eugène Viollet-le-Duc, *The Habitations of Man in All Ages*, translated by Benjamin Bucknall (Ann Arbor, MI: Gryphon Books, 1971), p. 394.
44 Rykwert, *On Adam's House in Paradise*, p. 192.
45 E. Baldwin Smith, *Egyptian Architecture as Cultural Expression* (New York: D. Appleton-Century Company, 1938), p. 11.
46 Anthony Vidler, *The Architectural Uncanny*, p. 117.
47 Wolfgang Hermann, *Laugier and Eighteenth-Century French Theory* (London: A. Zwemmer Ltd., 1962), pp. 48–9.
48 See Odgers, Samuel and Sharr, eds, *Primitive: Original Matters in Architecture*, p. 3.
49 Samir Younés, *The True, The Fictive, and the Real: The Historical Dictionary of Architecture of Quatremère de Quincy* (London: Andreas Papadakis Publishers, 1999), p. 82 (italics in original).
50 Harries, *The Ethical Function of Architecture*, p. 112.
51 Bachelard, *The Poetics of Space*, p. 33.
52 Younés, *The True, The Fictive, and the Real: The Historical Dictionary of Architecture of Quatremère de Quincy*, pp. 21, 37, 82, and 171.
53 According to Harries, "The primitive hut has played in architectural theory much the same part that the social contract has played in political theory," and "We are still not done with his primitive hut." Harries, *The Ethical Function of Architecture*, pp. 114–15.
54 As Rykwert states, the primitive hut will "retain its validity as a reminder of the original and therefore essential meaning of all building for people; that is, of architecture. It remains the underlying statement, the irreducible, intentional core." Rykwert, *On Adam's House in Paradise*, p. 193.
55 Rykwert, *On Adam's House in Paradise*, p. 193.
56 Dripps, *The First House*, p. 7.

Chapter 4 – Sacred domesticities: houses for divinity, divinity of home

1 His full name and title were Fitzroy Richard Somerset, 4th Baron Raglan.
2 E. Baldwin Smith, *Egyptian Architecture as Cultural Expression*, p. 12.
3 E. Baldwin Smith, *Architectural Symbolism of Imperial Rome and the Middle Ages* (Princeton, NJ: Princeton University Press, 1956), pp. 180–1.

4 Smith, *Egyptian Architecture as Cultural Expression*, p. 29.
5 Mircea Eliade, *The Sacred and the Profane: The Nature of Religion*, translated by Willard R. Trask (San Diego, CA: Harcourt Brace Jovanovich, Publishers, 1957), p. 58. See also, Norman Crowe, *Nature and the Idea of a Man-made World*, p. 42.
6 Lord Raglan, *The Temple in the House* (New York: W.W. Norton & Company, Inc., 1964), pp. ix and 2–7.
7 E. Baldwin Smith, *The Dome: A Study in the History of Ideas* (Princeton, NJ: Princeton University Press, 1950), p. 6.
8 Coomaraswamy, *Essays in Early Indian Architecture*, p. 109.
9 In "late Latin *doma* meant 'house,' 'root,' and only at times 'cupola.'" In the Middle Ages and Renaissance *domus dei* described the "house of god." Smith, *The Dome,* p. 5.
10 See Smith, *The Dome*, p. 86.
11 The inner ring depicts twenty-four ancestors, from Adam to Jacob; the outer ring, the fifteen children of Jacob.
12 Crowe, *Nature and the Idea of a Man-made World*, pp. 42–6.
13 William Chambers, *A Treatise on Civil Architecture in which the Principles of that Art are Laid Down and Illustrated by a Great Number of Plates Accurately Designed and Elegantly Engraved by the Best Hands* (London: 1759).
14 The evolution of wooden to stone structures is a popular and credible theory. Adam Hardy has suggested the same for the architecture of the Indian subcontinent where temples often replicated the wooden constructions of "huts, shrines, palaces and city gates," but points out that their lineage is not direct. Adam Hardy, *The Temple Architecture of India* (Chichester, UK: John Wiley & Sons, Ltd., 2007), p. 74.
15 Spiro Kostof, *A History of Architecture: Settings and Rituals* (New York: Oxford University Press, 1985), pp. 99–100.
16 Similar theories have been presented regarding Chinese courtyard houses, palaces, and temples. According to Knapp and Lo, "The Chinese house has more in common with the Chinese temple than with other architectural forms." Ronald G. Knapp and Kai-Yin Lo, eds, *House, Home, Family: Living and Being Chinese* (Honolulu: University of Hawaii Press, 2005), pp. 13–14.
17 J.G. Davies, *The Origin and Development of Early Christian Church Architecture* (New York: Philosophical Library, 1953), p. 3.
18 Michael Peppard, *The World's Oldest Church: Bible, Art, and Ritual at Dura-Europos, Syria* (New Haven: Yale University Press, 2016), pp. 16–20.
19 Davies, *The Origin and Development of Early Christian Church Architecture*, pp. 17–18.
20 Davies, op. cit., p. 31.
21 Robert Hillenbrand, *Islamic Architecture: Form, Function and Meaning* (New York: Columbia University Press, 1994), p. 39.
22 Hillenbrand, *Islamic Architecture*, p. 40.
23 See Joseph Rykwert, *On Adam's House in Paradise*, p. 127.
24 Ananda K. Coomaraswamy, *The Door in the Sky: Coomaraswamy on Myth and Meaning*, R. P. Coomaraswamy, ed. (Princeton, NJ: Princeton University Press, 1997), p. 175.
25 Coomaraswamy, *The Door in the Sky*, p. 177.
26 See Hardy, *The Temple Architecture of India,* pp. 56–8.
27 George Michell, *The Hindu Temple: An Introduction to Its Meaning and Forms* (Chicago: The University of Chicago Press, 1977), p. 61.
28 For a succinct summary of Chinese motivations and practices, see Knapp and Lo, *House, Home, Family*, pp. 99–102.
29 According to Juan Eduardo Campo, entering the traditional Islamic house required proper demonstrations of respect because it was the domain of women. Juan

Eduardo Campo, "The Domestications of Islam in Modern Egypt: A Cultural Analysis," in Chiara Briganti and Kathy Mezai, eds, *The Domestic Space Reader*, p. 40.
30 Cicero, *De Natura Deorum, Book II: 67.*
31 From Ovid, *Fasti*, see Clive Knights, "The Spatiality of the Roman Domestic Setting: An Interpretation of Symbolic Content," in Michael Parker Pearson and Colin Richards, eds, *Architecture and Order: Approaches to Social Space*, p. 125.
32 According to Cicero, the word *penates* is derived from *penus*, a store for food in the innermost part of the house. Cicero, *De Natura Deorum, Book II: 68.*
33 Knights, "The Spatiality of the Roman Domestic Setting," Pearson and Richards, eds., *Architecture and Order: Approaches to Social Space*, p. 134.
34 Knights, op. cit., p. 119.
35 Xiao Hu, "Boundaries and Openings: Spatial Strategies in the Chinese Dwelling," *Journal of Housing and the Built Environment*, Vol. 23, 2008, pp. 353–66.
36 Amos Rapoport, *House Form and Culture*, p. 41.
37 Paul Oliver, *Dwellings: The Vernacular House Worldwide*, pp. 171–2.
38 Oliver, op. cit., p. 180.
39 Oliver, op. cit., p. 174.
40 Oliver, op. cit., p. 174.
41 Rapoport, *House Form and Culture*, p. 51. According to Rapoport, Pawnee villages were also celestial symbols.
42 Peter Nabakov and Robert Easton, *Native American Architecture*, pp. 88–9.
43 Nabakov and Easton, op. cit., pp. 123–5.
44 Nabakov and Easton, op. cit., p. 30.
45 Nabakov and Easton, op. cit., pp. 30–1 and pp. 380–3.
46 Nabakov and Easton, op. cit., pp. 82–6.
47 Kostof, *A History of Architecture*, p. 147.
48 Leon Battista Alberti, *On the Art of Building in Ten Books*, translated by Rykwert, Leach, and Tavernor. See also Robert Tavernor, *On Alberti and the Art of Building* (New Haven, CT: Yale University Press, 1998).
49 According to Alberto Pérez-Gómez, it never developed into a specific building type, but instead was a "representation of significant action, apart from formal or stylistic considerations." Alberto Pérez-Gómez, *Built Upon Love: Architectural Longing after Ethics and Aesthetics* (Cambridge, MA: The MIT Press, 2006), p. 131.
50 Crowe, *Nature and the Idea of a Man-made World*, p. 114.
51 The sacred mirror, sword, and jewel were originally enshrined there, objects related to the creation myth of Isanagi and Izamami, and a resurrection myth featuring Amaterasu and her brother Susa-no-o. In the former myth, the brother and sister gods thrust the "jewel spear" into the ocean and as it was removed its drips created the Japanese islands. In the second mythical story, Amaterasu retreated into a cave after the trickery of her brother, which plunged the world into darkness. The world is resurrected only after she is lured out by dances reflected in a mirror.
52 William Coaldrake, *Architecture and Authority in Japan* (London: Routledge, 1996), p. 27.
53 Roxana Waterson, "The House and the World: The Symbolism of Sa'Dan Toraja House Carvings," *Anthropology and Aesthetics*, No. 15, Spring 1988, pp. 34–60.

Chapter 5 – House tombs: domestic abodes and memorials

1 Cicero, *On Living and Dying Well* (New York: Penguin Books, 2012), pp. 22–3.

2 However, Guthrie argues that there was no unanimity of belief in Greco-Roman culture regarding the afterlife. W.K.C. Guthrie, *Orpheus and Greek Religions: A Study of the Orphic Movement* (New York: W.W. Norton & Co., Inc., 1966), p. 148.
3 Louise Ropes Loomis, ed., *Plato: Apology, Crito, Phaedo, Symposium, Republic*, translated by B. Jowett (Roslyn, NY: Walter J. Black, Inc., 1942), p. 480.
4 Michel Ragon, *The Space of Death: A Study of Funerary Architecture, Decoration, and Urbanism,* translated by Alan Sheridan (Charlottesville: University Press of Virginia, 1983), p. 20.
5 According to E. Baldwin Smith, there was "more fear than love" in Egyptian death rites. E. Baldwin Smith, *Egyptian Architecture as Cultural Expression*, p. 26.
6 Ragon, *The Space of Death*, p. 3.
7 Mircea Eliade, *Symbolism, the Sacred and the Arts,* Diane Apostolos-Cappadona, ed. (New York: Continuum, 1992), p. 122.
8 Karsten Harries, *The Ethical Function of Architecture*, p. 293.
9 Harries, op. cit., p. 293.
10 Lindsay Jones, *The Hermeneutics of Sacred Architecture, Volume II, Hermeneutical Calisthenics: A Morphology of Ritual-Architectural Priorities* (Cambridge, MA: Harvard University Press, 2000), p. 153.
11 According to Michel Ragon, "The tomb is a second house… but… is also a sort of antechamber between this world and the next, a place of passage." Ragon, *The Space of Death*, p. 19.
12 Jones, *The Hermeneutics of Sacred Architecture, Volume II*, p. 180.
13 Ragon, *The Space of Death*, p. 26.
14 Herodotus wrote that the Egyptians considered their homes temporary, but their tombs permanent dwellings. James Stevens Curl, *A Celebration of Death: An Introduction to Some of the Buildings, Monuments, and Settings of Funerary Architecture in the Western European Tradition* (New York: Charles Scribner's Sons, 1980), p. 2.
15 Smith, *Egyptian Architecture as Cultural Expression*, p. 27.
16 Martin Bommas, "The Mechanics of Social Conventions Between the Living and the Dead in Ancient Egypt," in Maureen Carroll and Jane Rempel, *Living Through the Dead: Burial and Commemoration in the Classical World* (Oxford: Oxbow Books, 2011), p. 160.
17 Francis D.K. Ching, Mark Jarzombek, and Vikramaditya Prakash, *A Global History of Architecture* (Hoboken, NJ: John Wiley & Sons, Inc., 2011), pp. 20–1.
18 Harries, *The Ethical Function of Architecture*, p. 310.
19 According to Ragon, "This idea of the tomb continuing the house, in the familiarity of everyday life, was perhaps carried to the furthest limit by the Etruscans." Ragon, *The Space of Death*, p. 58.
20 According to Curl, "The plan of the necropolis is not unlike that of the Roman city of Ostia." Curl, *A Celebration of Death*, p. 40.
21 Curl, op. cit., p. 36.
22 Curl, op. cit., p. 40.
23 Howard Colvin, *Architecture and the Afterlife* (New Haven, CT: Yale University Press, 1991), p. 22.
24 Ronald G. Knapp and Kai-Yin Lo, *House, Home, Family: Living and Being Chinese*, p. 24.
25 Knapp and Lo, op. cit., p. 24.
26 According to Knapp and Lo, Chinese tombs "provide some of our best evidence of residential architecture." Knapp and Lo, op. cit., p. 20.
27 Rodney Castleden, *The Stonehenge People: An Exploration of Life in Neolithic Britain 4700–2000 BC* (London and New York: Routledge, 1990), p. 5.

28 Ian Hodder, "Architecture and Meaning: The Example of Neolithic Houses and Tombs," in Pearson and Richards, eds, *Architecture and Order*, p. 77.
29 Hodder, "Architecture and Meaning: The Example of Neolithic Houses and Tombs," p. 77.
30 Castleden, *The Stonehenge People*, pp. 158–62.
31 Aubrey Burl, *Prehistoric Avebury* (New Haven, CT and London: Yale University Press, 2002), pp. 95–6.
32 Aubrey Burl, *Neolithic Avebury*, p. 95.
33 Hodder, "Architecture and Meaning: The Example of Neolithic Houses and Tombs," p. 80.
34 Castleden, *The Stonehenge People*, p. 185.
35 As outlined in an early nineteenth-century study by H.C. Yarrow, *North American Indian Burial Customs*, completed in 1878 but first published by Eagle's View Publishing Company, Ogden, UT, 1988. See also, A. Martin Byers, *The Ohio Hopewell Episode: Paradigm Lost and Paradigm Gained* (Akron, OH: University of Akron Press, 2004).
36 William F. Romain, *Mysteries of the Hopewell: Astronomers, Geometers, and Magicians of the Eastern Woodlands* (Akron, OH: University of Akron Press, 2000), p. 158.
37 What Byers describes as the "laying-in" process where the body was first placed in a charnel house, followed after an interval of time by removal and either cremation or deposition.
38 Christopher Carr and D. Troy Case, *Gathering Hopewell: Society, Ritual and Ritual Interaction* (New York: Springer, 2006), p. 468.
39 In Eliade's words, "the pre-eminently shamanic technique is the passage from one cosmic region to another – from center to the sky or from earth to the underworld." Mircea Eliade, *Shamanism: Archaic Techniques of Ecstasy*, translated by Willard Trask (Princeton, NJ: Princeton University Press, 1964), p. 259.
40 Carr and Case, *Gathering Hopewell*, p. 42.
41 Burl, *Prehistoric Avebury*, pp. 127–8.
42 Mircea Eliade, *History of Religious Ideas, Vol 1, From the Stone Age to the Eleusinian Mysteries,* translated by Willard R. Trask (Chicago, IL: University of Chicago Press, 1978) p. 124.
43 Jones, *The Hermeneutics of Sacred Architecture, Volume II*, p. 159.
44 Carr and Case, *Gathering Hopewell*, pp. 42–5.
45 Romain, *Mysteries of the Hopewell*, p. 157.
46 Aubrey Burl, *Prehistoric Avebury,* p. 104.
47 Perhaps a reference to Orphic beliefs that presented life as a trial, during which original sin and sinful acts needed to be expiated to gain the heaven of an eternal life. Cicero, *On Living and Dying Well*, p. 20.
48 Curl, *A Celebration of Death*, p. 43.
49 Khaled Diab, "Egypt's Tombs for the Living," *The Guardian*, January 23, 2011. See also, Juan Eduardo Campo, "Domestication of Islam in Modern Egypt: A Cultural Analysis," in Chiara Briganti and Kathy Mezai, eds, *The Domestic Space Reader*, pp. 40–4.
50 Ragon, *The Space of Death*, p. 55.
51 Diab, "Egypt's Tombs for the Living."
52 The documentary film "El Velador" ("The Night Watchman"), by Natalia Almada, depicts the cemetery through the eyes of its caretaker.
53 Adolf Loos, from "Architecture," in Adolf Loos, *On Architecture*, Adolf and Daniel Opel, eds, translated by Michael Mitchell (Riverside, CA: Ariadne Press, 1995), p. 84.

54 Ragon, *The Space of Death*, p. 15.
55 According to Lefebvre:

> "Only through the monuments, through the intervention of the architect as demiurge, can the space of death be negated, transfigured into a living space which is an extension of the body; this is a transformation, however, which serves what religion, (political) power, and knowledge have in common."
>
> Henri Lefebvre, *The Production of Space*, translated by Donald Nicholson-Smith (Oxford: Blackwell, 1991), p. 221.

56 Lefebvre, *The Production of Space*, p. 235.

Chapter 6 – Materializing the immaterial: the house as a means of self-exploration and expression

1 Henri Lefebvre, *The Production of Space*, pp. 222–4.
2 In legends and art, he is depicted living in a tub at the Temple of Cybele, in Athens.
3 See Kazi K. Ashraf, *The Hermit's Hut: Architecture and Asceticism in India* (Honolulu: University of Hawaii Press, 2013).
4 Gaston Bachelard, *The Poetics of Space*, p. 32 (italics in original).
5 The preponderance of contemporary books on rustic cabins indicates their continued popularity and advancing mythology regarding their merits and promises.
6 Henry Beston, *The Outermost House* (New York: Random House, 1928), p. 8.
7 Beston, *The Outermost House*, pp. 5–6. In 1964, the house was designated a National Literary Landmark. However, in 1978, it was destroyed in a storm.
8 As a nature writer who built and occupied a rustic hut, Beston has routinely been compared with Thoreau, an association, however, he rejected.
9 Beston, *The Outermost House*, pp. 5–6.
10 Anne Morrow Lindbergh, *Gift from the Sea* (New York: Random House, 1955), p. 25.
11 Anne Morrow Lindbergh, *Against Wind and Tide: Letters and Journals, 1947–1986*, Reeve Lindbergh, ed. (New York: Pantheon Books, 2012), p. 39. Her daughter, Reeve Lindbergh, who never saw the Captiva cottages, states:

> I have thought of it as a one-room cottage. However, I know that she had guests visiting her at various times – her sister, a close friend from New York, even my father! – but whether she had a guest room, or simply shared her own room at those times, I do not know. She spent part of several winters or early springs there, referring to Captiva and the little house on the beach in her journals from March of 1948 through March of 1951. I'm not sure that she went back after that year.
>
> Email message to author, March 18, 2016.

12 Lindbergh, *Gift from the Sea*, p. 27.
13 Lindbergh, *Against Wind and Tide*, p. 42. According to Reeve Lindbergh:

> What I was told by my mother herself was that she began the book on Captiva, and worked on it there during the times she visited, especially when she was alone – no visitors – but that it was finished in Connecticut, in terms of being pulled together, shaped, and edited as a finished manuscript for Pantheon Books. I'd say Captiva, the house where she stayed, and those quiet winter periods were really the inspiration and the occasion for the book, while her

Connecticut home was the place where it could begin to come into being as a finished publication.

Email message to author, March 20, 2016.

14 Lindbergh, *Gift from the Sea*, p. 34.
15 See Paul Wijdeveld, *Ludwig Wittgenstein: Architect* (Cambridge, MA: The MIT Press, 1994).
16 Pablo Neruda, *Memoirs*, translated by Hardie St. Martin (New York: Farrar, Straus and Giroux, 1976), p. 140.
17 Pablo Neruda, *100 Love Sonnets*, translated by Stephen Tapscott (Austin: University of Texas Press, 1986), p. 3.
18 Neruda, *100 Love Sonnets*, p. 113.
19 Neruda, op. cit., p. 199.
20 Jung devotes a chapter in his autobiography to his "confrontation with the unconscious." Jaffe, ed., *Memories, Dreams, Reflections*, pp. 170-99.
21 Aniela Jaffé, ed., *Memories, Dreams, Reflections by C.G. Jung,* translated by Richard and Clara Winston (New York, NY: Random House, 1961), p. 224. Jung also writes, "I had in mind an African hut where the fire, ringed by a few stones, burns in the middle, and the whole life of the family revolves around the center." Jaffé, ed., p. 223.
22 Jaffé, *Memories, Dreams, Reflections*, p. 226.
23 Jaffe, p. 225 and 237.
24 For additional descriptions and analysis of Jung's house in Bollingen, see Thomas Barrie, *The Sacred In-between: The Mediating Roles of Architecture*, pp. 64–79; Robert Mugerauer, *Interpreting Environments: Tradition, Deconstruction, Hermeneutics* (Austin: University of Texas Press, 1995), pp. 15–28; Witold Rybczynski, *The Most Beautiful House in the World* (New York: Viking, 1989), pp. 191–2; and Theodore Ziolkowski, *The View from the Tower: Origins of an Antimodernist Image* (Princeton, NJ: Princeton University Press, 1998), pp. 131–48.
25 This essay, originally titled without the commas, was first presented as a paper at a conference in Darmstadt to an audience of mostly architects, engineers, and philosophers, including Hans Scharoun. Adam Sharr, *Heidegger for Architects* (London: Routledge, 2007), p. 36.
26 In this context, even though both men evidence significant idealistic and romantic inclinations, Heidegger is clearly the more revisionist.
27 Karsten Harries discusses Heidegger's valorizing of the Black Forest farmhouse as a Bachelardian "dream house" that represented "being at home in the world." Karsten Harries, *The Ethical Function of Architecture*, p. 203.
28 See Gertrud Heidegger, ed., *Martin Heidegger: Letters to His Wife, 1915–1970,* translated by R.D.V. Glasgow (Cambridge: Polity, 2008), pp. 85–6.
29 This was first presented as a radio address in 1934 and later a newspaper article. Adam Sharr, *Heidegger's Hut* (Cambridge, MA: The MIT Press, 2006), p. 63.
30 As Sharr argues, "The farmhouse was a clock of sorts, each sacred place demarcated in time through physical presences and absences." Sharr, *Heidegger's Hut*, p. 67.
31 Sharr, op. cit., p. 64.
32 Thomas Sheehan, ed., *Heidegger: The Man and the Thinker* (New Brunswick, USA, Transaction Publishers, 2010) p. 28.
33 Sheehan, ed., p. 28.
34 Until his colleagues at Freiburg University granted him emeritus status in 1951.
35 Heidegger, "Building, Dwelling, Thinking," in Leach, *Rethinking Architecture: A Reader in Cultural Theory*, p. 108.

36 Neil Leach, *Rethinking Architecture: A Reader in Cultural Theory*, p. 120.
37 Adam Sharr writes:

> To the philosopher the farmhouse traced its resident's understanding of situation: their physical situation denoted by the building's particular relationship with the weather and seasons, configured with respect to the sun, snow and wind; but also their broader situation, paced out in rites and routines between birth and death.
>
> Sharr, *Heidegger's Hut*, p. 68.

38 Sharr, *Heidegger for Architects* (London: Routledge, 2007), p. 70.
39 Sharr states, "To properly engage with Heidegger's writings, it is necessary to engage in detail with his life at Todtnauberg and its conditions." Sharr, *Heidegger's Hut,* p. 7.
40 Henry David Thoreau, *Walden* (Roslyn, NY: Walter J. Black, Inc., 1942), p. 114.
41 It has been suggested that he was influenced by reformist ideas of his time regarding the virtues of country cottages and fashionable notions about "the summerhouse, the literary hermitage, and the wilderness retreat." See William Barksdale Maynard, "Thoreau's House at Walden," *Art Bulletin*, Vol. 81, No. 2, June 1999, pp. 303–25. However, a counterargument is that Walden was a challenge to the nostalgic country houses promoted by Andrew J. Downing and others. Marlyn R. Chandler, *Dwelling in the Text: Houses in American Fiction* (Berkeley: University of California Press, 1991), p. 24.
42 Henry David Thoreau, *Journal, Volume 2: 1842–1848*, Robert Sattelmeyer, ed. (Princeton, NJ: Princeton University Press, 1984), p. 155.
43 From the chapter in *Walden* entitled "Where I Lived and What I Lived For."
44 William Ellery Channing writes in his biography of Thoreau, "Some fancied because he moved to Walden he left his family. He bivouacked there, and really lived at home, where he went every day." William Ellery Channing, *Thoreau the Poet-Naturalist* (New York: Biblo and Tannen, 1966), p. 24.
45

> "Remembering what he had said so boastfully at his college graduation, he determined to reverse the Biblical instruction and, after working one day a week, to rest six, though rest would be merely a euphemism. Those six days of each week he would devote to writing and the observation of nature."
>
> Walter Harding, *The Days of Henry Thoreau: A Biography* (New York: Dover Publications, Inc., 1962), p. 179.

46 Thoreau, *Walden* p. 390.
47 Thoreau, op. cit., p. 457.
48 Thoreau, op. cit., p. 380.
49 Thoreau, *Walden*, pp. 135–6.
50 From the chapter in *Walden* entitled "Solitude."
51 From the chapter in *Walden* entitled "Visitors."
52 Thoreau, op. cit., pp. 390–1.
53 Or, in the words of William Ellery Channing, a "natural stoic." Channing, *Thoreau the Poet-Naturalist*, p. 11.
54 Thoreau, *Journal, Volume 2: 1842–1848*, pp. 181–2.
55 Chandler, *Dwelling in the Text*, p. 28.
56 Thoreau, op. cit., p. 398.
57 Thoreau, op. cit., p. 299.
58 Thoreau, op. cit., pp. 564–5.
59 From the "Conclusion" of *Walden*.

60 Sharr also suggests, "For architecture, Heidegger's hut-inspired thinking about dwelling and place seems to have become a zero-sum game, whatever it gives, its associations can also take away." Sharr, *Heidegger's Hut,* pp. 7 and 112.
61 Assessments and characterizations of Thoreau himself have ranged from an authentic and principled voice of conscience, to a humorless misanthrope and sanctimonious scold.
62 In the case of *Walden*, this began when the Concord School of Literature and Philosophy was founded in 1879, a group that championed Thoreau's writings and whose gatherings included visits to Walden Pond.
63 He is also quoted as saying, "You think philosophy is difficult enough, but I can tell you it is nothing to the difficulty of being a good architect." Mugerauer, *Interpreting Environments*, p. 8.
64 Naming it La Sebastiana, "messy hair," was purportedly inspired by Matilde Urrutia's hair.
65 Pablo Neruda, *Fully Empowered*, translated by Alastair Reid (New York: Farrar, Straus and Giroux, 1967), pp. 49–53.
66 From Heidegger, "The Origin of the Work of Art," in Leach, ed., *Rethinking Architecture*, p. 119.
67 From the chapter in *Walden* entitled "Economy." Thoreau also opined in "Economy," "True, there are architects so called in this country, and I have heard of one at least possessed with the idea of making architectural ornaments have a core of truth, a necessity, and hence a beauty, as if it were a revelation to him. All very well perhaps from his point of view, but only a little better than the common dilettantism. A sentimental reformer to architecture, he began at the cornice, not at the foundation." Thoreau, *Walden*, p. 70 (italics in original).
68 Thoreau, *Walden*, p. 270.
69 Ralph Waldo Emerson's eulogy for Thoreau on May 9, 1862, first published in the *Atlantic Monthly*, 1862.
70 The three essays that address the architectural implications of human existence, "The Thing," "Building, Dwelling, Thinking," and "Poetically Man Dwells," were written in a post-war Germany experiencing a severe housing crisis, but remain aloof from its effects and remedies. At the end of "Building, Dwelling, Thinking," he does mention "today's housing shortage," and his essay can be understood, at least in part, as a challenge to instrumental approaches to address it.
71 Alan D. Holder, *Thoreau's Ecstatic Witness* (New Haven, CT: Yale University Press, 2001), pp. 34–5.
72 Gertrud Heidegger, ed., *Martin Heidegger: Letters to His Wife,* p. 139.
73 Brooks Atkinson, ed., *The Complete Essays and Other Writings of Ralph Waldo Emerson* (New York: The Modern Library, 1950) p. 42.

Chapter 7 – Domestic ideologies: Modernism, postmodernism, and the house

1 Marshall Berman, *All That is Solid Melts into Air* (New York: Penguin Books, 1982), p. 6.
2 Renata Hejduk and Jim Williamson, *The Religious Imagination in Modern and Contemporary Architecture: A Reader* (New York and London: Routledge, 2011), p. 3.
3 Colin Rowe, *The Architecture of Good Intentions: Towards a Possible Retrospect* (London: Academy Editions, 1994), p. 42.

4 Charles Jencks and Karl Kropt, eds, *Theories and Manifestoes of Contemporary Architecture* (Chichester, UK: Academy Editions, 1997), p. 7.

5 Rowe adds:

> These are very embarrassing themes for the would-be rationalist either to recognize or discuss: and preferably, they should be invisible. For areas where both belief and rationalism are loudly proclaimed, quite often the would-be rationalist is never, very seriously, agnostic. Simply, he believes and fails to observe the irony of his bland conviction.
>
> Rowe, *The Architecture of Good Intentions*, p. 32.

6 Michael Benedikt, "Shiva, Luria, Kahn," in Hejduk and Williamson, eds, *The Religious Imagination in Modern and Contemporary Architecture*, p. 33.

7 Walter Gropius, Bruno Taut, and Adolf Behne, "New Ideas on Architecture," in Ulrich Conrads, *Programs and Manifestoes on 20th-century Architecture* (Cambridge, MA: The MIT Press, 1971), p. 46.

8 "De Stijl Manifesto I", in Conrads, *Programs and Manifestoes*, p. 39.

9 Bruno Taut, "A Programme for Architecture" (1918), and "Daybreak" (1921), in Conrads, *Programs and Manifestoes*, pp. 41 and 63.

10 Louis Sullivan, *Kindergarten Chats* (New York: Dover Publications, 1979), p. 224.

11 Rowe, *The Architecture of Good Intentions*, p. 33.

12 In Mies van der Rohe's words, "Form is not the aim of our work, but only the result." Quoted in Rowe, *The Architecture of Good Intentions*, p. 21.

13 Theodor W. Adorno, "Functionalism Today," in Neil Leach, ed., *Rethinking Architecture: A Reader in Cultural Theory*, p. 9.

14 See Rowe, *The Architecture of Good Intentions*, p. 11.

15 As Rowe suggests, "The modern building, though generally alleged to be symbolically neutral, was more often than not, quite assiduously saturated with iconic content." Rowe, *The Architecture of Good Intentions*, p. 46. Charles Jencks more explicitly stated that even the most rational modernists were "inadvertent symbolists." Charles Jencks, *The Language of Post-Modern Architecture* (London: Academy Editions, 1987), pp. 19–20.

16 The house, which later became a museum housing his collection of art and antiquities, also displays architectural approaches, spatial compositions, and details that were to find full expression in later commissions.

17 See Hilde Heynen, "Modernity and Domesticity," in Hilde Heynen and Gülsüm Baydar, eds, *Negotiating Domesticity: Spatial Productions of Gender in Modern Architecture* (London: Routledge, 2005), p. 15.

18 Rowe, *The Architecture of Good Intentions*, p. 20.

19 Frank Lloyd Wright, from the chapter "Organic Architecture," in *The Natural House* (New York: Horizon Press, 1954), pp. 13–30.

20 Frank Lloyd Wright, *The Living City* (New York: Horizon Press, 1958), pp. 23–7.

21 See Karsten Harries, *The Ethical Function of Architecture*, p. 248.

22 Wright, *The Natural House*, p. 29.

23 For example, H.H. Richardson's practice was in his house in Brookline, MA. See David Zan Zantan, "Frank Lloyd Wright's Kindergarten," in Christopher Reed, ed., *Not at Home: The Suppression of Domesticity in Modern Art and Architecture* (London: Thames and Hudson, 1996), pp. 92–7.

24 Frank Lloyd Wright, "Declaration of Independence. T-Square and Triangle Verses," from *The Architectural Forum*, January 1938, front piece.

25 Paul Goldberger, from an address at the Hull House Museum, March 1, 2001. See also Kenneth Frampton, *Modern Architecture: A Critical History* (London: Thames and Hudson, 1980), pp. 57–63.
26 Schröder built the house after the death of her husband and lived there with her children. Rietveld also lived there at one time.
27 Alice Friedman, *Women and The Making of the Modern House: A Social and Architectural History* (New York: Harry N. Abrams, Inc., 1998), p. 66.
28 Wright, *The Natural House*, p. 27.
29 Le Corbusier, from the chapter "The Engineer's Aesthetic and Architecture," in *Towards a New Architecture*, pp. 16–24.
30 Le Corbusier, *Towards a New Architecture*, p. 18 (italics in original).
31 Le Corbusier, *Towards a New Architecture*, p. 12.
32 Le Corbusier, op. cit., p. 219.
33 Le Corbusier, op. cit., p. 82.
34 Matthew Nowicki, "Origins and Trends in Modern Architecture," first published in *The Magazine of Art*, November 1951, pp. 273–9.
35 Le Corbusier, *Towards a New Architecture*, p. 89.
36 Harries, *The Ethical Function of Architecture*, p. 151.
37 Le Corbusier, "Précisions sur un état présent de l'architecture et de l'urbanisme," quoted in Beatriz Colomina, ed., *Sexuality and Space* (New York: Princeton Architectural Press, 1992), p. 114.
38 Rowe, *The Architecture of Good Intentions*, p. 71.
39 Reyner Banham, *The Architecture of the Well-Tempered Environment* (Chicago: The University of Chicago Press, 1984), p. 143.
40 Reed, ed., *Not at Home*, p. 16.
41 Phillip Webb designed the wing. However, when Georgiana Burne-Jones lost her baby from scarlet fever, they withdrew and the project was never realized.
42 Schindler published a short article entitled "A Cooperative Dwelling," in *T-Square*, Philadelphia, February 1932, pp. 20–1.
43 See Robert Sweeney and Judith Sheine, *Schindler, Kings Road, and Southern California Modernism* (Berkeley: University of California Press, 2012), p. 14.
44 Richard Neutra and his wife then had a try at the new domestic arrangements after Neutra became Schindler's partner, but left in 1930. Pauline later returned to live in a seperate wing, and she and Schindler lived there until their deaths.
45 Phillip Johnson, "The Seven Crutches of Modernism," first published in *Perspecta: The Yale Architectural Journal*, Vol. 3, 1955, pp. 40–4.
46 David Whitney and Jeffrey Kipnis, eds, *Phillip Johnson: The Glass House* (New York: Pantheon Books, 1993), pp. xii–xiii.
47 In Johnson's words "The Glass House stylistically is a mixture of Mies van der Rohe, Malevich, the Parthenon, the English Garden, the whole Romantic Movement, the asymmetry of the 19th Century." From a 1991 interview by the National Trust for Historic Preservation.
48 The juxtaposed Brick House was as enclosed as the Glass House was open, prompting speculation that each represented complementary sides of Johnson's open and closeted sexuality. Friedman, *Women and the Making of the Modern House*, p. 152. http://theglasshouse.org/explore/brick-house/overview/
49 In Johnson's 1950 essay in *Architectural Review*, he cited sources for the Glass and Brick Houses as diverse as Le Corbusier, Mies van der Rohe, Karl Friedrich Schinkel, and Auguste Choisy. Whitney and Kipnis, eds, *Phillip Johnson: The Glass House*, p. xiii.

50 Robert Venturi, *Complexity and Contradiction in Architecture* (New York: Museum of Modern Art, 1966), p. 16.
51 *Complexity and Contradiction in Architecture*, p. 16.
52 Frederic Schwartz, ed., *Mother's House* (New York: Rizzoli, 1992), p. 39.
53 In Venturi's description it was big and small, complex and simple, open and closed and good and bad. Venturi, *Complexity and Contradiction in Architecture*, p. 118.
54 Like modernism, deconstructivist architecture was introduced to the public through an exhibition at the Museum of Modern Art – both exhibitions co-chaired by Phillip Johnson. Peter Eisenman was one of the seven architects featured in the 1988 exhibition.
55 According to Derrida, "If modernism distinguishes itself by striving for absolute domination, then postmodernism might be the realization or the experience of its end, the end of the plan for domination." Jacques Derrida, "Architecture Where Desire May Live," in Leach, ed., *Rethinking Architecture*, p. 207.
56 See Joan Ockman, "Between Utopias and Ideologies," in Cynthia C. Davidson, *Eisenman/Krier: Two Ideologies* (New York: Monacelli Press, 2004), p. 10.
57 Peter Eisenman, *Houses of Cards* (New York: Oxford University Press, 1987), p. 150.
58 Suzanne Frank, *Peter Eisenman's House VI: The Client's Response* (New York: Watson-Guptill Publications, 1994), p. 7.
59 Frank, *Peter Eisenman's House VI*, p. 21.
60 Frank op. cit., p. 11.
61 Frank, op. cit., p. 58.
62 Frank, op. cit., p. 23.
63 Frank, op. cit., p. 24.
64 Frank, op. cit., p. 49.
65 Frank, op. cit., p. 62.
66 Alain de Botton, *The Architecture of Happiness*, p. 164.

Chapter 8 – Domestic cultures: the twentieth-century house and suburb

1 Robert Fishman, *Bourgeois Utopias: The Rise and Fall of Suburbia* (New York: Basic Books, Inc., Publishers, 1987), p. 11.
2 According to Robert Fishman, "The true center of this new city is not in some downtown business district but in each residential unit." Fishman, *Bourgeois Utopias*, p. 185.
3 Alain de Botton, *The Architecture of Happiness*, p. 107.
4 Malcolm Kelsall, *The Great Good Place: The Country House and English Literature* (New York: Columbia University Press, 1993), p. 7.
5 According to Richard Gill, "To Penshurst" is a "panegyric to the country house," where the "natural order of landscape," reflects the "human order of life inside the house." Richard Gill, *Happy Rural Seat: The English Country House and the Literary Imagination*, (New Haven: Yale University Press, 1972), pp. 227–28. Jonson's description of the fecund world of nature surrounding the country house has been compared to Martial's praises of Faustinius' villa at Baiae. Kelsall, *The Great Good Place*, p. 15.
6 William Macdonald and John A. Pinto, *Hadrian's Villa and Its Legacy* (New Haven, CT: Yale University Press, 1995), pp. 3–6.
7 See John Archer, *Architecture and Suburbia: From English Villa to American Dream House, 1690–2000* (Minneapolis: University of Minnesota Press, 2005), pp. 35–6.

8 Kelsall, *The Great Good Place*, p. 20.
9 Leon Battista Alberti, *De re aedificatoria: Book IX, Ch. 2,* translated by Cosimo Bartoli and James Leoni (London: Alec Trianti Ltd., 1755), p. 189.
10 From Pliny's *Letters on the Tuscan Villa*, first century CE.
11 Andrea Palladio, *The Four Books of Architecture: Book II, Ch. XII* (New York: Dover Publications, Inc., 1965), p. 46.
12 It was named the Villa Capra after its subsequent owners.
13 Kenneth Jackson, *Crabgrass Frontier: The Suburbanization of the United States* (New York: Oxford University Press, 1985), p. 18.
14 James S. Ackerman calls it more a *belvedere* than a villa. James S. Ackerman, *Palladio* (Baltimore, MD: Penguin Books, Inc., 1966), p. 70. See also, James S. Ackerman, *The Villa: Form and Ideology of Country Houses* (Princeton, NJ: Princeton University Press, 1990), pp. 106–7.
15 Robert Tavernor, *Palladio and Palladianism* (London: Thames and Hudson, 1991), p. 78.
16 Alberti, *De re aedificatoria*, p. 189.
17 Palladio, *The Four Books of Architecture*, p. 46.
18 See Archer, *Architecture and Suburbia*, pp. 58–62.
19 Kelsall, *The Great Good Place*, p. 14.
20 Its allusions have been credited to Virgil's *Aeneid,* Christianity, sexuality and chastity, and even its owner and creator Henry Hoare's own life. There have even been parsed arguments regarding which passages from the *Aeneid* were monumentalized. See Stephanie Ross, *What Gardens Mean* (Chicago: The University of Chicago Press, 1998), pp. 63–5 and 73–80.
21 See Archer, *Architecture and Suburbia*, pp. 218–21.
22 See Fishman, *Bourgeois Utopias*, pp. 91–2.
23 It was not without its critics, one of whom wrote in 1844, "And thus at the very moment when the engines are stopped, and the counting houses are closed, everything which was the thought – the authority – the impulsive force – the moral order of this immense industrial combination, flies from the town, and disappears in an instant. The rich man spreads his couch amidst the beauties of the surrounding country, and abandons the town to the operatives, publicans, mendicants, thieves, and prostitutes, merely taking the precaution to leave behind him a police force, whose duty it is to preserve some little of material order in this pell-mell of society." Quoted in John J. Parkinson-Bailey, *Manchester: An Architectural History* (Manchester: Manchester University Press, 2000), p. 38.
24 See Ian Bradley, *The Call to Seriousness: The Evangelical Impact on the Victorians* (New York: Macmillan Publishing Co. Inc., 1976), pp. 145–54.
25 See Catherine Hall, "The Early Formation of Victorian Domestic Ideology," in Sandra Burman, ed., *Fit Work for Women* (New York: St. Martin's Press, 1979), p. 25. See also, Fishman, *Bourgeois Utopias*, pp. 51–62.
26 According to Catherine Hall, "Central to these new ideas was an emphasis on women as domestic beings, as primarily wives and mothers. Evangelicalism provided one crucial influence on this definition of home and family." Hall, "The Early Formation of Victorian Domestic Ideology," in Sandra Burman, *Fit Work for Women*, p. 15.
27 William Wilberforce, *A Practical View of Christianity*, Kevin Charles Belmonte, ed., (Peabody, MA: Hendrickson Publishers, Inc., 1996), pp. 226–7.
28 Quoted in Ford K. Brown, *Fathers of the Victorians: The Age of Wilberforce* (Cambridge: Cambridge University Press, 1961), p. 27.

29 Fishman, *Bourgeois Utopias*, p. 3.
30 The early suburbs benefitted from proximity to London, and regular and efficient transportation.
31 John R. Gillis, *A World of Their Own Making: Myth, Ritual, and the Quest for Family Values,* p. 110.
32 Commons surrounded by houses of prominent townspeople were to find their own expressions in the New England colonies.
33 Jefferson's rural villa, unlike its Roman and English predecessors of which he was aware, was envisioned as an income-producing farm (though often not a successful one). Like his English contemporaries, Jefferson was an amateur, gentleman architect. For a full discussion of Jefferson and his influences see Ackerman, *The Villa,* pp. 185–211.
34 Archer, *Architecture and Suburbia*, p. 49.
35 Henry Wotton, *The Elements of Architecture* (London: Gregg International Publishers, 1969), pp. 82–3.
36 John Ruskin, *The Seven Lamps of Architecture* (New York: Dover Publications, Inc., 1989), p. 182.
37 John Ruskin, "Of Queen's Gardens," from *Sesame and Lilies*, in Dinah Birch, ed., *John Ruskin: Selected Writings* (Oxford: Oxford University Press, 2004), pp. 158–9.
38 Fishman, *Bourgeois Utopias*, p. 122.
39 Claudia Stokes, *The Altar at Home: Sentimental Literature and Nineteenth-century American Religion* (Philadelphia: University of Pennsylvania Press, 2014), p. 127.
40 Archer, *Architecture and Suburbia*, pp. 251 and 177.
41 Archer, op. cit., p. 181.
42 See Archer, op. cit., pp. 221–4.
43 According to Robert Fishman, "If there was a single plan that expresses the idea of the bourgeois utopia, it is Olmsted's Riverside." Fishman, *Bourgeois Utopias*, p. 129.
44 According to William Whyte, the new suburbs "bear a resemblance to such utopian ventures as the Oneida Community or the Fourier settlements." William H. Whyte, Jr., *The Organization Man* (New York: Simon and Schuster, 1956), p. 282.
45 They differ however from the twentieth-century suburbs that followed in that they envisioned self-contained and self-sufficient communities. The nineteenth-century social reformer Ebenezer Howard, credited with founding the garden city movement in England, also viewed the countryside as preferable for building a new society. Letchworth, designed by Raymond Unwin according to Howard's principles, was an early and important prototype that paired housing, shared greenspaces, and industry.
46 Quoted in Jackson, *Crabgrass Frontier*, p. 231.
47 Andrew J. Downing, *The Architecture of Country Houses: Designs for Cottages, Farm-Houses, and Villas* (New York: D. Appleton & Co., 1850), pp. 268–9. See also, Archer, *Architecture and Suburbia*, p. 208.
48 One of the first was Chestnut Hill, outside of Philadelphia, which was conceived by a railroad executive in the late 1870s as a means to access land for sale and profit. Here, along with a country club, a resort hotel, and an episcopal church, large houses were set back from the street on large lots.
49 The Interstate Highway Act of 1956 envisioned as an over 42,000-mile system of limited access highways was soon and regularly expanded. Conceptualized by a committee appointed by Dwight Eisenhower, its goals were to create a national system of convenient, safe, and efficient roads while also providing high-volume roads for the evacuation of cities in case of a nuclear attack. Funded by the Highway Trust Fund and funded by gas taxes, which were kept separate from other tax

revenues and were non-divertible to other areas, it essentially guaranteed a nearly constant expansion of the nation's roads and their upkeep.

50 According to Kenneth Jackson, "Suburbia has become the quintessential achievement of the United States; it is perhaps more representative of its culture than big cars, tall buildings, or professional football." Jackson, *Crabgrass Frontier*, p. 4.

51 Lynn Spigel, "The Suburban Home Companion: Television and the Neighborhood Ideal in Postwar America," in Beatriz Colomina, ed., *Sexuality and Space* (New York: Princeton Architectural Press, 1992), p. 193.

52 *The Money Pit,* starring Tom Hanks and Shelley Long, and released in 1986, is a remake of the novel that *Mr. Blandings Builds His Dream House* was based on.

53 Other characters include the teenagers, Wally, the older brother, and Eddie Haskel, who serves as the foil for expected behaviors of the time.

54 Its predominant themes were more subtly (or subversively) delivered by another popular program, *The Munsters*, which aired from 1964 to 1966, and was produced by the creators of *Leave It to Beaver*. Even though the characters of the house are very different from the Cleavers – the characters play roles of "monsters" – it presented the same conventions and domesticity as its predecessor. The Munsters are an otherwise typical suburban family who, in their struggles to fit in with the social norms of suburbia, illustrate their virtues.

55 The reconsiderations of the unitary norms and virtues of suburban domesticity were perhaps presaged by an episode of *I Love Lucy*, the television show that aired from 1951 to 1957, entitled "Lucy Wants to Move to the Country," when Lucy and Desi move to the suburbs of Connecticut. The episodes that follow highlight the loneliness and dislocation they feel, eventually tempered by, among other things, their former neighbors Fred and Ethel joining them.

56 Ackerman, *The Villa*, p. 9.

57 Daphne Spain reminds us, "Dwellings reflect the cultural values as well as the technological and geographic characteristics of the societies in which they are built." Daphne Spain, *Gendered Spaces* (Chapel Hill: University of North Carolina Press, 1992), p. 111.

58 Ackerman, *The Villa*, p. 30.

59 The expression "self-made man" was popularized by the Kentucky senator Henry Clay in a speech of 1832.

60 It is ironic that *prestige* is from the Latin *praestigiae*, which refers to "illusions," as in magic tricks.

61 And, even though multi-family housing is common in suburbia, it is often physically, by its location in peripheral areas, determined by zoning, and culturally, "invisible."

62 Fishman, *Bourgeois Utopias*, p. 4.

Epilogue – Making a home in the world

1 Gaston Bachelard, *The Poetics of Space*, p. 51.

2 Leon Battista Alberti, *On the Art of Building in Ten Books,* translated by Rykwert, Leach, and Tavernor, p. 23.

3 This statement appeared in numerous writings and forms, beginning in 1961. Van Eyck's house as city and city as house analogy was published in a number of forms, the best known being the Tree and Leaf diagram of 1965.

4 Leon Battista Alberti, *On the Art of Building in Ten Books*, translated by Rykwert, Leach, and Tavernor, p. 23.

5 Alberti, *On the Art of Building in Ten Books*, translated by Rykwert, Leach and Tavernor, p. 140.
6 Casper Pearson states "Unsurprisingly, both the house and the city use the division and arrangement of space to impose a moral order." Caspar Pearson, *Humanism and the Urban World: Leon Battista Alberti and the Renaissance City* (University Park: The Pennsylvania State University Press, 2011), pp. 88–90.
7 Aldo van Eyck, "Place and Occasion," in Vincent Ligtelijn and Francis Strauven, eds, *Aldo van Eyck: Collected Articles and Other Writings, 1947–1998* (Amsterdam: Sun Publishers, 2008), p. 471.
8 van Eyck, *Aldo van Eyck: Collected Articles and Other Writings*, p. 447.
9 van Eyck, op. cit., p. 447.
10 van Eyck, op cit., p. 426.
11 van Eyck, op cit., pp. 428–9.
12 van Eyck, op cit., p. 442.
13 In the words of Norman Crowe, "As a community's counterpart to the family hearth, the hearth of the polis reinforced the unity between the citizen, the family, and the community." Norman Crowe, *Nature and the Idea of a Man-made World*, p. 114.
14 Henri Lefebvre, *The Production of Space*, p. 247.
15 Hannah Arendt presented the Greek city of *polis* and *oikos* to argue that the common good is best served when private concerns are not confused with public policies. Hannah Arendt, *The Human Condition*, p. 183.
16 Herman Hertzberger, *Lessons for Students in Architecture* (Rotterdam: 010 Publishers, 2005), p. 172.
17 *Midnight in Paris*, 2011, written and directed by Woody Allen.
18 John R. Gillis, *A World of Their Own Making: Myth, Ritual, and the Quest for Family Values,* p. xv.
19 Jonathan Franzen, *The Discomfort Zone: A Personal History* (New York: Farrar, Straus and Giroux, 2006), pp. 23–4.
20 Juhani Pallasmaa, "Identity, Intimacy and Domicile: Notes on the Phenomenology of Home," from David N. Benjamin, ed., *The Home: Words, Interpretations, Meaning, and Environments* (Aldershot: Avebury, 1995), p. 131.
21 Marcel Proust, a passage at the end of *In Search of Lost Time*.
22 Emmanuel Levinas, *Between Totality and Infinity*, p. 153.
23 Hegel writes, "Art no longer affords the satisfaction of spiritual needs which earlier ages and nations sought in it, and found in it alone, a satisfaction that, at least on the parts of religion, was most intimately linked with art." He continues:

> In all these respects art, considered in its highest vocation, is and remains for us a thing of the past. Thereby it has lost for us genuine truth and life, and has rather been transferred into our *ideas* instead of maintaining its earlier necessity in reality and occupying its highest place.
>
> G.W.F. Hegel, *Aesthetics: Lectures on Fine Art, Vol. 1*, translated by T.M. Knox (Oxford: Clarendon Press, 1975), pp. 10–11.

24 Karsten Harries, *The Ethical Function of Architecture*, p. 357. Marshall Berman reflected that while the freedom and autonomy of modern art was welcomed by some, "The freedom it confers is the freedom of a beautifully formed, perfectly sealed tomb." Marshall Berman, *All That Is Solid Melts into Air*, p. 30.
25 From a House of Commons speech on November 11, 1947.
26 Blaise Pascal, *Thoughts*, translated by A.J. Krailsheimer (New York: Penguin Books, 1987), p. 89.

INDEX

Page numbers followed by f indicate figures.
Page numbers followed by n indicate note numbers.